For Jeremy Noakes

# World War Two

## A military history

Jeremy Black

Routledge
Taylor & Francis Group

LONDON AND NEW YORK

First published 2003
by Routledge
2 Park Square, Milton Park, Abingdon, Oxon, OX14 4RN

Simultaneously published in the USA and Canada
by Routledge
270 Madison Ave, New York NY 10016

*Routledge is an imprint of the Taylor & Francis Group*

Transferred to Digital Printing 2006

Typeset in Bembo by Taylor & Francis Books Ltd

*British Library Cataloguing in Publication Data*
A catalogue record for this book is available from the British
Library

*Library of Congress Cataloging in Publication Data*
Black, Jeremy.
World War Two / Jeremy Black.
Includes bibliographical references and index.
1. World War, 1939–1945 I. Title: World War 2. II. Title.

D743 .B488 2003
940.53 –dc21                    2002156182

ISBN  0–415–30534–9 (hbk)
ISBN  0–415–30535–7 (pbk)

# Contents

*Preface*                                                      xi
*List of abbreviations*                                       xvi

1  Background                                                    1

2  Initial attacks                                              31

3  The war widens                                               74

4  Attacks held, 1942                                          109

5  Mounting Allied pressure, 1943                              129

6  Defeating the Axis, 1944                                    161

7  The fall of the Axis                                        206

8  Contexts                                                    226

9  Struggle reviewed                                           266

*Selected further reading*                                    291
*Index*                                                        293

# *Preface*

It is always helpful to explain what a book is about, not least for a subject that is so extensively and ably covered in the available literature. This book is a military history, primarily operational in its scope, and deliberately written with the interests of students in mind. It draws heavily on my experience of teaching military history at the University of Exeter, and will most appropriately be judged by those and other students.

The audience in part shapes the approach, not least the decision to keep notes to a minimum. The approach also owes much to a prominent recent work, Joanna Bourke's *The Second World War: A People's History* (Oxford, 2001). Although well written, engaged and conceptually up-to-date, with a particularly impressive focus on the experience of ordinary people and the remembrance of war, Bourke's treatment of the subject is one that I have reacted against. Her book displays the demilitarisation of war, a tendency that is all too frequent in the secondary literature, not least the absence of sufficient discussion of issues such as military capability. Bourke suggests that the treatment of the conflict as 'just another story of battles and strategies will dilute its horror. The sanitization of the war in some military history is dangerous. Mass slaughter becomes a bland recital of "body counts".... A similar process of dehumanization enabled atrocious behaviour to take place during the war'.[1] The many who follow a different approach are explicitly compared to the brutal Soviet dictator Josef Stalin, a surprising view that is part of a dangerous appropriation of the subject.

As far as 'body counts' are concerned, it is instructive to note Samuel Griffith's conclusion in his study of Guadalcanal, where he

was wounded: 'In the cold perspective of history, the relative importance of a military campaign is not judged by statistics...it is the
ultimate effect which the battle, or connected series of battles, exerts
on the conduct and result of the war that should be considered'.[2]
Furthermore, from the perspective of a 'People's History', it might
be reasonable, as Bourke does, to consider the Eastern Front in large
part in terms of atrocities and resistance; it is also necessary to give
due weight to the course and explanation of conflict on that Front,
in particular giving due weight to recent re-evaluations of Soviet
fighting quality and operational effectiveness.[3]

More generally, my essential approach is operational, with a stress
on war as a military activity. A focus on campaigns and battles of
course faces many problems. There is a misleading tendency in operational history to attribute to winners all the skills of vision, strategic
know-how, preparation and back-up, whereas losers tend to lose
because they lose. I hope I have made sufficient reference to chance,
and used terms such as 'perhaps' or 'maybe' enough.

A focus on campaigning can also lead to a failure to note the
constraints within which the military operated. For example, in
March 1944, the British Chiefs of Staff responded to pressure from
Winston Churchill, the Prime Minister, that they plan for a year's
campaigning to restore British power in Malaya and Singapore,
which had been conquered by Japan in the winter of 1941–2, before
British forces were switched to join the Americans in the Pacific in
attacking Japan:

> This assumes a flexibility which would not, we fear, prove
> practicable. The administrative preparations for whatever
> operations may be decided upon, whether in the East or in
> the West, will be on a vast scale, if indeed not beyond our
> power, to make these preparations in both areas. There is
> thus no question of retaining indefinitely an option in this
> matter. It is essential to make a decision within the next
> three months as to which policy is to be adopted, and to
> adhere to it.[4]

The organisation of my book is essentially chronological, and an
attempt has been made to cover all the major fields of conflict,

although the balance between them is open to discussion. I would in particular like to have devoted more space to the war in China. This conflict may not have contributed greatly to the defeat of Japan, but it is important to give due weight to the longest struggle of the war, one that directly involved millions of combatants and civilians and that helped mould the history of post-war China, and thus the post-war world. Figures for Chinese casualties are particularly tentative, but they may have been about 2.5 million military and 7.5 million civilians.

More generally, each of the chapters could have been expanded to the length of several books with scant difficulty. Yet, compression has its values, while I am unconvinced that long books aid comprehension. All too often they are read only in part, and that is particularly true of footnotes. These have been kept to a minimum in this book. The secondary literature should be approached through the notes and the section on 'Selected further reading'.

A chronological organisation has its weakness, not least the danger of repetition, and, again, leads to issues of balance, but it helps lessen the danger of a smoothing out of the conflict as attention is concentrated on the major clashes. It is useful, for each year of the war, to remember the range of combat zones, a range that, on land, included, for example, Finland in 1939–40, Laos and Cambodia in 1940, Iraq in 1941, Madagascar in 1942, and the Norwegian Arctic and Borneo in 1945. More centrally, a chronological approach precludes a thematic focus that can lead to an underplaying of the simultaneity of conflict in different spheres, with all the problems of coordination and allocation of resources that these posed for planners and leaders.

That does not, however, end the problem of how best to prioritise and organise material within each chapter. Here there is a danger of national priorities, if not prejudices, playing a role. In particular, it is difficult for Western writers to give sufficient weight to operations on the German Eastern Front with the Soviet Union, particularly after German defeat by Soviet forces in the battle of Kursk in 1943, because, thereafter, there does not appear to be comparable drama to the battle for Moscow in 1941 or that for Stalingrad in 1942, and the fate of the war on the Front – Soviet success – appears preordained. That, however, does not lessen its importance for the course of the war or its interest for military historians.

A word of explanation is necessary about the quotations from the writings of Major General J.F.C. 'Boney' Fuller (1878–1966). Although his Fascist political sympathies were reprehensible, it is useful that one of the leading military thinkers of the age[5] commented on the war as it developed, and did so without the constraints of an official position.

There is a danger in my approach that the motivation and experience of individual soldiers receives insufficient attention. However, I am not convinced about the value of the weight some writers place upon personal experience, whether of place or of combat. Aside from the serious issue of selective memory, such experience can lead to an excessive focus on what may well be an atypical perception.

Yet, at the same time, wars are fought and press upon individuals as well as units and civilians, and loss and suffering are personal as well as collective. When reading in works such as these about lines being breached, or reserves deployed, flanks turned, or the struggle in the air, or at sea, won (and lost), it is important to remember that people's lives were at stake and that, however trained or motivated, individuals reacted in very different ways to the strains and pain of conflict. More than 21 million combatants died and over 38 million civilians, although there have been very varied figures, reflecting, in particular, very different estimates for Soviet and Chinese casualties.

I wish to underline my conviction that this was a moral struggle, an unfashionable statement for an historian to make, not least in an age in which many intellectuals are in thrall to aspects of postmodernism, or at least cultural relativism. Many others doubt the validity of such a description as applied to World War Two. I am also concerned by attempts, outside academe, to neglect or minimise Axis responsibility for the struggle, and was much struck in Japan in 1998 when students walked out of a lecture at Tsukuba University on the causes of war when I mentioned Pearl Harbor in terms of Japanese aggression. I have no doubt that the Soviet regime was a vile and genocidal dictatorship that matched that of the Nazis, and I can understand why those who suffered Soviet conquest or Allied bombing might feel that there was an equivalence between the sides. They are wrong, just as those who take the same view on World War One are wrong. It is not only that the Germans in both World Wars and the Japanese in World War Two were aggressors who sought conflict, but also that their regimes extolled war as a higher good. Those who fought them and those who died, a multitude that included several of my relatives, were engaged in a just and necessary struggle and were victims of malign forces.

I would like to pay tribute to the wealth of fine scholarship I have read while working on this book, and to thank Kristofer Allerfeldt, Stan Carpenter, Theodore Cook, Evan Davies, David Hall, Russell Hart, Michael Neiberg, Nick Smart and an anonymous reader for commenting on an earlier draft. Lisa Williams has proved an exemplary copy-editor. I have benefited from invitations to lecture on World War Two at Pearl Harbor and at both the Joint Forces Staff College and the Headquarters of Atlantic Command in Norfolk, Virginia. I would also like to recall those with whom I have travelled when visiting wartime sites, including my father, with whom I went round the soulless and bleak remains of a concentration camp, and my wife and children, with whom I visited invasion beaches where sultry skies and bathers gave no clues to lives lost in the shallows and sands.

It is a great pleasure to dedicate this book to my colleague (and next-door neighbour in the department at Exeter), Jeremy Noakes, on his retirement. A justly renowned scholar, Jeremy is also a man of great culture and wit, and as keen to open a decent bottle as to comment wryly on the latest idiocies of politically correct cant in our profession. He will be sorely missed.

## NOTES

1   J. Bourke, *The Second World War: A People's History* (Oxford, 2001), pp. 6–7.
2   S.B. Griffith, *The Battle for Guadalcanal* (Urbana, Illinois, 1963), p. 244.
3   See, in particular, D.M. Glantz, 'The Red Army at War, 1941–1945: Sources and Interpretations', *Journal of Military History*, 62 (1998), pp. 595–617; A. Hill, 'Recent Literature on the Great Patriotic War of the Soviet Union 1941–1945', *Contemporary European History*, 9 (2000), pp. 187–97.
4   L.H. Alanbrooke 6/3/9.
5   B.H. Reid, J.F.C. *Fuller: Military Thinker* (1987) and *Studies in British Military Thought: Debates with Fuller and Liddell Hart* (Lincoln, Nebraska, 1998).

# *Abbreviations*

| | |
|---|---|
| BBC | British Broadcasting Corporation |
| BL | British Library |
| GATT | General Agreement on Tariffs and Trade |
| LH | London, King's College, Liddell Hart Centre for Military History |
| MP | Member of Parliament |
| NATO | North Atlantic Treaty Organisation |
| PRO | London, Public Record Office |
| RAF | Royal Air Force |
| USAAF | United States Army Air Forces |
| USSR | Union of Soviet Socialist Republics |
| WO | War Office |

Unless otherwise stated, place of publication is London.

# CHAPTER ONE

# *Background*

World War Two is an umbrella term for a number of closely related struggles that, nevertheless, each had their own cause, course and consequences. Seen from the perspective of Italy or Iran, Japan or Jamaica, it can look very different. This chapter looks at two aspects of the background: first the causes of the conflict, and, secondly, the military background in terms both of the lessons drawn from World War One and of inter-war developments in military capability and doctrine on land, sea and air.

## Causes of war

World War Two is commonly dated to 1939, the year in which Germany invaded Poland on 1 September, leading, in response, to declarations of war by Britain and France on 3 September, followed by the Dominions of the British Empire, Canada, for example, on 10 September. This is an appropriate beginning for the conflict in Europe, but, in Asia, the parallel struggle stemming from Japanese aggression and imperialism began in 1931 with an invasion of Manchuria, the most industrial province of China.

### *Japan*

In the case of Germany and Japan, the essential cause of conflict was a refusal to accept existing territorial and political arrangements, a willingness, indeed, at times, eagerness, to use force to effect change, and a refusal to accept multilateral and collective arrangements and

1

solutions. Thus, the Japanese, who were but one of the outside powers that had benefited from the weakness of China from the late nineteenth century in order to seize territory and gain commercial concessions, were not interested in discussing additional gains with the other outside powers. Instead, they regarded them, particularly the British, as competitors and treated them with active hostility.

Japan treated China as if the largely unconstrained imperialist expansionism of the decades prior to 1914, which had seen the Japanese make gains as a result of wars with China (1894–5) and Russia (1904–5), was still in force. Right-wing nationalism became much stronger in Japan in the 1930s, in part as a consequence of stresses resulting from the Slump and the subsequent global economic crisis. Such nationalism was particularly powerful in the military and was linked to a strong racist contempt for the Chinese. Having conquered Manchuria from its semi-independent warlord in 1931–2, the Japanese pressed on, in large part because of the determination of imperialists in the Kwantung army in Manchuria, who were increasingly successful in pushing Japan in a militaristic direction. They were helped by the absence of hostile foreign intervention, and by the lack of other conflicts to absorb their attention. There was a series of operations in northern China, including the overrunning of Rehe (Jehol) in 1935. In 1937, the Japanese launched what became an all-out war of conquest in China, although it was formally termed an incident and had begun as an unexpected clash at the Marco Polo Bridge near Beijing when Japanese night manoeuvres were fired upon. Unlike in 1931, the Chinese Kuomintang (Nationalist) government (with its capital at Nanjing) responded to subsequent Japanese moves, helping to resolve differences over policy in Japanese policymaking circles and ensuring that full-scale war broke out.[1]

## Germany

In Europe, the determination to force through change was pushed hardest by Adolf Hitler (1889–1945), who became German dictator in 1933. A megalomaniac with few inhibitions about pursuing his goals, Hitler sought to remould Germany and Europe. This entailed a militarisation of Germany, the discarding of the Versailles Peace Settlement of 1919 that had followed German defeat in World War

One (1914–18), as well as of the compromises of diplomacy and international agreements, and a willingness to resort to war in order to create the Aryan-dominated Europe he sought. Control and direction of foreign and military policy within Germany were monopolised by Hitler: the system he created, as he destroyed the democracy of the Weimar period, lacked effective institutional and political restraints or the facility to offer any reasonable range of policy options that might encourage restraint.

Hitler's long-term views interacted with the short-term opportunities and anxieties presented by international developments. However, opportunities and anxieties do not exist in the abstract, but are sensed and created, and Hitler's views largely conditioned the process. As a long-term goal, Hitler wanted to extirpate what he (inaccurately) regarded as the Jewish-dominated Communist Soviet Union, which he felt would secure his notions of racial superiority and living space. This was to be accompanied by the annihilation of the Jews, the two acts creating a Europe that would be dominated by the Germans, who were to be a master race over the Slavs and others.

This agenda began with the violent suppression of political and economic freedoms, organisations and groups within Germany, including strikes, left-wing parties and Jews, but there was also psychological and practical preparation for war, which Hitler saw as a necessary, and even positive force, the last a view that looked back to the nineteenth-century attitudes that had helped lead to World War One. Indeed, in many respects, Hitler's views represented the refraction of pre-1914 right-wing nationalist and racist views through the prism of German defeat and the disintegration of Habsburg (Austrian) hegemony over part of Slavic Europe. Hitler aspired to reverse the earlier defeat, and to recreate an acceptable (ie. German-dominated) Europe, specifically by controlling Eastern Europe, where *Lebensraum* (living space) was to be pursued. To achieve his goals, Hitler sought to end the threat of a war on two fronts, as Germany had faced for most of World War One. To him this required not peace on one front, but rather a rapid victory. This was to be achieved by obtaining the goal that had eluded Germany in 1914: defeating France and reaching an agreement with Britain.

To achieve his ends, Hitler rapidly increased German military spending and the size of the armed forces, and took control of the military high command. From the low base of 100,000 troops permitted under the Versailles settlement, he, on 1 October 1934, ordered a trebling of army size, as well as the creation of an air force, which had been illegal under the Versailles terms. On 7 March 1936, troops were sent into the Rhineland, unilaterally abrogating the demilitarisation of Germany's western frontier provided for under the Locarno Pact. The Four-Year Plan, initiated the same year, was designed to ensure self-sufficiency, by import-substitution plans, which would secure Germany's readiness to go to war in four years and reduce her vulnerability to blockade. Yet again, this reflected the experience of World War One, in which British naval power had enforced a strict maritime blockade on Germany, harming her war economy and hitting food supplies.

## Appeasement

Far from responding forcefully against the successive breaches of the Versailles settlement, Britain and France took a largely passive position. In hindsight, this encouraged Nazi expansionism, but, at the time, it was not generally seen in such a stark light. Initially, the British and French governments hoped that Hitler would be tamed by the responsibilities and exigencies of power, or that he would restrict his energies to ruling Germany. There was also a feeling in Britain that the Versailles terms had been overly harsh on Germany and that it was, therefore, understandable that Hitler should press for revision. It was anticipated that German revisionism could be accommodated, and that Hitler would prove to be just another episode in European power politics, rather like Napoleon III in the mid-nineteenth century. Both Britain and France were unsure whether the Soviet Union, the sole Communist state and also a great power, was not a more significant threat to the European system than Nazi Germany. In 1920, a Soviet invasion of Poland had only been thwarted with considerable difficulty. There was some support in conservative circles for the view that a strengthened Germany might keep the Soviet Union at bay.

Furthermore, pacifism was strong in both Britain and France, in large part in response to the massive casualties in World War One. Fiscal restraint limited rearmament, although, outside Europe, both powers used troops to sustain their imperial interests. This military commitment, however, both lessened the forces available for operations in Europe and led to priorities in force structure, doctrine, training and weaponry that were not appropriate for fighting the German military. Furthermore, the very limited nature of Anglo-French military co-operation over the previous decade and their lack of military and political preparedness for war with Germany were understood by contemporaries as a poor basis for joint action, and neither felt that it was in a position to act on its own.

Hitler pressed on to occupy Austria on 12 March 1938, uniting it with Germany in the *Anschluss* (union) of the following day. This was seen as more than a revision of the Versailles settlement. It was a fundamental redrawing of the map of Europe, and one that opened the way for more radical changes. Opposition to *Anschluss* in Austria had been limited, but Hitler's subsequent goals were ones that could only be achieved by serious intimidation, if not conflict.

Hitler then turned on Czechoslovakia (modern Czech Republic and Slovakia). Created out of the Austro-Hungarian empire after World War One, it included parts of Bohemia and Moravia where there was a majority of ethnic Germans – the Sudetan Germans. This was unacceptable to Hitler, who sought the union of all Germans in one state, although, for him, that was only a prelude to further gains. He was also determined to destroy Czechoslovakia, a democratic state that looked to other great powers for support. France, in particular, had followed an active policy of negotiating agreements in Eastern Europe that were designed to support the states of the region against Germany and the Soviet Union. Hitler's threat to attack Czechoslovakia, and the concern that this would cause a major war, led to the satisfaction of his territorial demands in a settlement negotiated with Britain, France and Italy, the Munich agreement of 29 September 1938. This was seen as the apogee of the policy of appeasement, the term used to describe the satisfaction of the demands of the dictatorships.

The policy of appeasement rested on the belief that it was possible to reach mutually acceptable settlements with the dictators. There was a muted response to Japanese aggression in Manchuria and to the Italian dictator Mussolini's conquest of Abyssinia (Ethiopia) in 1935–6. The British government thought it both necessary and feasible to negotiate with Hitler, and it took time for the government to appreciate that this was both impossible and, indeed, dangerous. Hitler wanted Germany to be a superpower, was happy to destroy both the balance of power and collective security in order to achieve this goal, and aimed at a new world order.

Nevertheless, it is too easy in hindsight to criticise the British and French leaders of the period and, in condemning appeasement, to underrate their difficulties, not least their genuine and understandable fear of causing a second 'Great War'. Even if mobilised, Britain could do little in Central or Eastern Europe to stop Hitler. Commenting on the German threat to Austria, Harold Nicolson had noted in 1934, 'We cannot send the Atlantic fleet to Linz [in Austria]'. In 1938, the British service chiefs urged caution. They were conscious of Britain's numerous global commitments and warned about the dangers of becoming entangled in major military action on the Continent. Concern about German aerial capability, particularly the threat of bombing, reinforced this caution, as did warnings from British and French intelligence about German military capabilities.

Dominion leaders, such as the Prime Minister of Canada, Mackenzie King, also urged caution, while the American government under Franklin Delano Roosevelt made clear its unwillingness to play a role in limiting German expansion: American policy towards Europe was resolutely isolationist and this gravely weakened the option of collective security as the USA was the world's leading economy. Lesser European powers, including Denmark, Ireland, Norway, Sweden and Switzerland, also failed to lend support to the opposition to Hitler.

Anglo-French fears may have been excessive given the weaknesses of the Nazi regime, not least a lack of enthusiasm among the German generals for either Hitler or war. Lieutenant-General Ludwig Beck, the Chief of the General Staff, who had protested without success at the occupation of Austria, prepared a coup in the event of war breaking out, and felt undermined by the Munich agreement: he had resigned in August. The German army and air force (*Luftwaffe*) were not prepared for a major war, and were far less powerful than they were to be a year later. As yet, developments in German tank capability were limited. Indeed, the strength of

German armour when Poland was attacked in 1939 owed much to the seizure of Czech tanks and military-industrial capacity.

The ability of Czechoslovakia to resist successfully in 1938 would have been lessened by the hostility towards the Czech-dominated government of much Slovak opinion, as well as that of other minority groups, particularly Germans and Hungarians. Furthermore, the country's elongated shape and the length of its common border with Germany made it vulnerable to a bisecting attack. There were good fortifications along much of the common border, but they did not extend to cover adequately its extension following the *Anschluss*. A successful defence of the country would have depended on international support, not only attacks by Britain and France on Germany's as yet poorly fortified western frontier, but also backing from Poland and, even more, the Soviet Union. The latter two, however, were not in a situation to mount a major offensive against Germany, Poland had aggressive goals towards Czechoslovakia of its own, and Anglo-French forces were not ready to attack.

The Munich agreement led to a great increase in German influence in Eastern Europe, as other powers responded to the apparent weakness of Britain and France. France had supported Yugoslavia and Romania, and provided arms for their military, but, after Munich, both powers moved towards Germany. Eventually, on 15 March 1939, Hitler destroyed his Czech victim, seizing Bohemia and Moravia, and was able to do so without encountering armed resistance, because Czechoslovakia had been much weakened by internal dissent between Czechs and Slovaks, and by the Munich agreement, which resulted in its loss of frontier fortifications in the areas annexed by Germany.

The Germans also benefited greatly from the failure of the Eastern European powers to unite against her. This disunity was the result of attempts to gain the territories they felt they had lost unfairly, or should have gained, as part of the Versailles settlement. Hungary and Poland had used the Munich crisis to make gains at Czechoslovakia's expense in 1938, and, in March 1939, Hungarian forces occupied Ruthenia, the easternmost part of Czechoslovakia, overcoming popular opposition. Similarly, a failure of Scandinavian unity was seen in 1939–40, in response, first, to growing German power and, subsequently, to the German attack on Denmark and Norway: Sweden provided assistance to neither.

Also in March 1939, the Germans bullied Lithuania into ceding the city of Memel (Klapeida), where there was a vocal German minority, plus the surrounding area. In intimidating the other powers in 1938, Hitler benefited from their fear of war. In many respects, the Munich agreement was part of the legacy of World War One and the desire to avoid a repetition of its heavy casualties.

### The coming of war

Germany may have been weaker than was thought, but Hitler, nevertheless, was determined to gain his objectives. Once he seized Bohemia and Moravia and renounced all the guarantees he had earlier made in the Munich agreement, the situation was transformed. It was now clear that Hitler's ambitions were not restricted to bringing all Germans under one state. Neville Chamberlain, British Prime Minister from 1937 until 1940, and the architect of Munich, lost confidence in negotiating directly with Germany.

Instead, at the prompting of Lord Halifax, the Foreign Secretary, Chamberlain sought to create a collective-security alliance system capable of intimidating Hitler and of deterring him from further aggression. Despite the resulting guarantees of British support to Poland and Romania, Hitler persisted with his plan for an attack on Poland, which blocked German expansion to the east. He believed that Britain and France would not fight, especially after he secured a non-aggression pact with the Soviet leader Josef Stalin, signed on 23 August 1939, that reflected the failure of Britain and France to negotiate an alliance with the Soviet Union. Such an alliance would have been incompatible with the anti-Soviet policies of the Polish government, and this reflected, and, in turn, exposed, the weakness of the British diplomatic offensive in Eastern Europe. The Nazi–Soviet Pact made it unlikely that, should deterrence fail, Poland would be able to resist attack successfully, and it encouraged Hitler to press forward with his plans for Poland. He was keen on conflict and determined not to be thwarted of it, as he had allowed himself to be in 1938. In turn, the Poles were determined not to make concessions. The British Chiefs of Staff had advised that it would not be possible to offer Poland any direct assistance, although Gamelin, the French Chief of Staff for National Defence, had told the Poles that France would. The German attack on Poland on 1 September 1939 led Britain and France to declare war two days later.[2] Winston Churchill, a harsh critic of appeasement, who now entered the Cabinet as First Lord of the Admiralty, told the House of Commons on 3 September:

> This is not a question of fighting for Danzig or fighting for Poland. We are fighting to save the whole world from the pestilence of Nazi tyranny and in defence of all that is most sacred to man. This is no war for domination or imperial aggrandisement or material gain; no war to shut any country out of its sunlight and means of progress. It is a war, viewed in its inherent quality, to establish on impregnable rocks, the rights of the individual, and it is a war to establish and revive the stature of man.

## Military background

Some of the conflicts that together were to constitute World War Two had been planned for years. This was particularly true of war between Japan and the USA and between France and Germany. Others had received far less prior attention. The idea that the USA would have to fight Germany by invading first North Africa, then Italy, and then France was totally outside her experience in World War One, and had not been prepared for. The idea of Britain and the Soviet Union allying against Germany appeared improbable when discussed in 1939.

Whether or not individual conflicts had been adequately prepared, there had been, over the two previous decades, an attempt to digest what were seen as the lessons of World War One, and then a response to subsequent developments, particularly in weaponry but also in doctrine and tasking. Like all major conflicts, World War One could be variously interpreted, and this, in part, reflected personal, factional and institutional interests and the politics of military doctrine. The range of investment options in weaponry and force structure increased with the additional claims of air power and armour, creating inter-service disputes over the division of limited resources.

Tasking was also an issue. It is important to remember that the term 'inter-war', with its suggestion of the need to prepare for World War Two, is misleading, especially for the 1920s. Even in the 1930s, the configuration of powers in a major war was still very unclear, and this had implications for strategy, and thus for desirable force structure. In the 1920s, with the Soviet Union checked by the Poles, German armed forces limited by the Versailles Treaty, and Balkan tensions containable without war, the most pressing military problems for Britain, France and the USA appeared to be imperial: colonial rebellion in the case of the first two (for example in Syria and French Morocco for the French), and within the informal American empire in the Caribbean and Central America for the third.[3]

In none of these cases did the 'lessons' of World War One appear particularly pertinent, because there seemed little reason to prepare for conflict with another major power. Nevertheless, there was an attempt among military thinkers to focus on the supposed lessons. In doing so, the emphasis among some commentators, who were to be seen as particularly influential for the future, was on the potential of mechanised warfare, rather than the successes of the infantry–artillery co-operation that had, in fact, played a crucial role in Allied, largely British, success on the Western Front in 1918.

The British experience is enlightening. In the last stages of the war, J.F.C. Fuller, a British colonel, had devised 'Plan 1919', an operational scheme for the defeat of Germany in 1919 based on a large-scale tank offensive designed to penetrate deep into opposing territory, rather than simply supporting an infantry attack on the front line. Fuller saw this deep penetration as leading to the disintegration of opposition cohesion, as well as an attendant demoralisation that would compromise fighting quality. This offensive strategy, by its impetus, was designed to provide effective protection for the attacking power.

Following Fuller, Basil Liddell Hart, an ex-army officer turned military correspondent and ardent self-publicist, developed notions of rapid tank warfare; although he also argued that the infantry retained an important offensive role. Publicly expressed in his pieces for the *Daily Telegraph* and *The Times*, Liddell Hart's ideas also had an influence on British armoured manoeuvres in the 1930s, while he and Fuller were cited by the Inspector of the Royal Tank Corps in his report to the 1926 army committee on the reorganisation of the cavalry.

Liddell Hart was particularly keen to advocate advances that did not entail frontal attacks: the 'indirect approach' that emphasised manoeuvre, not attrition. In *The Decisive Wars of History* (1929), he pressed the case for attacking the enemy where they were not expecting it, and for mechanised forces bypassing the flanks of enemy armies in order to hit their communications and bases, a theme he returned to in *The British Way of Warfare* (1932).

Liddell Hart and others claimed that his ideas, as well as reports of British manoeuvres, influenced German *Blitzkrieg* tactics in World War Two.[4] This was an exaggeration, as these tactics were a development of mechanised warfare itself and of the offensive tactics employed by the Germans in 1917–18, and also drew on the emphasis on an effective combined arms doctrine developed under Hans von Seeckt, Commander-in-Chief of the *Reichswehr* (German army) in 1920–6.[5]

In Britain, Germany, the Soviet Union, the USA and elsewhere in the inter-war period, there was intellectual enquiry about the nature of war-winning, attempts to develop operational doctrine, and concern about ensuring manoeuvrability and what would later be termed 'deep battle'. There was also much interest in the potential of tanks, mechanised transport, and air-to-land and air-to-sea warfare, and in the enhanced communication capability offered by radio. In the Soviet Union, Marshal Mikhail Tukhachevsky, the talented commander of the Red Army, was interested in mechanised warfare and seizing the offensive, and was responsible in 1932 for the creation of mechanised corps.[6]

The Spanish Civil War of 1936–9 seemed to offer the possibility of testing out new weaponry and tactics and of learning military lessons. It also prefigured the war of ideologies that World War Two became. Germany, Italy and the Soviet Union played a supporting role in the conflict, each sending troops and supplies, the first two to the right-wing Nationalist rebels under Franco, the last to the left-wing Republican government. Other powers followed the conflict with close attention. In Spain, although to a more limited extent than is often imagined, the Germans used close air-support tactics and aircraft, including dive-bombers. They found that this required an effective ground–air liaison system, and developed one. These tactics were to be important in the early stages of World War Two.[7]

Nevertheless, in practice, ideas advanced further than technological capability and resource availability, as was to be shown in the early land campaigns in World War Two. A lack of allocated industrial capacity and/or funds was a major factor, and, in part, reflected the severity and global span of the Depression of the 1930s. The lack of funds was particularly apparent in the USA, which was to be the global military power of World War Two and which had the largest economy in the world in the 1930s. Limited expenditure on the American military, which reflected a lack of public and political will, led to inadequate manpower and resources, as well as a failure to stage major manoeuvres, and thus ensure operational training. However, there were also limitations, if not deficiencies, in areas of doctrine and equipment. For example, tank warfare was given little role and no independence under the National Defence Act of 1920. Instead, tanks were allocated to the infantry, an allocation only challenged in 1931 when light tanks were assigned to the cavalry. It took the fall of France to the Germans in 1940 to lead to the rearmament of the American army and to inspire the creation of the United States Armored Force, although the navy had already begun to rearm (but not to expand). Prior to 1940, the American army had made a serious attempt to assess the lessons of World War One, and also devoted much attention to the military education of officers, but the failure to develop combined army doctrine affected the army in the early stages of World War Two. In preparation for independence from the USA, an army of Filipino conscripts had been created in the Philippines, but it lacked funds, equipment and adequate training, and its deficiencies were to be cruelly exposed by the Japanese when they attacked in 1941–2.[8]

New weaponry, related operational doctrines and the character of military thought in the inter-war period are generally considered in light of what was to happen in World War Two, but, before becoming too judgemental, it is also necessary to note the lack of clarity about what constituted military progress, the variety of responses, and the roles of political suppositions. Lesson-learning and doctrinal innovation sound far more clear cut and easier than was the case; so also with the evaluation of the process.[9] This can be seen with tank offensives. Enthusiasm for tanks in fact became more contained than it had been in the 1920s, and this was not foolish. By the 1930s, both Fuller and Liddell Hart had come to appreciate that tank offensives could be blunted by an effective defence, as, indeed, was to be shown in World War Two.

Such defences were to cast a shadow over the claims made for tank offensives, but that had only a limited impact on popular perceptions. More generally, there was, and is, the problem of assessing 'anti-'strategies and tactics. They tend to lack the appeal of action and apparent decisiveness seen in the offensive. Investing in the defensive can be seen as defeatist, if not anachronistic. This is underlined by the success of German offensive tactics, operations and strategy in 1939–41, and the corresponding failure of the defensive, particularly of the Maginot Line, the French fortress system constructed along the German border in 1930–5. More positively, however, a focus on defence can also be seen as a way to try to lessen the impact of the offensive, and, in this view, can be seen as prescient, or even forward-looking. The Maginot Line limited the geographical range of the likely German offensive, and was far less important in France's failure than a mistaken strategy and an inability to respond adequately to German breakthrough. Nevertheless, the Maginot Line is used as a form of shorthand for a foolish French doctrine.[10]

### Mechanisation

Aside from the likely response by the defence, mechanisation posed problems of doctrine and training, as well as of equipment procurement and maintenance, both of which were costly. Nevertheless, it appeared to have much to offer if the methods of World War One were to be supplanted. There was a search for a limited war that could be effective, as opposed to what was presented as the ineffective total conflict seen in World War One. The search for a doctrine of rapid victory through utilising the operational possibilities of the new weaponry was, at once, a desire to respond to the apparent possibilities of the weaponry and to avoid the devastation and prolonged struggle of World War One, with all the military, economic and social costs that entailed. At the level of control, the inter-war emphasis on such operations suggested that war would be entrusted to trained, regular forces, rather than to mass armies.

Inter-war mechanisation of armies led to greater focus on the combination of firepower and mobility. Changes and new doctrine made static field defences seem limited and the past form of mobility, cavalry, appear redundant. The horse was increasingly replaced by the motor vehicle. Surviving cavalry units sought to adapt. Most were mechanised. By 1939, the Polish cavalry, about 10 per cent of the Polish army, was armed with anti-tank weapons and heavy machine guns, and was trained to fight dismounted, the horses being employed in order to change position after an action, in short, for mobility, not shock action, although, again, a misleading image, that of Polish cavalry charging German tanks, is employed in order to suggest the anachronism of Polish warmaking and the inevitability, for technological reasons, of its failure.

The Polish example underlines the difficulty of deciding what lessons to draw from recent conflict, and also indicates the role of military politics in the development of doctrine and organisation. The Polish victory over Russia in 1920, not least at Komarów, the last cavalry battle in Europe, led to a mistaken confidence in the continued value of the methods used then. For this reason, but, in part, also because of a lack of financial resources and industrial productive capacity, the Poles did not match the mechanisation of the German and Soviet armies in the 1930s. General Wladyslaw Sikorski, who had been Minister of War in the 1920s, pressed the value of mechanised warfare and the tank, but he was out of favour with Marshal Josef Pilsudski, who was dictator in 1926–8 and 1930–5. Although, in the late 1930s, the Polish military came to understand the value of armour, they were too far behind their rivals.[11]

The Poles, however, were far from alone in only slowly appreciating the developing potential of land operations. The British had lost the hard-earned all-arms concepts that had clearly emerged at the end of World War One and had failed to integrate tank with infantry training. This left both vulnerable: tanks to anti-tank guns and infantry to mobile opponents. British infantry tactics were not adequate to the challenge of war with Germany. Reflecting the experience of 1918, artillery remained more important to British thinking, and, in this, they were correct.[12]

The importance of integrating different arms was amply displayed, in August 1939, in the last major clash before the outbreak of World War Two in Europe. Clashes between the Japanese Kwantung Army in Manchuria and the Soviet Union, both directly and, also, thanks to its dominance of (Outer) Mongolia, escalated from May 1939, as both sides launched major air raids. In July, Japanese forces twice invaded Mongolia. Concern that this might lead to an advance into Siberia led Stalin to appoint General Georgi Zhukov to command a counter-offensive. On 19–20 August 1939, the Soviets attacked in the battle of Khalkhin-Gol/Nomonhan, advancing into Manchuria and encircling and destroying the Japanese forces in the contested frontier area, with heavy Japanese casualties. Zhukov's success reflected numerical superiority, the availability of effective tanks and his skill in combining the different arms.[13]

This Soviet offensive did not lead to a major conflict, because the Nazi–Soviet Pact and the outbreak of war in Europe convinced both sides that they had more to gain from settling the dispute, which they did with a ceasefire that became effective on 16 September. The Japanese defeat encouraged a caution in 1941 when Hitler's attack on the Soviet Union created the possibility for an additional Japanese attack. Zhukov's plan reflected Soviet interest in the 1930s in the concept of 'deep operations'. This was more defined than German ideas of mechanised warfare, which had a more improvised character.

### Navies

In naval power, there was also a lack of clarity about the lessons of World War One, and there was controversy over the potency of different weapons systems in any future war. The respective merits of air power, from both aircraft carriers and shore-based sites, surface gunnery, and submarines were all extensively discussed, as well as their likely tactical and strategic combinations. Although some theorists argued that battleships were now obsolete in the face of air power and submarines, big surface warships had a continued appeal, and not simply for the European powers. Indeed, there was opposition to a stress on carriers becoming the key capital ships; and, in the 1930s, both the Americans and British put a major emphasis on battle fleet tactics based on battleships.[14] So also did the Japanese. Under the Marusan Programme of 1937, they began to build the *Yamato* and *Musashi*, which were to be the most powerful battleships in the world. In the USA, keels were laid for four comparable 45,000-ton battleships in 1941, and seven were projected at over 60,000 tons each. As battleships remained central to American and Japanese naval thinking, proponents of other weaponry had to explain how their recommendations, such as carriers and submarines, would effectively combine with battleships. Proponents of mass naval aviation met serious opposition from supporters of battleships in Japan in the 1930s. The Germans built large surface warships once the Versailles limitations on the German fleet were broken in 1935; while Stalin, who wanted to build up a large surface fleet, investigated the possibility of buying American battleships.

The role of battleships was enhanced by the absence of a major change in their design comparable to those in the late nineteenth century and the 1900s. With the arrival of the dreadnoughts in the 1900s, battleship architecture had reached a new period of relative stability: the USS *Texas* (BB-35) of 1914 and *Nevada* (BB-36) of 1916 participated in the D-Day bombardment in 1944. There was still great interest in battleship big guns, both for ship destruction and for shore bombardment. The vulnerability of capital ships to air and submarine attacks was appreciated, although not its extent. Air spotting for naval gunfire developed in the 1930s. In addition, certainly for the Germans and Soviets, but, also, more generally, there was an interest in large capital ships for prestige reasons. Yet this factor, like institutional conservatism, should not be used to criticise interest in battleships as anachronistic.

What is more questionable is the interest of both Germany and the Soviet Union in large capital ships, because geographical factors ensured that access to the oceans would be very difficult. Indeed, World War One had suggested that the German fleet would find it difficult to challenge the larger British fleet effectively in the North Sea. In the event, in World War Two, geographical constraints were to be altered when Germany conquered Norway and France in 1940, and thanks to the use of air attacks on warships, but the decision to invest in large surface ships can still be seen as a mistake. They brought scant strategic benefit in the war, although they were operationally important to the conquest of Norway. The lesson of 1870 – that Germany could defeat France even though the French navy was stronger – was to be repeated in 1940, while in World War Two, as in World War One, it was to be submarines that offered Germany the strongest strategic card at sea.

As with other weapons systems which did not remain static, there were considerable efforts to strengthen battleships in order to increase their resistance to air attack. Armour was strengthened, outer hulls added to protect against torpedo attack, and anti-aircraft guns and tactics developed.

## *Carrier warfare*

Naval air power altered more radically than battleships in the interwar period. In the 1920s, the difficulties of operating aeroplanes in bad weather and the dark, their limited load capacity and range, and their mechanical unreliability all remained serious constraints, but improvements were made, particularly in the 1930s. Developments in aircraft and carrier aviation, such as arrester hooks for landings, helped ensure that carriers, rather than seaplanes or airships, were seen as the way to apply air power at sea, and made it easier to envisage using carriers as the basis for operational and strategic tasks. Aside from developments in aircraft carriers, there were also marked improvements in naval aircraft. In the 1920s, water-cooled aircraft engines were replaced by the lighter and more reliable air-cooled engine. The manoeuvrability, speed and range of carrier aircraft all improved. In 1927, Japanese Naval War College war games included a carrier attack on Pearl Harbor, the forward base of the American Pacific Fleet. The Americans and Japanese made major advances with naval aviation and aircraft carriers. The Japanese completed an experimental carrier in 1922, and had six carriers by 1940.

Britain, Japan and the USA were the only combatants to operate fleet carriers during World War Two. Germany, Italy and the Soviet Union did not build aircraft carriers in the inter-war period, and France had only one, a converted dreadnought-type battleship. The

German Plan Z of 1938, approved by Hitler in January 1939, included the building of eight carriers (four by 1948), but work on completing the only one that was launched ceased in 1943. Germany thus lacked the added range that such carriers offered, while Mussolini preferred to rely on Italy as a natural aircraft carrier in the Mediterranean and refused to let the navy have its own air arm. German or Soviet carriers would have offered easy targets for attack as they made their way through the restricted waters of the North Sea and Baltic. The main sphere of German air attack on shipping, the Mediterranean in 1941–2, was vulnerable to attack by surface bases and the Germans were reliant on the alliance with Italy for these. In addition, the Germans did not have a tradition of naval aviation.

Nevertheless, the lack of emphasis on carriers also reflected the politics of force structures. Hermann Göring, head of the *Luftwaffe*, stopped the navy from having its own air arm and had scant interest in army–navy co-operation. In contrast, Britain's carrier construction gave an important added dimension to her naval superiority over other European powers. These carriers were to help extend the range of British naval activity, particularly in the Mediterranean, but, also, for example, in supporting the invasion of Madagascar in 1942 and more generally, in operations in the Indian Ocean.

Whereas, however, naval air power in Britain lacked a separate institutional framework, because embarked aircraft and their necessary shore support were placed under the RAF between 1918 and 1937, and the RAF was primarily concerned with land-based aeroplanes and had little time for their naval counterparts, in the USA there was a very different situation thanks to the Bureau of Aeronautics of the American navy. This stimulated the development of effective air–sea doctrine, operational policies and tactics. The Americans benefited from the development of dive-bombing tactics in the 1920s and, subsequently, of dive-bombers. These proved more effective than aircraft launching torpedoes, although they were also vulnerable to anti-aircraft fire and to fighter planes escorting shipping. The stand-off guided-weapons technology of the close of the century, that was to enable planes to fire rockets and bombs from a considerable distance, had not yet been developed. As a result, naval air attacks were risky operations that tended to lead to high loss rates.

The development of specialised planes for carriers was pushed by Japan and the USA. The Japanese Zero had a great range, which brought important tactical and operational advantages, but, from 1942, in the Corsair, and 1943, in the Hellcat, the Americans had good carrier fighters. The Japanese also had effective torpedoes.[15]

## Submarines

The use of submarines also excited considerable interest among naval planners in the inter-war period, and there were major developments in the range of torpedoes. The size, speed and range of submarines all improved. The American S class of 1918–21, with a range of 5,000–8,000 miles at a surface speed of 10 knots, was replaced by the B class (12,000 miles at 11 knots). They were followed by the P boats of 1933–6, the first American submarines with a totally diesel-electric propulsion, and then by the *Gatos*, introduced in 1940: double-hulled, all-welded-hull submarines with a range of 11,800 miles and a surface speed of 20–5 knots. By the time of the Japanese attack on Pearl Harbor in 1941, the American navy had 111 submarines in commission, while the Japanese had sixty-three ocean-going submarines. The Japanese Type 1 submarines had a range of 24,400 nautical miles at 10 knots and carried supplies for sixty days. In the event of war with the USA, the Japanese planned to use their submarines to hit American warships advancing into the western Pacific. They intended to use long-range submarines with a surface speed of 24 knots, which would be able to act as a major preliminary component in fleet action. In the event, their submarines failed to fulfil expectations, which was unsurprising as exercises in 1939 and 1940 had indicated important deficiencies.[16]

Partly due to Hitler's interest in battleships, Germany only had fifty-seven submarines at the outset of World War Two. The USSR had the largest submarine fleet, and Italy the second largest; neither was to make much of an impact. Indeed the Soviet fleet, most of which was based in the Baltic and Black Seas, played little role in the war. Much of it was destroyed in the German advance, particularly as a result of air attack. The major naval base in the Black Sea, Sevastopol, was captured by the Germans in 1942, while the Baltic fleet was greatly affected by the German and Finnish advance on

Leningrad. The Soviets had not built up a major Pacific fleet. There were also serious operational limitations with the Soviet navy.

## Naval planning

Aside from shifts in weaponry, the possible geostrategic character of any future major conflict ensured there would be different requirements to those in World War One: as ever, issues of capability have to be considered alongside tasking. In addition to the focus in the earlier conflict on fleet engagements in the confined waters off north-west Europe and submarine warfare in the North Atlantic, it would be necessary to plan for the vast expanses of the Pacific, in which World War One operations had been far ranging but on a relatively trivial scale. Whereas the Japanese had had experience of land and sea operations in East Asia and adjoining waters, their role in seizing German overseas territories in World War One had not prepared them for conflict with the USA. The Japanese were to cite the example of their total defeat of a Russian fleet at Tsushima in 1905 as a precedent for war with the USA, but it was misleading: the Russians had not had the capacity to produce rapidly a fresh fleet, while the Americans were able to do so. Thus a 'decisive' battle could at best be only a short-term victory for the Japanese.

American and British concern about Japan mounted in the 1920s and, even more, in the 1930s, with Japanese expansionism at the expense of China, as well as an increase in the size of its navy. This affected Britain and the USA, powers with both Atlantic and Pacific commitments. In response, Britain developed Singapore as a base. In the event of war with Japan, the bulk of the British fleet was to be sent there.

The Americans had a strong commitment to the independence of China and also a major territorial presence in the western Pacific: the Philippines, Guam and Samoa. This led to planning for war with Japan, planning that was a bridge from the naval thought of the pre-1914 Mahanian period to the strategy pursued in World War Two. Plan Orange of 1924 called for the 'through ticket': a rapid advance directly from Hawaii to Manila, the capital of the Philippines, a decisive battle, and then starving Japan by blockade. The naval base at Pearl Harbor on the Hawaiian island of Oahu was greatly developed.

This plan was succeeded in the mid-1930s by greater interest in a slower process of victory that would entail seizing the Japanese islands in the Pacific – the Marshalls, Carolines and Marianas – which they had gained in the World War One treaty settlement. Seizing these would provide the Americans with forward bases, and deny them to the Japanese. Without control of this area, it was argued, a naval advance to the Philippines would be unsuccessful. The development of naval weaponry had led to this more cautious approach, not least the problems posed by a lack of long-range scouting planes capable of finding carriers that might, otherwise, wreck a superior fleet.[17]

After World War One, there had been an attempt to control the size and type of fleets and to fix ratios of capital ship tonnage, as an important aspect of the drive for force limitation in that period. The Washington Naval Treaty of 1922 and the London Naval Treaty of 1930 created a negotiated regime that, however, could not be sustained in the face of growing international competition. In 1935, in the Second London Naval Conference, Japan demanded higher naval ratios than she had gained in 1922. The American rejection of Japanese naval superiority in the Pacific led to the collapse of the conference, the unilateral Japanese disavowal of existing limits, and the launching of the Marusan Programme of shipbuilding, which was designed to achieve superiority over the British and American fleets.[18]

In the *Zengen Sakusen* (Great All-Out Battle Strategy), the Japanese focused on the successive use of submarines, long-range shore-based bombers, carrier-based dive-bombers, and destroyer night-time torpedo attacks against the advancing American fleet, leading up to engagement by the Japanese battleships. This policy encouraged battleship construction, as well as a policy of seizing Pacific islands in the event of war, so as to provide airbases. The assumption that there would be a major battle in the western Pacific led to a pattern of ship design that put the emphasis on fighting characteristics, especially speed and armament (guns and torpedoes), rather than range. This affected their ability to operate in the actual conditions of World War Two. By then Japanese planning had altered. In place of separating vulnerable carriers, there was a conviction of the value of massed air power at sea, and thus of a carrier group, while, from early 1940, the Japanese were carrying out exercises involving torpedo-planes against warships. The Japanese created an independent carrier force on 1 April 1941.

As in land warfare capability, the achievements of the Axis powers at sea were less than their ambitions and rhetoric might suggest; and this was to prove an important, though not determinant, factor in the forthcoming conflict. By 1940, the Japanese fleet was only 7:10 relative to the American, while the Japanese had failed to fulfil their plans for airfield construction on the islands they already controlled. However, the Americans were outnumbered in the Pacific. The Vinson–Trammel Act of March 1934, followed by the 'Second Vinson Act' of May 1938, had set out to rearm the American navy and to remedy an earlier situation in which there had been a failure to construct even what was allowed by the Naval Conferences.

Even so, the situation did not really alter until after 19 July 1940, when Congress passed the Two-Ocean Naval Expansion Act, which was designed to produce a fleet that would enable the Americans to wage naval war against both Germany and Japan. It provided for the building of a truly massive additional complement: 18 fleet carriers, 11 battleships, 6 battle cruisers, 27 cruisers, 115 destroyers and 43 submarines. Most of these ships, however, were not due for completion until 1946–8.

Confidence in American naval strength, as well as a concern to help prevent the collapse of Britain, led, in 1940–1, to growing naval assertiveness that included the handing over to Britain of fifty old destroyers in return for the use of strategic British naval bases, as well as a role in escorting convoys against German submarine attack in the western Atlantic. The movement of the American Pacific Fleet from San Diego to Pearl Harbor in 1940 was a deterrent gesture stemming from fear of Japanese adventurism but one, instead, that provoked it.

The development of the German and Italian navies in the 1930s suggested that both powers would contest European waters. The British were aware that any war would bring the threat of both air and submarine attacks on their communications. The February 1934 report of the Defence Requirements Sub-Committee of the Committee of Imperial Defence noted of the navy: 'The greatest potential threat lies in the acquisition of submarines and aircraft by

Germany.'[19] They were prepared for a far more varied conflict than would result from a German battle fleet offensive alone. Concern about the possibility of Italian naval attacks in the Mediterranean was a factor in British planning at the time of the Ethiopian crisis of 1936.

### Air warfare

Air power threatened to change, if not transform, conflict on land, and indeed war in general. The role of air power in World War One had led to a major interest in developing its potential, which accorded with a more general fascination with the transforming character of flight.[20] Air power was seen as a war-winning tool, and also as the best way to avoid the drawn-out attritional character of conflict on the ground. Advocates such as the Italian Guilio Douhet, in his *Il Dominio dell' Aria* (1921), and the American William Mitchell, in *Skyways* (1930), claimed that air power could deliver effective total war. Nakajima Chikuhei made similar claims in Japan.

Pressing for air forces to be independent, rather than under army or naval command, Douhet argued that they should attack enemy communications, economies and populations rather than fighting forces. Claiming that wrecking enemy morale would create a demand for peace, Douhet pressed for the use of gas and incendiary bombs against leading population centres. A firm advocate of strategic bombing as the best way to harm an opponent's ability to wage war, Mitchell also pressed for an independent air force.[21]

It was anticipated that civilian targets would play a major role in future conflict. The impact on public morale of German raids on London in World War One seemed an augury. Fuller predicted that fresh raids in another conflict would lead to popular demands for surrender. The threat from bombing was emphasised in *Flying* (1933) by Major-General James E. Fechet, former head of the American Air Corps, and *War from the Air: Past–Present–Future* (1935), *War over England* (1936) and *The Menace of the Clouds* (1937) by Air Commodore L.E.O. Charlton. In response, air defence became a major issue with its own doctrine, technology and organisation.

The emphasis on strategic bombing influenced some, but not all, air forces. British airmen argued that bombers would be able to destroy opposing economies and, more particularly, that large bombers would be able to fight off fighter attack and thus not require fighter escorts.[22] As a result, the Royal Air Force (RAF) had twice as many bombers as fighters for most of the inter-war period. These bombers were seen not only as likely to be effective in war, but also as a deterrent against attack. Priorities were not changed until 1937. The American Air Corps Tactical School developed a policy of high-flying daylight precision bombing designed to damage an opponent's industrial system. This later greatly influenced American policy in World War Two, but, in practice, precision was to be difficult to achieve,[23] and it also took a very long time to work out what were the key targets to hit in a modern industrial war machine.

Meanwhile, seeking a strategic bombing force that could act as a deterrent and also as a strategic threat, Germany had initially led in the development of the four-engine bomber: the 'Ural' or 'Amerika' bomber. However, only prototypes were built. The capability to produce the engines necessary for the planned heavy bombers was lacking. In 1937, the four-engined bomber programme was abandoned. In 1939, Britain and America were the only countries with bombers in production suitable for strategic bombing.

Strategic air power had captured the imagination of many, sowing fears that the bombing of civilian targets would be decisive in a future war. This affected British thinking at the time of the Munich crisis in 1938. In practice, as World War Two was to show, Douhet had exaggerated the potential of bombing (as well as underestimating the size of bomber forces required to give effect to his plans), and underplayed the value of tactical air support. In addition, the concentration on air defence affected the allocation of scarce resources.

The inter-war use of air power had already suggested that it might be less effective than its protagonists claimed, but the conflicts of the 1920s and 1930s, for example the use of aircraft against insurgents in Morocco and Iraq, offered only limited guidance because they did not happen between equally balanced air forces, while rapid technological developments soon made equipment outdated. The conflicts were also inadequately analysed. The spectacular terror bombing of civilian targets in the Spanish Civil War, particularly Madrid (1936), Guernica (1937) and Barcelona (1938), by German and Italian planes sent to help Franco's Nationalists, did not actually play a significant role in the result of the conflict. The war, nevertheless, suggested to the Germans that large long-range bombers were not necessary in order to have an impact, but in Britain the ability to learn lessons from the war about air support was limited by inter-service rivalry and the nature of air-force culture. In particular, there was, in Britain and elsewhere, resistance to the possibilities of ground-support operations on the part of those committed to strategic bombing. Lessons were also not drawn from the Sino-Japanese War. The battle of Shanghai in 1937 showed that Chinese losses made during the day could be regained at night, when Japanese air power was impotent.

Leadership decisions, service culture and politico-military tasking determined doctrine and force structure. After Hitler came to power, there was a major emphasis in Germany on the *Luftwaffe* (air force), which absorbed about 40 per cent of the defence budget in 1933–6. However, Hermann Göring, Air Minister and Commander-in-Chief of the *Luftwaffe*, as well as a prominent Nazi, was not interested in the less glamorous side of air power, such as infrastructure, and was less than careful in his appointments. Ernst Udet, whom he made Technical Director, was overly interested in dive-bombing. Göring's concern for the prestige of high plane numbers encouraged an emphasis on twin-engined bombers, not longer-range four-engined aircraft. Furthermore, the search for a force structure that would make what was termed by a journalist *Blitzkrieg* (lightning war) a success, a search made necessary by Hitler's preference for quick wars, led to a lack of support for strategic bombing, which was seen, instead, as a long-term solution. There was no coherent doctrine underlying *Blitzkrieg*, but it entailed no obvious requirement for a strategic bombing force, and no doctrine of strategic air power was developed by the Germans, although, for the long-term, Göring sought such a force.

More generally, the German air industry did not develop sufficiently to support an air force for a major conflict. There were problems with the availability of aviation fuel for the air force, and also a preference for numbers of planes as opposed to a balanced expenditure that would include investment in infrastructure, for example logistical provision, especially spares.[24]

In France and the Soviet Union, the stress was on tactical doctrine and force structure, rather than strategic bombing. Both Britain and France devoted attention to fighter defence in the late 1930s, seeing this as a necessary response to German power. They were able to take advantage of the marked improvement in the flying standards and combat characteristics of planes in the inter-war period, an improvement that reflected the general advance in aviation. This was particularly so for fighters in the mid- and late 1930s, as wooden-based biplanes were replaced by all-metal cantilever-wing monoplanes with high-performance engines capable of far greater speeds, for example the American P36 Hawk, German Messerschmitt 109 and Soviet I16 Rata. The range and armament of fighters and the range, payload and armament of bombers all increased.[25]

Improvements in fighters began to undermine the doctrine of the paramountcy of the bomber. The introduction of radar on the eve of the war was another blow to the latter. The British developed two effective and nimble monoplane fighters, the Hawker Hurricane and Supermarine Spitfire, and, alongside early warning radar, they were to help rescue Britain, in 1940, from the consequences of devoting too much attention to bombing.[26] However, the British still had to overcome the poor tactics based on a tight vic (V-formation) of three planes. In contrast, the Germans had developed a more flexible two-aircraft *Rotte* formation.

Another important inter-war development, which stemmed from the increasing size of planes, was greater interest in the use of airborne troops. A number of powers, especially Germany and the Soviet Union, trained parachute and glider-borne units. There were also developments in air transport: in 1935, the Soviets moved a 14,000-strong rifle division by air from near Moscow to the Far East, while, in 1937–8, they practised dropping artillery and tanks by parachute. In the event, the greatest use of such troops was to be by Germany in 1940–1 and by Britain and the USA in 1944. As yet, the nature of technology did not permit the greater flexibility that was to be offered from the 1950s by helicopters.

The potential of air power also led to a growing interest in jet aircraft, rocketry and space flight, especially in Germany and the Soviet Union. The Soviet Katyusha multiple rocket launcher was one result. Known as 'Stalin's Organ', the rockets were fired in volleys, with the launchers moved on trucks. They were therefore a particularly mobile weapon.

In 1930, Frank Whittle, an RAF officer, patented the principles that led to the first gas-turbine jet engine, which he first ran under control in 1937. His innovation was rapidly copied, and the Germans, in 1939, and the Italians, a year later, beat the British jet into the air. The jet fighter, however, arrived in service too late to affect the course of the war. In 1944, the British brought Meteors and the Germans Me262 into service, and the Allies found that the speed of the latter (540 mph) made it difficult to tackle, but the Germans had insufficient numbers, and the plane also had problems, both with the engines and with an inadequate rate of turn.

World War Two was to see an extensive use of air power. It was possible to manufacture, supply and man large numbers of aircraft without the high cost that advanced electronics and other factors were to lead to by the 1980s. Thus the characteristics of planes were particularly opportune during World War Two. The major improvements made in aircraft and associated technology during the 1930s ensured that they were far more useful than during World War One, but, as yet, their specifications had not improved to a degree that was to inhibit their use. A similar point could be made about naval air power and also about airfields.

## Conclusions

War planning prior to World War Two responded to shifts in doctrine, force structure and weaponry, but was primarily set by the strategic transformations resulting from changes in political goals and alliances.[27] Both were to be of major importance in 1939–41, and to underline the unpredictability of developments. In 1939, Hitler initially fought alone. His eventual ally in the Polish campaign, although not in war with Britain and France, was the Soviet Union, not his Axis allies, Italy and Japan. Allied (i.e. anti-Axis) concern about Soviet policy was to lead to planning in the winter of 1939–40 for intervention to help the Finns against the Soviets, as well as a French scheme for the bombing of the Soviet oil wells at Baku. Thus planning had to be devised to cope with unexpected and rapidly changing contingencies. It also had to cope with the need to give effect to plans in a rapidly changing military environment in which opposing capability was far from clear or fixed. There were also the problems of achieving combined arms effectiveness, more specifically co-operation between armour and infantry, as well as between ground forces and air power, and, in some spheres, the added factor of naval commitments, possibilities and strength. These difficulties should be remembered before resorting to the all-too-easy course of blaming the defeated for the choices they made.

## NOTES

1 B.A. Shillony, *Revolt in Japan: The Young Officers and the February 26, 1936 Incident* (Princeton, 1973); L. Young, *Japan's Total Empire: Manchuria and the Culture of Western Imperialism* (Berkeley, 1998).

2 G.L. Weinberg, *The Foreign Policy of Hitler's Germany, 1937–39* (Chicago, 1980); W. Murray, *The Change in the European Balance of Power, 1938–1939: The Path to Ruin* (Princeton, 1984); D.C. Watt, *How War Came* (1989); R.A.C. Parker, *Chamberlain and Appeasement: British Policy and the Coming of the Second World War* (London, 1993); P.M.H. Bell, *The Origins of the Second World War in Europe* (2nd edn, Harlow, 1997); P.W. Doerr, *British Foreign Policy, 1919–1939* (Manchester, 1998); I. Lukes and E. Goldstein (eds), *The Munich Crisis, 1938: Prelude to World War II* (London, 1999).

3 D. Omissi, *Air Power and Colonial Control: The Royal Air Force 1919–1939* (Manchester, 1990); N. Shepherd, *Ploughing Sand: British Rule in Palestine, 1917–1948* (Piscataway, New Jersey, 2000); H. Schmidt, *The United States Occupation of Haiti, 1915–1934* (New Brunswick, New Jersey, 1971).

4 J.P. Harris, *Men, Ideas and Tanks: British Military Thought and Armoured Forces, 1903–1939* (Manchester, 1995); A. Danchev, *Alchemist of War: The Life of Basil Liddell Hart* (London, 1998); A. Gat, *British Armour Theory and the Rise of the Panzer Arm: Revisiting the Revisionists* (London, 2000).

5 J.S. Corum, *The Roots of Blitzkrieg: Hans von Seeckt and German Military Reform* (Lawrence, 1992); R.M. Citino, *The Path to Blitzkrieg: Doctrine and Training in the German Army, 1920–1939* (Boulder, 1999).

6 R. Simpkin, *Deep Battle: The Brainchild of Marshal Tukhachevskii* (London, 1987); S.W. Stoecker, *Forging Stalin's Army: Marshal Tukhachevsky and the Politics of Military Innovation* (Boulder, 1998).

7 M. Alpert, 'The Clash of Spanish Armies: Contrasting Ways of War in Spain, 1936–1939', *War in History*, 6 (1999), pp. 331–51; J. Corum, 'The Spanish Civil War: Lessons Learned and Not Learned by the Great Powers', *Journal of Military History*, 62 (1998), pp. 313–34.

8   D.E. Johnson, *Fast Tanks and Heavy Bombers: Innovation in the US Army, 1917–1945* (Ithaca, 1998); W.O. Odom, *After the Trenches: The Transformation of US Army Doctrine, 1918–1939* (College Station, 1999); B.M. Linn, *Guardians of Empire: The US Army and the Pacific, 1902–1940* (Chapel Hill, 1997).

9   A.R. Millett and W. Murray (eds), *Military Effectiveness II. The Interwar Period* (Cambridge, 1988); H.R. Winton and D.R. Mets (eds), *The Challenge of Change: Military Institutions and New Realities, 1918–1941* (Lincoln, 2000).

10  A. Kemp, *The Maginot Line: Myth and Reality* (1981); R.A. Doughty, *The Seeds of Disaster: The Development of French Army Doctrine, 1919–1939* (Hamden, 1985); M.S. Alexander, *The Republic in Danger: General Maurice Gamelin and the Politics of French Defence, 1933–1940* (Cambridge, 1992).

11  A. Suchcitz, 'Poland's Defence Preparations in 1939', and P.D. Stachura, 'The Battle of Warsaw, August 1920, and the Development of the Second Polish Republic', in P.D. Stachura (ed.), *Poland Between the Wars 1918–1939* (Basingstoke, 1998), pp. 109–10, 54–5.

12  B. Bond, *British Military Policy Between the Two World Wars* (Oxford, 1980).

13  A. Sella, 'Khalkhin-Gol: The Forgotten War', *Journal of Contemporary History*, 18 (1983), pp. 658–67; A. Coox, *Nomonhan: Japan against Russia 1939* (Stanford, 1985).

14  J. Sumida, ' "The Best Laid Plans": the Development of British Battle-Fleet Tactics, 1919–1942', *International History Review*, 14 (1992), pp. 682–700.

15  C.G. Reynolds, *The Fast Carriers: The Forging of an Air Navy* (New York, 1968); G. Till, *Air Power and the Royal Navy, 1914–1945* (London, 1989); T. Wildenberg, *Destined for Glory: Dive Bombing, Midway, and the Evolution of Carrier Airpower* (Annapolis, 1998); T.C. Hone, N. Friedman and M.D. Mandeles, *American and British Aircraft Carrier Development, 1919–1941* (Annapolis, 1999).

16  N. Polmar and D. Carpenter, *Submarines of the Imperial Japanese Navy 1904–1945* (1986).

17  E.S. Miller, *War Plan Orange: The US Strategy to Defeat Japan, 1897–1945* (Annapolis, 1991), p. 175.

18  S.E. Pelz, *Race to Pearl Harbor: The Failure of the Second London Naval Conference and the Onset of World War II* (Cambridge, Massachusetts, 1974); E. Goldstein and J.H. Maurer, *The Washington Naval Conference: Naval Rivalry, East Asian Stability, and the Road to Pearl Harbor* (Ilford, 1994).

19  PRO. CAB. 16/109 fol. 9.

20  P. Fritzsche, 'Machine Dreams: Airmindedness and the Reinvention of Germany', *American Historical Review*, 98 (1993), pp. 685–709.

21  C. Segrè, 'Giulio Douhet: Strategist, Theorist, Prophet?', *Journal of Strategic Studies*, 15 (1992), pp. 69–80; A.F. Hurley, *Billy Mitchell: Crusader for Air Power* (New York, 1964); J.J. Cooke, *Billy Mitchell* (Boulder, Colorado, 2002).

22 M. Smith, ' "A Matter of Faith": British Strategic Air Doctrine Between the Wars', *Journal of Contemporary History*, 15 (1980), pp. 423–42.

23 S.L. McFarland, *America's Pursuit of Precision Bombing 1910–1945* (Washington, 1995).

24 E.L. Homze, *Arming the Luftwaffe: The Reich Air Ministry and the German Aircraft Industry 1919–39* (Lincoln, 1976); J. Corum, *The Luftwaffe: Creating the Operational Air War, 1918–1940* (Lawrence, 1997).

25 J. Buckley, *Air Power in the Age of Total War* (London, 1999), pp. 109–10.

26 S. Ritchie, *Industry and Air Power: The Expansion of British Aircraft Production, 1939–1941* (London, 1997).

27 C.M. Bell, *The Royal Navy, Seapower, and Strategy Between the Wars* (Stanford, 2000).

# CHAPTER TWO

# *Initial attacks*

### War in China

The first major series of attacks was launched not by Germany, but by Japan. On 18 September 1931, Japanese soldiers blew up part of the South Manchurian railway near Shenyang (Mukden). This incident served as the basis for an advance north and west from the established Japanese sphere of influence in southern Manchuria, moving forward along the railways and seizing major positions. Manchuria fell in a five-month campaign. Japanese expansion was helped by the fact that Manchuria was ruled not by the Kuomintang (the Chinese Nationalist government) but by an autonomous warlord, Chang Hsueh-liang. Furthermore, the centre of Kuomintang power was Nanjing, in central southern China, not the ancient capital of Beijing, which was close to Manchuria. There, the Japanese proved able not only to defeat conventional forces, but also to check large guerrilla forces from 1931. The Japanese renamed Manchuria Manchukuo and, in 1934, made Pui Yi Hsüan-t'ung, the last Manchu Emperor, the puppet emperor of the state.

Having seized Manchukuo, the Japanese army developed it as a military and industrial base effectively outside civilian control, and with the build-up of coal- and iron-based heavy industry which served as the basis for a powerful military-industrial complex. This was used to support expansionism in China and to strengthen Japan in the event of war with the Soviet Union, a possibility greatly feared (and anticipated) in Japanese army circles. The Japanese had intervened in the Soviet Far East during the Russian Civil War that had followed the Communist seizure of power in 1917.

The willingness of the Soviet Union, hitherto the dominant power in north Manchuria, where it had intervened in force in 1929, to cede its interests before the Japanese advance was also important to the consolidation of the Japanese position in Manchuria. In 1935, the Soviets withdrew to the frontier on the Amur River, although relations remained tense. In 1938 and 1939, the Soviets were willing to clash with Japan on Manchuria's frontiers: at Changkufen (August 1938) and Nomonhan Bridge (May 1939). In the first, the Japanese suffered from poor coordination between armour, infantry and artillery,[1] and, in the second, the Japanese were seriously beaten. This increased their army's concern about Soviet intentions.

In 1937, when full-scale war broke out with China, the Japanese initially captured Beijing and Tientsin, but the war then broadened out, not least because the navy's attempt to seize Shanghai in August was firmly resisted and the army intervened in strength to provide assistance. Bitter fighting led to the destruction of the best Nationalist units and to the fall of Shanghai on 11 November. The Japanese then advanced on Nanjing, which fell on 13 December after a heavy air attack. They also overran the northern provinces of Hopei, Shansi and Inner Mongolia, defeating badly-led but numerous opposing forces.

The ports of Amoy, Swastow and Canton, as well as the Yellow River valley, and Wuhan and other cities on the middle Yangtze, followed in 1938, and the island of Hainan in February 1939. The 1938 campaign had joined the Japanese positions in northern and central China, as well as gaining important commercial positions, although it had not proved possible to encircle and destroy the principal Chinese forces. The 1939 campaign added important coastal positions as part of an attempt to separate China from foreign links. It reflected Japanese amphibious capability, which had earlier been seen in Shanghai. Japanese-ruled Formosa (Taiwan) proved a useful local base for operations against the Chinese coast. In addition, from Hainan, the Japanese could threaten French Indo-China.

The Japanese were helped by the extent to which many Chinese did not fight. Some Chinese warlords were unwilling to risk their troops. On a number of occasions, German advisers prepared defensive positions only to find that their Chinese defenders fled when the Japanese approached. More generally, there was a lack of cohesion in the Chinese response that reflected the local ties of warlords and most troops.

Little information is available on Japanese operations, specifically on policymaking as opposed to what happened on the ground. In operational terms, the Japanese showed that it was not necessary to introduce mass mechanisation in order to conquer large tracts of territory. Lacking raw materials and industrial capability, Japan was technologically behind the European powers in various aspects of military innovation, such as the use of tanks and motorised transport. This led to a greater stress on 'spirit' over material, for example with an emphasis on the use of bayonets and swords in attack.

'Spirit', however, did not suffice in China, not least because, ironically, the Japanese underrated the extent of nationalist determination in China. Despite expanding their army from 408,000 troops in 1937 to 2.08 million in 1941, and stationing over 1.5 million of these troops in China and Manchuria (the latter in large part to deter Soviet attack, but also to counter continued guerrilla activity), the Japanese lacked the manpower to seize all of China. In addition, resistance continued. The Chinese military had been badly affected by successive defeats, losing well-trained units and equipment; and most of what was left was indifferently trained and led badly, and, also, lacked equipment, especially adequate artillery, let alone motorised transport and air support. Nevertheless, Japanese drives on Changsa in the summers of 1939 and 1940 and in January 1942 failed, and it was not captured until a renewed drive in 1944. Railway junctions played a particularly important role in campaigning due to the lack of motor transport. The Japanese were affected by the problems of transporting sufficient food as Chinese forces cleared the countryside of supplies.

Furthermore, what she did seize had cost Japan a great deal in resources, particularly raw materials. Even within occupied areas, Japanese control outside the cities was limited and episodic. Japanese military leaders were surprised, and frustrated, by their failure to impose victory. It proved far easier to destroy the Chinese navy in 1937 and to deploy overwhelming force against cities, the nodes of the transportation system, than it was to fight in rural areas. There, the ratio of strength and space told against the Japanese, particularly when their opponents, most notably the Communists, employed guerrilla tactics, moved into the rural areas of northern China and hit Japanese communications. In addition, the movement of Japanese troops from Manchuria into China in 1937 led to a revival in partisan operations in Manchuria. In the Hundred Regiments Offensive in north China in August–December 1940, the Communists hit Japanese communications hard. This challenged the Japanese 'point-and-line' pattern of occupation.

The Japanese also failed to win over sufficient Chinese support. The Japanese had added to Manchukuo in 1933 and 1935, and also established the 'Provisional government of the Republic of China' in north China in 1937, and 'the Reformed government of the Republic of China', based at Nanjing, in 1938. These states organised puppet forces, but the Japanese found them of limited value and treated them with suspicion.[2]

Japanese conquests in China indicated a lesson that Hitler would have done well to consider before attacking the Soviet Union in 1941: that high-visibility gains did not necessarily lead to overall victory. Ishiwara Kanji, chief of the Operations Division of the General Staff, had warned that an invasion of China would lead to an intractable commitment, with victory unobtainable and withdrawal impossible, but more aggressive views had prevailed. He was transferred from the General Staff in September 1937, and the attempt he encouraged to secure foreign mediation was abandoned in January 1938 when the Japanese ministry announced that the Kuomintang government was not an acceptable participant in peace talks. This was a sign that they intended to create their own puppet government in China, although, throughout, there was a lack of clarity about Japanese goals. The lack of agreement and clarity helped to thwart both the peace initiatives towards the Kuomintang in late 1937 and the summer of 1940, as well as the attempt to benefit from the defection, in December 1938, of Wang Ching-wei, a rival of the Kuomintang's leader Chiang Kai-shek. After difficult negotiations, he eventually became the President of the Nanjing-based 'Reformed government', but the Japanese could not decide how much power to allow him, and this discredited his government.[3]

Japanese campaigns in China also showed that brutality did not work, a lesson that their racialism prevented both Japan and Germany from learning. The massacre by Japanese troops of large numbers of civilians (the approximate number is controversial) after the capture of Nanjing on 13 December 1937, including using people for bayonet practice, as well as mass rapes, the culmination of barbarous Japanese conduct during their advance up the Yangtze, did not break Chinese morale. Instead, it testified to an emerging immoral and callous attitude within the Japanese military.[4] This was further seen in the 'kill all, loot all, burn all' campaign launched in response to the Hundred Regiments Offensive in China in 1941, a campaign whose methods strengthened Chinese resistance and made a compromise peace less likely.

The Japanese were helped by rivalry between the other two major forces in China, who, between them, ruled most of the half of the Chinese population who remained outside Japanese control: the Kuomintang and the Communists, a rivalry that led to regional conflicts, as in 1940. This rivalry enabled the Japanese to maintain what were in effect local truces with both, although these were not formalised, and were challenged by both guerrilla operations and the harsh Japanese response. There was to be no major change in China until after the USA entered the war at the close of 1941. American policymakers saw China as a base from which Japan could be attacked: it was closer to unoccupied China than to American bases in the Pacific. The Americans attempted to develop airbases in Kuomintang-controlled China and to build up the Kuomintang army as an offensive force. This policy, in turn, led to Japanese offensives in 1942 and 1944.[5]

## The conquest of Poland

In Europe, World War Two began in 1939 with a dramatic example of military effectiveness. The Germans lost fewer than 15,000 dead in a *Blitzkrieg* that led to the rapid defeat of Poland, a state with armed forces totalling over 1 million men, although all bar 370,000 were reservists. The Germans greatly outnumbered the Poles in aeroplanes, tanks and other mechanised vehicles, enjoyed the initiative, and benefited from the long and vulnerable nature of the Polish frontier and the dispersed position of the Polish army, most of which was infantry. The Polish air force was rapidly destroyed, a crucial step in the German offensive. The Germans benefited from launching surprise attacks that destroyed some of the Polish planes on the ground, although the extent of these losses has been exaggerated and many Polish planes were lost in aerial combat. The rapid opening by the Germans of improvised airfields behind their advancing forces countered the short range of their aircraft and helped the *Luftwaffe* provide close air support.

In a rapid German ground offensive that began on 1 September, and reflected the political pressure for a speedy victory and the need to win before the British and French could attack on the Western Front, the cohesion of the Polish army was destroyed: German armoured forces broke through, isolated and enveloped their dispersed military formations. In order to signal their determination not to match the fate of the Czech Republic in 1938, the Poles had defended the full extent of their borders, rather than concentrating in the heart of Poland to provide defence in depth and respond to German thrusts separately. Their deployment helped the German penetration and encirclement strategy. The German armour was also helped by the flat terrain of most of Poland, as well as by the dryness of the soil and the roads following the summer. In addition, the Polish army was weak in tanks and in anti-tank guns and training.

By forcing the Poles into a one-sided war of manoeuvre, the Germans put them at a tremendous disadvantage, and Polish positions were successively encircled. Inner and outer pincers created by German columns closed, isolating Polish armies, and making it difficult for them to maintain supplies or launch counterattacks. Confidence in the latter enabled the German armour to advance ahead of the marching infantry and with exposed flanks. This, however, was a risky technique, especially when the Poles were able to counteract the disorganisation and fear that came from German attack, and the Germans also faced problems with supplies, particularly the supply of fuel. Nevertheless, they were able to cope with the problems that occurred and to regain momentum. Rivers were crossed and major Polish cities rapidly fell. Brest-Litovsk (though not its citadel) to the east of Warsaw fell on 14 September.

Despite brave resistance, including a temporarily successful coun-terattack on the Bzura River on 9–12 September (to which the Germans rapidly responded), the German victory was total and rapid. The Bzura counterattack was quashed by German tank rein-forcements. However, as an important indication of the limitations of armour, a tank advance into Warsaw on 9 September was stopped in street fighting by Polish anti-tank guns and artillery. This contributed to the heavy losses of German tanks (in part through wear and tear) in the campaign.

A successful, although poorly executed, Soviet invasion of eastern Poland from 17 September, in co-operation with the Germans, and, along the entire length of the frontier, against limited resistance from the few Polish forces in the region, had helped complete the picture of Polish vulnerability. The Soviets captured Lvov on 22 September: the Germans had earlier failed to encircle it in time. The Soviet inva-sion removed strategic depth from the Polish defence and, in particular, the opportunity of weakening German pressure by dispersing their troops.

The Germans had not conquered eastern Poland by the time the Soviets invaded, and, although much of the Polish army had been lost, or was encircled, prior to the invasion, the Poles were still hopeful of organising a bridgehead near the River Dniester and the Romanian frontier. The Soviet invasion led, instead, to a decision to retreat into Romania. Soviet and German forces joined on the upper Dniester on 20 September, cutting off the line of retreat.

Warsaw still resisted, but it was under heavy artillery and air attack and short of food and ammunition. This led to the surrender of the unconquered city on 27 September. The last Polish troops stopped fighting on 6 October. In their campaign, the Germans killed 70,000 Polish troops and took 694,000 prisoners. Another 100,000 escaped into Romania.[6]

Hitler had turned the defeat of Poland into an opportunity for better relations with the Soviet Union. They shared a common brutality and a willingness to use slaughter to achieve their goals. The Germans and the Soviets at once began to kill Poland's natural leaders and intelligentsia in order to further their ends of creating a ductile slave population. In addition, several thousand Jews were killed by the Germans during, or soon after, the conquest, while the remaining Jews were obliged to live in ghettos where they were subject to harsh conditions, especially limited food. Those who tried to leave were killed.[7]

Britain and France had entered the war in support of the Poles, but, due to limited preparedness and to military and political caution, were unable to provide assistance. The French needed two weeks to get their artillery out of storage. In September 1939, they advanced, but with only nine divisions, and only five miles, despite the weakness of the opposing German forces, and then fell back after Warsaw fell. This failure to help Poland further increased German influence in Eastern Europe, particularly in Bulgaria and Hungary.

The British forces sent to France were small, short of equipment, particularly tanks, transport, artillery, small arms and ammunition, and poorly trained for conflict with the Germans. Due to the fiscal situation, there had been no large-scale army manoeuvres for several years. Command and control systems were inadequate. The movement of the British force was too late to have any impact on the war in Poland. The main troop landings began at Cherbourg on 10 September and it was not until 3 October that units began to take over part of the front line from the French. Winston Churchill, the First Lord of the Admiralty, advocated the dispatch of a fleet to the Baltic specially prepared to resist air attack, but this rash idea, which would have exposed the fleet to air attack in confined waters, was thwarted by his naval advisers.

The unwillingness of the Germans to try to translate initial victories into a widely accepted peace ensured that the cessation of offensive operations with the fall of Poland did not lead to an end to conflict. Despite Hitler's Reichstag speech of 6 October 1939, calling for peace with Britain and France, no real effort was made to negotiate one. Hitler could not be trusted and was planning to attack in the west, although he had to delay until after the winter. In November 1939, he rejected a Belgian–Dutch peace approach.

Britain and France were anyway determined to fight on in order to prevent German hegemony. Sceptical about Germany's ability to sustain a long war, and confident that, as in World War One, the Allied forces in France would be able to resist attack, Chamberlain hoped it would be possible to intimidate Hitler by a limited war through blockade. The strategy was intended to put such pressure on

Germany that either Hitler would be forced to negotiate, or it would lead to his overthrow.

Hitler's response was an attack on France, *Fall Gelb* (Operation Order Yellow), ordered from October, but not eventually launched until May 1940. Hitler argued that Germany enjoyed a window of opportunity thanks to being more prepared for war than Britain or France, but he feared that the latter would be able to build up their strength. Hitler was also eager to profit from the ability Poland's defeat offered for Germany to fight on only one front, and thus to revert to the opportunities for success she had enjoyed in the Wars of German Unification in 1864–71. More specifically, he was worried that the Allies would be able from France to bomb the nearby Ruhr, Germany's leading industrial zone. The victorious campaign in Poland had helped to consolidate the position of German generals who favoured rapid armoured advance and had enhanced Hitler's self-confidence as a great strategist, but bad weather in the severe winter of 1939–40, caution on the part of the German High Command and the need for preparations delayed the attack on France.

Military activity on the Western Front was very limited in the interim, leading to its description as *Sitzkrieg* or 'Phoney War'. The Anglo-French forces failed to respond to German success in Poland with a training regime able to respond to *Blitzkrieg*; instead training was conventional, and there was little preparation for mobile tank warfare, although more than was subsequently to be alleged. Nor was there the anticipated bombing war between the combatants.[8]

## Conflict in Scandinavia

Instead, most fighting in the winter of 1939–40 unexpectedly took place in Finland. Soviet aggression had led, first, to the demand of major frontier changes and a thirty-year lease of Hanko for use as a military base that would leave Finland strategically bereft, and, then, to the staging by the Soviets of an incident on 26 November 1939 that offered them a pretext for invasion four days later.

Despite being numerically superior, and having complete control of the air and far more artillery and ammunition, the Soviets suffered serious defeats, especially at Tolvayarvi and Suomussalmi in

December. Their strategy was poor, characterised by an inadequate coordination of advancing forces, an underestimation of the fighting quality and mobility of the Finns, and Stalin's serious exaggeration of Soviet military capability and failure to commit adequate resources at the outset. Soviet inflexibility contrasted with the flexibility of the Finns, who used ski battalions. This enabled the Finns to avoid the dependence on roads that characterised the Soviets, and helped the Finns to encircle Soviet columns.

The Soviets were not adequately prepared for winter operations. Their equipment was not protected against cold and ice and there was a lack of winter camouflage. The importance of environmental factors was shown by the contrast with the situation in Poland. There, the Germans had been able to use their overwhelming superiority in armour, but, in Finland, the Soviets could not do so successfully. Instead, the Finns exploited the unsuitability of terrain and climate for armour, destroying large numbers of Soviet tanks with Molotov cocktails: petrol bombs thrown by hand. Finnish morale was also higher.

Soviet deficiencies in Finland indicated the need to match equipment and doctrine to circumstances. The Soviet army was trained for conflict in open country, but this was of scant value in forested regions, where vehicles were forced to rely on roads that were vulnerable to ambush. The same was, later, true for tanks in the forested terrain of the Indo-Burmese frontier, although in central Burma there were open plains suited to tanks. On the Burma–India frontier and in Finland, the bulk of the terrain was impenetrable to vehicles, which led to a focus on roads from which it was difficult to deploy. This led to a vulnerability to flank attacks. Similar problems were to be revealed by fighting in cities, although, in cities, there were more routes of approach.

More, however, was involved in the initial Soviet failure in Finland than terrain and training. The Soviet army also proved unable to implement its doctrine and to operate in a flexible fashion. In particular, there was a lack of coordination between the various arms and an inability to implement strategic plans effectively. Thus, control of the air was not employed to decisive strategic, operational or tactical effect, although there was some important re-supply of isolated units, helping them to fight on even when encircled; while the Soviet failure to coordinate infantry and tank advances left the latter vulnerable to Molotov cocktails.

Eventually, in January 1940, the Soviets reorganised their forces. They then overwhelmed the Finns with numbers, continuing to press on the Finns north of Lake Ladoga while focusing the attack in the south. There, in February and March, they used their superior artillery to smash their way through the fortified Mannerheim Line, although only with considerable difficulty. The Finns were forced by a treaty of 12 March to cede territory as the price of peace. This cut short British plans to stage a euphemistic 'uninvited landing' in Norway as a prelude to sending troops to help the Finns.

These plans had an unrealistic air, as the determination of both Norway and Sweden to remain neutral in the Russo-Finnish Winter War greatly limited British options, while the British were not really prepared for winter conflict. The plans also reflected the extent to which the Soviet Union was identified with Germany, although it was not in fact at war with Britain and France. Nevertheless, the pact between the two countries led to a large-scale supply of Soviet economic resources to the Germans. This encouraged French thoughts of air attacks on the Soviet oilfields at Baku, and an expedition to Thessaloniki in Greece in order to contest any German and/or Soviet advance into the Balkans.

Soviet casualties in the war with Finland were about 392,000 men. The combination of deficiencies in the Winter War campaign with those in the attack on Poland in 1939 stimulated demands for military reform in the Soviet Union; pressure that was accentuated by evidence of German success. An evaluation of the campaign led, in May 1940, to the issue of Order No. 120 by the Supreme Military Soviet. This pressed for changes, including better training, more fluid infantry tactics and better all-arms coordination. This was part of the action–reaction cycle of responses to problems that was so important to military capability during World War Two.

Perhaps more significantly, the Winter War contributed to a misleading impression of Soviet incompetence that influenced Hitler's attitudes when he attacked in 1941. As far as more general lessons were concerned, the conflict apparently demonstrated both the degree to which resources did not dictate outcomes and the extent to which they did in the end. In reality, neither was true. In

February 1940, the Soviets were able to focus the conflict on the Karelian Isthmus and to employ appropriate artillery-support tactics in order to breach the Finnish positions.[9]

The Soviet Union's other campaign in 1940 – the occupation of the independent Baltic States of Estonia, Latvia and Lithuania, as agreed with Hitler – was far less difficult than that in Finland. The Soviets met scant resistance from vastly outnumbered and disunited forces that lacked any international support. The common border between Germany and the Soviet Union, established by their joint attack on Poland, was now lengthened, as Lithuania had had a border with Germany. The advance of the Soviet border in 1939 and 1940 undermined Soviet military defences, as there was not sufficient time to implement a new defensive scheme before the German attack in 1941. On the other hand, the Soviets had considerably deepened the area that the Germans would have to conquer. The Soviets also intimidated Romania into ceding Bessarabia and northern Bukovina, again with Hitler's grudging agreement.[10]

In April 1940, other neutrals were also attacked. Anxious to preempt the danger of British moves, and keen to establish submarine bases from which to attack British shipping, the Germans, in Operation *Weserübung*, invaded Denmark and Norway: Denmark was to be occupied in order to improve German ability to operate in strategic Norway, in particular by gaining airfields.

Denmark rapidly fell on 9 April to a surprise attack in which the Germans made effective use of their air power. Airborne troops, including the first parachute assault, complemented those landed by ship, while other units advanced overland. The Danish military was weak and poorly prepared, and intelligence reports of a forthcoming attack were largely ignored. Resistance was speedily overcome.

In Norway, the Germans largely relied on amphibious landings. Oslo, however, was captured by airborne troops, although only after much confusion and the loss of the *Blücher*, a heavy cruiser escorting a planned amphibious landing. The ability to take advantage of the seizure of the airfield in order to compensate for the blocking of the landing, and to airlift in troops, was symptomatic of the responsiveness of the German command structure. The fall of Oslo on 9 April was a powerful psychological blow to Norwegian resistance. As a sign that the German policy of terror would not be restricted to

Eastern European conquests, the Germans, on 9 April, threatened to shoot Norwegians who resisted, and followed up by shooting a number of civilians in order to demoralise the population.

Thanks both to tougher resistance and to Anglo-French intervention, Norway took longer to fall than Denmark, although the initial German success was decisive, as all major cities, harbours and military bases had been seized, and the cohesion of opposition shattered. The Germans lost about a quarter of their navy in the campaign, but, again, their air power made a major impact. It helped exacerbate the limitations of the Norwegian resistance and of the Anglo-French naval and land intervention. The failure of the poorly-directed British navy to prevent the initial landings or, subsequently that day, to disrupt them was a serious problem, and was part of a more general failure of naval management. The British were initially convinced that the Germans were planning to sail into the Atlantic. A *Luftwaffe* attack ended moves by the British surface fleet on invasion day, although British submarines had an impact. The possibility of naval action was shown on 10 and 13 April, when British warships sailed into Ofotfjord to wreck the German squadron that had attacked and occupied Narvik.

On land, however, the British suffered from inadequate training and equipment, and a lack of air cover and appropriate artillery. Despite terrain that was unsuitable for their attacks, the Germans proved better able to seize and maintain the initiative and to overcome successive defensive positions. As a result, the British were evacuated from Åndalsnes, south of Trondheim, on 1 May and from Namsos, to the north, on 2–3 May. The Germans then advanced north towards Narvik, where Allied forces were putting the isolated German garrison under great pressure: the town fell to the Allies on 28 May. The Allied attempt to delay the German advance on Narvik met with scant success, but that was not the decisive factor in German success. They were further helped by the distraction of their attack on the Low Countries and France on 10 May. The Allies evacuated the Narvik area, their last base, on 8 June. Next day, the Norwegian army accepted armistice terms. The Germans installed a puppet government under the Norwegian Nazi Vidkun Quisling: he became Minister President in 1942, although the *Reichskommissar* was a dominant figure. King Haakon VII and the elected government went into exile in Britain.

General Auchinleck, who commanded the Anglo-French expeditionary force to Narvik, attributed the German victory primarily to
air power:

> The predominant factor in the recent operations has been
> the effect of air power. In the operations which culminated
> in the evacuation of Bodo the enemy had complete initia-
> tive in the air, and used it, first, to support his troops –
> a) By low-flying attacks
> b) By bombing
> c) By surprise landing of troops by parachute and from
>    seaplanes.
> d) By supplying his advanced detachments by air.
>
> And, secondly, to deny us the use of sea communications in
> the narrow coastal waters in the theatre of operations.
>    The actual casualties caused to troops on the ground by
> low-flying attacks were few, but the moral effect of contin-
> uous machine-gunning from the air was considerable.
> Further, the enemy made repeated use of low-flying attacks
> with machine guns in replacement of artillery to cover the
> movement of his troops. Troops in forward positions
> subjected to this form of attack are forced to ground, and,
> until they have learned by experience its comparative
> innocuousness, are apt not to keep constant watch on the
> enemy. Thus the enemy was enabled on many occasions to
> carry out forward and outflanking movements with
> impunity...showed a very high degree of co-operation
> between his Air Force and his Army...the enemy's
> supremacy in the air made the use inshore of naval vessels of
> the type co-operating with this force highly
> dangerous...the first general lesson to be drawn is that to
> commit troops to a campaign in which they cannot be
> provided with adequate air support is to court disaster.[11]

The British navy had also been shown to be unable to cope effectively with German air power, and a doctrine of reliance on
anti-aircraft fire had been revealed as inadequate. Admiral Sir Dudley

Pound, the First Sea Lord, remarked: 'The one lesson we have learnt here is that it is essential to have fighter protection over the Fleet whenever they are within reach of the enemy bombers.'[12] The navy also took hard knocks from the German surface warships, particularly when covering the forces returning from Narvik. The vulnerability of aircraft carriers to surface ships was shown, on 7 June, when the *Glorious* was sunk by the *Scharnhorst*, although, in the event, that was the sole carrier ever sunk by battleships.

The Germans were also more effective at coordinating the different arms on both land and sea, and this was important to a campaign that revealed the potential of joint operations, and thus represented a paradigm shift in warmaking. German skills interacted with Allied deficiencies in a manner that provided opportunities for bold command decisions: the Germans both took these and could give successful effect to them.[13]

Although Churchill, the First Lord of the Admiralty, had backed a rash policy over Norway, his reputation as a resolute opponent of Hitler helped ensure that he succeeded Chamberlain as Prime Minister on 10 May: the latter was weakened by Conservative disquiet over the energy and style of his war leadership, harmed by poor man-management and discredited by failure in Norway. Churchill became Prime Minister in a coalition government and was to remain war leader until after the defeat of Germany.

The conquest of Denmark and Norway led the British to respond by occupying the Faeroes, a strategic Danish archipelago, in April 1940, and Iceland, a state under the Danish crown, its diplomatic relations handled by Denmark. Iceland declared independence from Denmark, and, in May, to ensure that the Germans could not intervene, the British landed troops. Greenland, a Danish colony, opted for self-government; the following April, a treaty with the Americans permitted the latter to establish airfields.

## The Fall of France

On 10 May 1940, the Germans attacked Belgium and the Netherlands, both hitherto neutral, as well as invading France. The Netherlands, whose military had had no experience of European conflict since the 1830s, fell most rapidly, in large part because of the speed of the German advance, especially the use of paratroopers, whose capture of bridges weakened the Dutch use of river and canal defences, and hit the morale of the poorly trained and commanded Dutch forces. German airborne landings denied the Dutch defence depth. Both the Dutch and the Belgians were weak in the air, and the Germans swiftly gained and used air superiority. Supported by air attacks and tank advances, the Germans retained the initiative and the Dutch army surrendered on 14 May. Heavy casualties caused by the bombing of Rotterdam on 14 May speeded the surrender. In response, the first British raid on the Ruhr was launched. A French force that had advanced through northern Belgium in order to support the Dutch was unable to sway the struggle there. Instead, German success against the Dutch led to a shortening of their front of advance in the north and increased the pressure on Belgian forces.

The crucial operation in the campaign, however, occurred further south. This German advance brutally exposed the military failure of the Anglo-French alliance, and, in particular, the quality of French military leadership. The French Maginot Line, the well-fortified position that covered the German frontier, was outflanked when, in Operation *Sichelschnitt* (Sickle-stroke), Army Group A, including seven panzer divisions, advanced through the supposedly impenetrable Ardennes in southern Belgium and pushed across the Meuse at Dinant and Sedan on 13 May, without waiting for large-scale infantry and artillery backing, although the crossings of Meuse were excellent examples of infantry river crossings and at Sedan some artillery was well forward. Poor Allied strategy and a major intelligence failure had led the Allies to move their strategic reserve into Belgium before they were aware of the main direction of the German attack; although to have abandoned Belgium would have been unacceptable politically, as well as risking the loss of part of the Allied order of battle.

This mistake ensured that they were unable to respond adequately to the German advance, as did their doctrine, particularly the failure to prepare for fluid defence in depth. The French attention to a continuous front greatly limited their ability to respond to the German breakthrough, and the British were tied to French strategy.[14] In addition, although the Norwegian campaign did not make the British Expeditionary Force in France any weaker, British attention had been overly focused on Scandinavia. A recent study concludes:

> the plan worked *because* it was so risky and thus so unexpected....Yet the plan also worked in the inevitable chaos of war because, when mistakes were made on both sides, the Germans generally recovered from these and the Allies did not'.[15]

The French forces that opposed the Meuse crossing were not élite units, and were not supported by sufficient artillery or airpower. The Allied armies were not well prepared for a major clash, and coordination between them was inadequate. During the winter's 'Phoney War', they, and particularly the French reserve divisions, had essentially followed a static regime that, in many cases, led to a situation of diminished readiness.

In contrast, the Germans made effective use of their massed mechanised forces, especially tanks, and of tactical air support, particularly Ju-87 (*Stuka*) dive-bombers, gaining the strategic, operational and tactical initiative against forces that were as numerous, disorientating opponents and sapping their will to fight. The Germans had rapidly achieved air superiority, inflicting heavy casualties on the Allied air forces.[16] The Vichy Court of Supreme Justice was to hold the French air force responsible for the military defeat in 1940. This was a political judgement, but it reflected the failure of the *Armée de l'Air* to match the *Luftwaffe* in planes and doctrine.

German panzer divisions proved operationally effective as formations, maximising the weapon characteristics of tanks. Handled well, as by the British in their counterattack near Arras on 21 May, Allied tanks could be effective, but, on the whole, the Germans controlled the pace of the armoured conflict, not least because their tank doctrine was more effective. Having caused heavy casualties, the British were finally stopped near Arras by an artillery screen.

The Germans were able to make the offensive work in both operational and tactical terms, amply displaying the tactical potential of an offensive spearheaded by armoured forces. Tanks could move across country, limiting the need to tie forward units to roads. The French had more tanks than the Germans in 1940, and their tanks were, for the most part, more heavily gunned and had more effective protection. The best French tank, the Char B, had far thicker armour than its German counterparts, which were vulnerable to both tank fire and anti-tank guns. However, French tanks were also somewhat slower and many had to turn in order to fire. Tanks with one-man turrets left the commander to be the gunner and the communicator. Their lack of radios also created problems for French tanks: communication was by signal flag, which made unit coordination harder. Aside from a poor overall strategy, the French failed to develop an effective doctrine for their armour. They persisted in seeing tanks, like artillery, as a support for infantry, and most French tanks, accordingly, were split up into small groups for use as mobile artillery, rather than being employed as armoured divisions for their shock value. Tactics and operational control and coordination were more important for German mobility, and thus success, than the actual technological capabilities of the weapon. When German and French tank forces first clashed – in Belgium on 13 May – the Germans were successful thanks to their offensive tactics.

Having crossed the Meuse, German tanks broke through to reach Abbeville on 20 May and the English Channel the following day, cutting off much of the mobile Allied forces to the north. The tempo of the attack was far greater than in 1918, but the Germans were also more successful in maintaining supplies for their advancing units. Superiority in the air helped them, not least by preventing effective Allied attacks on their advancing forces or supply lines.[17] The Allies had no equivalent to the *Stuka*, and the British and French air forces were outclassed and outnumbered by the German one. Army–air force co-operation was particularly bad for the British, and this ensured a lack of close air support, which had serious consequences for the campaign. The British were also short of anti-tank and anti-aircraft guns.

Nevertheless, the effectiveness of the *Blitzkrieg* has been exaggerated by commentators, who remain excessively under the spell cast by the sheer shock and drama of the German offensives, and have therefore overrated the impact on war of military methods which represented more of an improvisation than the fruition of a coherent doctrine, even among the Germans.[18] In 1940, as in 1939, much of the German army still walked. The potential of mechanised/motorised internal combustion engine-based weaponry and logistics was less fully grasped than talk of *Blitzkrieg* might suggest. The key element was the tactical and operational use of the armoured tip of the army, rather than its overall weight, although the quality of German infantry and artillery should not be underrated. More generally, alongside the well-trained regular divisions there were more numerous reserve divisions; their training and morale were less impressive.

Yet, it was the contrast at the decisive point of breakthrough that was crucial. There was a massive French intelligence failure and totally inadequate forces in the Ardennes, both aspects of a poorly-prepared army led by commanders who were not up to the task, and who certainly had only a limited understanding of mechanised warfare. The lack of adequate signals equipment and training made it difficult for the French to respond to developments. Morale was also important. German morale was high, but French morale, on the whole, was poor, and defeatism rapidly spread. When the French fought well, however, they were able to make an impact. At Gembloux on 14–15 May, the French artillery–infantry defence, particularly the French artillery, was effective.[19]

When the British counterattacked, they disrupted the German advance considerably. But much of the army was poorly trained, equipped (especially in anti-tank guns) and commanded, and, for some, their heart was not in the fight. The British were not adequately prepared for a fighting retreat in the face of a mobile opponent: transport, fuel and communications all proved insufficient. In the end, getting the army out of France became paramount.

Having reached the Channel, the Germans widened their bridge-head to the north, taking Boulogne on 23 May and besieging Calais. It held out until 27 May, while Lille did not surrender until 1 June. Both provided important distractions for the Germans closing in on the encircled Allied forces around Dunkirk.

Bravery, skill, luck and the not fully explained German halt on the Aa Canal on 24 May, which owed much to *Luftwaffe* pressure to take a leading role and to the need of German tanks for maintenance, helped the British save much of their army (but not its equipment), as well as many French troops, in the evacuation from Dunkirk on 27 May–4 June; 338,000 troops, mostly British, but including 110,000 French, were evacuated, with the British navy, which evacuated most of the troops (although private boats also took off an important number) taking serious punishment from German planes in the process. The British were helped by the survival of a pier that could be used for embarkation, as well as by the weather: 'By a twist of fate, or better yet a meander of the jet stream, neither of these two most-likely weather patterns dominated Flanders in late May 1940. Instead the one set of conditions that most favored the Allied evacuation persisted for days.'[20] Nevertheless, the German achievement had been far greater than in 1870–1 and 1914. Aside from defeating the British and the French, other German forces had overrun Belgium, which surrendered on 27 May, weakening the Dunkirk position.

In *Fall Rot* (Operation Order Red), launched on 5 June, the Germans also pressed south into France, overcoming strong resistance on the Somme and the Aisne. On 7 June, Rommel ignored the strongly held French defensive hedgehogs and advanced from the Somme towards the Seine. On 9 June, he reached the Seine. Further east, despite a French armoured counterattack on 10 June, the Germans crossed the Marne and captured Rheims the next day. The French army was heavily outnumbered, especially in armour, its morale had been badly hit by earlier defeats, and much of its equipment, including over half the tanks, had already been lost. The well-motivated Germans benefited from their training and equipment, but also from better generalship.

After the initial struggle, resistance rapidly collapsed. The Seine could no more be held than the Somme. The French government left Paris for Bordeaux on 10 June, and the Germans entered the capital four days later. They pressed forward on a number of axes. From Rouen, there were advances to Cherbourg (fell 19 June) and, via Rennes (18 June), to Brest (19 June). Talk of continued resistance from a Breton redoubt proved abortive. Cut-off Allied units were evacuated by sea from St Valéry-en-Caux (although a British division had to surrender there), Le Havre, Cherbourg, St Malo, Brest and St Nazaire, but others were captured.

From Paris, German forces advanced into the valley of the Loire, capturing Tours (18 June) and Nantes (20 June). Others, advancing south-east of Paris, captured Dijon on the 16th and pressed on towards the Swiss frontier and Lyons. The French forces in eastern

France – half a million strong – were trapped between Nancy and Belfort. There was also a political collapse in France. With the Commander-in-Chief, General Maxime Weygand, critical of the political system and pressing for an armistice, and Marshal Henri Pétain, the Deputy Prime Minister, also pessimistic about the future and opposed to fighting on, the Cabinet, on 15 June, agreed to find out what armistice terms the Germans would offer. This sold the pass. There would be no union with Britain, no guerrilla warfare, no retreat of the government to the North African colonies. On 16 June, Paul Reynaud resigned as Prime Minister, to be replaced by Pétain. The French asked for an armistice on 17 June and accepted German terms on the 22$^{nd}$, the Germans insisting on the symbolic step of their signature in the railway carriage at Rethondes in which the Germans had signed terms at the close of World War One. By then, German forces had captured Lyons (20 June) and Vichy (20 June). For less than 30,000 dead, the Germans had inflicted a rapid victory on a scale that enabled them to dictate radical terms.

Under the settlement, a new French government established on 10 July, headed by Marshal Pétain and based in Vichy, was left in control of south and part of central France, about 40 per cent in total, although Vichy France also was occupied by the Germans on 11 November 1942. Vichy was restricted to a 100,000-strong army, while 1.6 million French military personnel became German prisoners of war; 100,000 had died in the campaign. The parts of Alsace and Lorraine ruled by Germany from 1871 until World War One were annexed anew, while German control in the occupied zone in north and west France was intense. Hitler was interested in further breaking up France at the end of the war. From their refuge in London, the Free French under Brigadier-General Charles de Gaulle (1890–1970), called for continued resistance, but most of the French empire chose to follow orders from Vichy.

Germany's success in its seven-week campaign had transformed the strategic situation in Europe. Victory led Hitler to a conviction of his own ineluctable success, and that of the *Wehrmacht* under his leadership. Thanks to this victory, the Germans would clearly be able to fight on, and any successful challenge to them would now have to overcome German dominance of Western Europe. British air attacks on Germany would no longer be able to benefit from French airfields and friendly airspace. Vichy's control of Syria, Lebanon, Madagascar, French West Africa, particularly Senegal, Algeria, Tunisia, Morocco, French Guiana and French Indo-China, and a substantial fleet, also changed the global position, as it created the possibility of German penetration into the Middle East and Africa. It also appeared to clear the way for Italian expansion into Egypt, as the Italians would not have to worry about French forces in their rear in Tunisia. The willingness of the weak Vichy government in Indo-China to close the railway to Nanning in China in response to Japanese pressure in June 1940 was followed by the (coerced) acceptance of effective Japanese control in the north that September and in the south the following July.

## Britain under attack

More immediately, Britain's security was now at risk. The coastline from the Spanish border to the North Cape of Norway was now under the control of Germany, and, on 30 June, the Germans occupied the undefended Channel Islands, which were vulnerable to German air attack. Moved forwards into France, Belgium, the Netherlands and Norway, German airbases were now close to Britain, cutting the journey time of bombers and allowing fighters to escort them. German planes would not only be able to reach southern England. They could now easily reach the Midlands and Lancashire. From Brittany and Normandy, German planes could 'outflank', to the west, air defences focused on protecting south-east England.

Germany's air power and submarines threatened Britain's vital sea lines of communication and supply with the outside world, while Hitler planned Operation Sealion (*Seelöwe*), an invasion of southern England, although there was, initially, a lack of commitment that, in part, reflected his hope for a negotiated settlement. German attention was also diverted by growing interest in preparations for an invasion of the Soviet Union. On 19 July, Hitler offered peace, with Britain to retain her empire in return for her acceptance of Germany's dominance of the Continent.

Influential British politicians, particularly the Foreign Secretary, Lord Halifax, who had come close to succeeding Chamberlain, felt that such negotiations were desirable, and David Lloyd George, a former Prime Minister, thought that he might be able to succeed Churchill. He could well have proved, as Chamberlain warned, a British Pétain, not in terms of his politics but in terms of his willingness to settle with Germany.[21] Churchill's political position was vulnerable, not least because Chamberlain remained leader of the Conservative Party, but Churchill was determined not to surrender and not to negotiate with Hitler.

The *Luftwaffe* was instructed to help prepare the way for invasion, particularly by driving British warships from the Channel. The Norway campaign had indicated the vulnerability of amphibious operations to British naval power, and, although Italy's entry into the war had increased pressure on the British navy, enough warships remained in home waters to challenge any German naval attack. However, *Luftwaffe* commanders were increasingly concerned to attack the RAF and its supporting infrastructure in order to prepare the way for reducing Britain to submission by a bombing war on civilian targets, a strategy that would put the *Luftwaffe* centre-stage. The lack of clarity in the relationship between air attack and invasion affected German strategy, but there was also a lack of preparation for a strategic air offensive, because the Germans had not sufficiently anticipated its necessity. Furthermore, the schedule was too tight, with the need to invade before mid-September, when the weather was likely to become hostile.

In addition, the Germans suffered from a lack of sufficiently trained pilots, and from limitations with their planes and tactics. Their bombers' load capacity and range were too small, and their fighters were too sluggish (Me 110) or had an inadequate range affecting the time they could spend over England (Me 109), and the fighters were also handicapped by having to escort the bombers. The Germans also failed to understand the role of British radar and its place in the integrated air-defence system. Furthermore, they had lost many planes and pilots during the Battle of France. Despite these deficiencies, the Germans outnumbered the British on the eve of the battle. There had been heavy losses of British planes in the Battle of France, and the factories where new planes were being manufactured were now within range of German bombers.

Initial German attacks on the RAF and its airfields inflicted serious blows, particularly on pilot numbers, and it was a shortage of pilots, particularly trained pilots, rather than planes, that threatened Britain's survival. There was an acute crisis in late August and early September 1940. However, fighting over Britain, it was possible to recover pilots who survived being shot down, while the RAF also benefited from the support provided by radar and the ground-control organisation, as well as from able command decisions, good intelligence and a high level of fighting quality. The benefit of the ground-control organisation was seen in the higher ratio of *Luftwaffe* losses in the Battle of Britain compared to those during the air war over Dunkirk. Between 10 July and 31 October, the British lost 915 aircraft, the *Luftwaffe* 1,733, a disparity that, in part, reflected the vulnerability of bombers.[22]

The Germans switched, in early September 1940, in part because of faulty intelligence and, to a minor extent, in response to a British raid on Berlin on the night of 25–6 August, to bomb London and other cities in the Blitz. As a result, the pressure on the RAF diminished, although the strain on the population was heavy. The Germans were out to destroy civilian morale, but, although there were occasional episodes of panic, on the whole morale remained high.

On 17 September, Operation Sealion was formally postponed. Irrespective of the serious problems that would have faced any invasion, not least insufficient naval resources and preparation, it could not be allowed to go ahead without air superiority. Without that, it would be impossible to prevent the British navy from challenging any invasion attempt. Furthermore, air power would have provided the artillery for any invasion.[23]

Although the British had been greatly weakened by the Battle of France, much *matériel*, including large numbers of tanks, had been left behind in the evacuation from France and much of the army was poorly deployed and untrained to resist invasion, a German invasion of Britain was still a formidable task, not least because of a lack of German experience in large-scale amphibious operations. The invasion of Norway was no comparison, although it had showed that the British navy could not be relied upon to block an invasion. Furthermore, the British army had been considerably strengthened by the arrival of Canadian forces successfully convoyed across the Atlantic. The First Canadian Division, which was deployed in Surrey as a mobile reserve, was probably the best-equipped division in

Britain, although it lacked effective anti-aircraft guns.[24] In addition, any invasion would have been vulnerable to weather conditions.

Nevertheless, had the Germans landed they would not have faced the prepared defences encountered by the Allies in Normandy in 1944. Instead, the situation might have been more comparable to the Japanese landing in the Philippines in December 1941, although, by 24 July, Admiral Sir Dudley Pound, the First Sea Lord, could write about an invasion that 'tremendous strides have been made in the last six weeks in preparing the country for that possibility'.[25]

Unlike the Allies in Normandy, a German invasion would have been improvised and the units employed would have had scant time for re-supply after the invasion of France or for preparation. The Germans lacked the specialised tanks the British were to use on the invasion beaches in 1944, as well as specialised landing craft. Initially, the invasion force, which was intended to land between Hythe and Rottingden, with a parachute landing to cover the right flank, would have been supported by little armour. This would have helped the British contain and counterattack the bridgeheads, but, if those could be re-supplied – control of the sea again being the issue – then the situation would have been far more threatening. Furthermore, the German attack on Crete in 1941 showed how disruptive a parachute attack could be. Churchill told the House of Commons on 4 June 1940, 'we shall fight on the beaches, we shall fight on the landing grounds, we shall fight in the fields and in the streets, we shall fight in the hills; we shall never surrender'; but, if the first two had failed, it is difficult to see how resistance at his subsequent stages could have succeeded.

The failure of the *Luftwaffe* provides an appropriate opportunity to draw attention to more general problems with German warmaking. The planning and execution of the attacks on Poland, Norway and France had revealed flaws in strategy and command, as well as deficiencies in motorised infantry, logistics, artillery support and effective ground-support air power. The Germans had not been ready for a major war when conflict began in 1939, and, indeed, Hitler had been surprised by British and French entry into the conflict. The understandable swagger in German attitudes that followed the conquest of France paid insufficient attention to deficiencies in the German military and, more seriously, war economy.

German success owed much to making fewer mistakes than their opponents.

## Italy enters the war

In June 1940, the war spread in a new direction. Despite his alliance with Hitler, Mussolini had initially taken no part in the war, but, on 10 June 1940, after the French had been clearly defeated, he joined in because he feared that he would otherwise lose the opportunity to gain glory and territories. On 20 June, the Italians attacked the French in the Alps. Mussolini hoped to benefit from, and match, earlier German successes. Feeling that Italian greatness required domination of the Mediterranean and, therefore, British defeat, Mussolini sought gains from the British Empire and from France, and more power in the Balkans. On 19 June, he told Hitler that he wanted Corsica, Nice, French Somaliland and Tunisia from France, but all he got was Nice and Savoy: the Italian attacks had been held in the Alps by far smaller French forces. Casualties on both sides were light, but the Italians suffered more losses, and also the humiliation of being unable to defeat an already clearly beaten opponent. In part, this reflected the nature of the Alpine frontier, where the French had prepared defences to cover the few routes of advance. There was no opportunity for the Italians to emulate the mobile warfare of the Germans, nor indeed for them to use effectively their greater numbers.

Mussolini's ambitions were not based on a reasonable assessment of the capabilities of the Italian military machine, and this failure was to lead to a series of disasters. Greece was invaded from the Italian colony of Albania on 28 October 1940, but the invasion was repelled in November and the Greeks advanced into southern Albania. Mussolini's conviction that Italy would easily win was cruelly punctured. The poorly trained and commanded Italians were outfought by more resilient, better-trained and more motivated troops. Greek strategy was also far better and reflected superior generalship. Italian advantages in equipment, for example in aircraft, did not compensate, and were, in turn, vitiated by problems with command, communications and logistics. Italian counterattacks in Albania were thwarted in January and March 1941.[26]

Similarly, but more spectacularly, a poorly-prepared and commanded invasion of Egypt from the Italian colony of Libya by far greater forces (215,000 to 31,000 defenders) was mounted hesitantly, stalled, and was then routed by the British (a term, throughout, that, where appropriate, includes Dominion and Empire forces), who successfully counterattacked at Sidi Barrani (9–11 December 1940), and captured over 38,000 prisoners.[27] The Italians were then driven out of Egypt, before the British went on to conquer Cyrenaica (eastern Libya), taking large numbers of prisoners. The number of Italian families that soon had members as British prisoners gravely sapped confidence in the war within Italy.

The decision of Churchill to send tanks, that were a key part of Britain's strategic reserve, to Egypt was important to the success of the operation. It reflected his determination to strike at the Axis where possible, but also his confidence that an invasion of Britain would not come. The move was prefigured in 1758–9, when William Pitt the Elder, 1st Earl of Chatham, sent forces to conquer Canada despite the risk of a French invasion, that was, indeed, to be thwarted by the British navy .

The Italians were also defeated by British forces in Somaliland and Ethiopia. The campaign had begun with the Italian conquest of British Somaliland in August 1940: larger Italian forces were able to outflank well-defended British positions and the far less numerous British garrison was evacuated; the Italian casualty rate was eight times that of the British. Other Italian forces had moved across the Sudan border.

However, the following February, British forces (mostly from West, East and South Africa) outfought the Italians in Italian Somaliland and also displayed an ability to move rapidly in very difficult terrain. Let down by inaccurate intelligence about likely British plans, and poorly commanded, the Italians lacked the necessary ability to respond rapidly. Despite being more numerous, they were short of transport and psychologically, as well as operationally, immobile. Although the Italians had many planes, they were not used effectively, in contrast to those of the British. An undefended Mogadishu fell on 25 February 1941.

The Somaliland campaign prefigured that of the Japanese, at the expense of the British, in Malaya the following winter. The ability of boldly-advancing forces to disorientate and defeat a larger static opposition was shown to be the key to success, not the presence of tanks. Effective doctrine, well implemented by able commanders and impressive troops, brought victory, and could do so with few casualties for the attacker. This depended, however, on a capability gap: opponents had to fight less well and, crucially, to lack a well-deployed and directed mobile reserve.

Success in Somaliland encouraged the British invasion of Eritrea, British Somaliland and Ethiopia, with attacks being mounted from Sudan, Aden, Italian Somaliland (the main axis of advance into Ethiopia) and Kenya. The difficulty of obtaining supplies in the areas of operation was a major hindrance, as was the extent of territory, the terrain (including mountains over 10,000 feet) and the climate. The Italians put up a poor resistance in British Somaliland and eastern Ethiopia, and their commander, the Duke of Aosta, abandoned the capital, Addis Ababa, in order to concentrate his forces in more defensible positions. The Italian position had also been weakened by local opposition armed and encouraged by the British; although tribesmen hostile to Haile Selassie (the Emperor whom the Italians had defeated in 1935–6 when they conquered Ethiopia) backed the Italians.

In Eritrea, the Italians put up a firmer defence, taking particular advantage of the difficult terrain near Keren, where, despite air and artillery support, the British encountered considerable difficulty in February and March 1941. The well-led Italians, their morale higher than many other units the British had encountered, fought well and mounted numerous counterattacks. The British made a successful use of tanks in the valley bottom, but in the mountainous terrain they could only accomplish so much. Once, however, the crucial defensive position had been cleared on 26–7 March, the British rapidly captured the major towns in Eritrea: Asmara (1 April) and, with an air-supported assault, the port-city of Massawa (8 April).[28] The seizure of the port was important to British logistics.

The remaining Italian forces in East Africa were in the mountainous terrain of northern Ethiopia, and they put up a strong defence before surrendering – at Amba Alagi on 19 May, Wolchefit Pass on 27 September and Gondar on 28 November. Logistical problems and the heavy rains made British operations particularly difficult, affecting both ground advances and air support. Artillery proved especially important in British attacks on mountainous positions, and engineering skills in creating and improving routes and bridges.[29] The ability of the Italians to hold out until late in 1941 had a wider impact, as it delayed the transfer of British units to the Middle East.

Successful British attacks on the Italian fleet, involving both surface ships and aeroplanes, combined with the failure of the large Italian submarine force to make a major impact, ensured that Italy was as ineffective at sea as it was on land. Admiral Domenico Cavagnari, the Chief of the Italian Naval Staff, had planned a fleet able to seize control of both ends of the Mediterranean, so that it could operate on the oceans, but he adopted a far more cautious stance once war broke out.[30] Despite the success of individual units, the Italians alone were not to make a major impact on British naval strength. Instead, the British repeatedly took the initiative. The successful night attack by twenty-one torpedo planes on Italian battleships moored in Taranto on 11 November 1940 possibly inspired the Japanese attack on Pearl Harbor a year later; three battleships were badly damaged. On 28 March 1941, off Cape Matapan, thanks to torpedo aircraft, battleship firepower and ships' radar, the British sank three Italian cruisers and damaged a battleship.[31]

## Germany and the Balkans

From the outset, Italy had proved a poor ally to Germany, and this was a contributory factor (albeit a minor one) in Hitler's eventual failure. Hitler responded to Italian defeats, and to the possibility of weakening the British in the Mediterranean, by sending assistance to Mussolini. From January 1941, the dispatch of German planes to Sicily helped make the central Mediterranean hazardous for British shipping. British plans for amphibious attacks on Italian positions in the Mediterranean – Pantelleria or the Dodecanese – now seemed redundant. Furthermore, in North Africa, the British position was weakened from November 1940 by the dispatch of British supplies and aircraft to Greece to help against the Italians in Albania. German forces sent to Libya proved better than the British (and much better than the Italians) at mobile warfare and combined land–air operations, and drove the British back into Egypt in late March–June 1941. Rommel was a bold and effective commander of the German forces, while British tank–infantry–artillery co-operation was inadequate and British tanks were poor.

This was part of a major advance in German power around the Mediterranean. Already, in 1940, German support had been crucial in obliging Romania to cede the Southern Dobruja to Bulgaria (June) and Transylvania to Hungary (September), and had helped lead to the seizure of power by a Fascist dictatorship, which was followed by a growing German political, economic and military presence: German military missions arrived on 12 October. The Romanian oilfields at Ploesti were to be Germany's leading source of supply throughout the war. Mussolini found that the Balkans were increasingly under German influence. Turkey's proclamation of non-belligerency represented a renunciation of the Tripartite Treaty of Alliance with France and Britain (October 1939), which had provided for Turkish assistance to them if they had to come to the support of Greece or Romania. On 1 March 1941, Bulgaria joined the Axis and German troops began to enter the country in order to be able to threaten Greece. Hitler had decided that Italian failure required German intervention in Greece. In response to German demands, Yugoslavia joined the German alliance system on 25 March.

The Germans responded to an unexpected nationalist coup by the military in Yugoslavia on 27 March with an invasion in conjunction with Bulgarian, Hungarian and Italian forces, none of which, in fact, contributed much, apart from territory from which the Germans could operate. Virtually surrounded by these opponents, Yugoslavia was as vulnerable as Poland had been, and it fell rapidly. The Germans deployed six divisions against the 31-division-strong Yugoslav army, but (like the Poles in 1939) the Yugoslavs chose to resist attack on all parts of their country, instead of falling back to ensure a stronger defence, and the army was strung out along over 1,000 miles of frontier. As a result, only seven divisions fought the Germans. The attack was mounted, without ultimatum or declaration of war, on 6 April 1941. In Operation Punishment, the Germans advanced from Bulgaria, Romania, Hungary and Austria (since 1938 part of Germany). At the same time, German forces from Bulgaria invaded Greece. The attack on Yugoslavia included the terror-bombing of undefended Belgrade on 6 April in order to cause heavy civilian casualties: over 17,000 people were killed.

The initial German advances from Bulgaria rapidly took Skopje, the capital of the province of Macedonia (7 April), and Nis in southern Serbia (8 April). German armoured advances proved particularly effective in the absence of anti-tank guns. Advancing from Germany, other armoured forces captured Zagreb on 10 April and crossed the Drava River en route for Belgrade. The Germans benefited from the unwillingness of many Croats, including most of the Croat units in the military, to support what they saw as a Serb-dominated Yugoslavia. Belgrade surrendered on 12 April and, with resistance collapsing, the Germans advanced into the interior, taking Sarajevo on 16 April. Already, on 14 April, the Yugoslavs had requested an armistice, and three days later they capitulated. Italian forces invading from Italy and Albania helped overrun Dalmatia, but made little real contribution to the course of the campaign. Yugoslavia was partitioned, with German, Italian, Hungarian and Bulgarian territorial gains, an independent Fascist Croatia and a Serb puppet state. Fewer than 200 Germans had been killed in the invasion.

The Germans pressed on to conquer Greece, which they had also invaded on 6 April. As with Poland and Yugoslavia, the defence was weakened by an overly long perimeter, specifically the Metaxas Line that protected Thrace from Bulgaria but could not block German forces when they advanced via Yugoslavia. The British had sent an expeditionary force to help the Greeks, but with inadequate air support, and it was pushed back. The tempo of the German advance, especially its rapid use of airborne troops and armour, brought a decisive advantage, as did the effective use of ground-support aircraft. Thessaloniki fell on 9 April, successive defensive lines could not be held, Athens fell on 27 April, and the British withdrew their forces from the Peloponnese on 28–30 April. An Italian advance in Albania made scant difference to the campaign. German air attacks destroyed Greek warships.

Fuller argued that it was mistaken for the British to confront the German 'mechanised hordes' in the Balkans, and that 'to plunge into the Balkan bog before we can fully be supported by America is the height of folly'. He also suggested that there had been a serious violation of the concept of concentration of force due to intervention in

Eritrea rather than consolidating the gains in Libya. Fuller commented on Rommel's advance: 'like a ladder in a girl's stocking, our splendid desert campaign is running backwards up our strategical leg from its ankle to its knee'; and on Greece: 'We should have blitzed our enemy before he blitzed our allies. And if we were not in a position to do that, then we should never have gone to Greece at all.'[32] The dispatch of forces there had, indeed, greatly weakened the British in North Africa. Churchill, who had backed the policy for political reasons, in order to show that Britain was supporting all opposition to the Axis, swiftly recognised it as an error.

The Balkan campaign culminated with the capture of Crete by German parachute and glider troops that landed on 20 May 1941 and had captured the island by the 31st; although German losses (5,567 dead) were so great that Hitler ordered that no similar operation should be mounted in the future. Although warned of German plans by intelligence from ULTRA (deciphered German intercepts) material, the British defence was poorly prepared: much of the garrison had hastily retreated from Greece and was short of equipment, particularly artillery, and lacking in air support. The German success in seizing Maleme airfield provided a bridgehead for reinforcements. German air attacks hit the British attempt to reinforce, supply and, eventually, evacuate Crete by sea: the Mediterranean Fleet took many losses, including three cruisers and six destroyers sunk, although two German convoys en route for Crete to support Operation Mercury were intercepted.[33] Fuller fulminated in a heavily censored piece in the *Sunday Pictorial* of 8 June, 'Because we could not think cubically we expected a caterpillar crawl and got a dragonfly assault'. Criticism of Churchill increased, while the British Expeditionary Force gained the nickname 'Back Every Friday'. Admiral Cunningham, the British naval commander in the Mediterranean, feared that the Germans might press on to attack Cyprus and to deploy in Vichy-run Syria.[34]

## War at sea

The British navy was under wide-ranging pressure at this juncture. The German conquest of Norway and France ensured that the naval situation was totally different to that in World War One. The Germans now had access to bases and anchorages that made it harder for the British to enforce the blockade policy followed in World War One. In France, their bases included Brest, Lorient, La Rochelle and St Nazaire. Instead of using their surface fleet as a unit and providing a concentrated target, the Germans relied on raids by squadrons or individual ships designed, in particular, to attack Allied shipping and to divert British warships from home waters. These ships, however, were hunted down, the 'pocket battleship' *Graf Spee*, which had attacked shipping in the Atlantic, being damaged off South America in the battle of the River Plate (13 December 1939) with less-heavily gunned British warships, before scuttling there on the 17th.

The most spectacular of these raids, by the battleship *Bismarck* in May 1941, was designed to show that surface warships could make a major impact on North Atlantic shipping. British bombers had failed to find the *Bismarck* in Norwegian waters, but she was spotted by patrolling British warships in the Denmark Strait, between Iceland and Greenland, on 23 May. The following day, the *Bismarck*, and her sister ship, the cruiser *Prinz Eugen*, encountered a British squadron sent to intercept her south-west of Iceland. Ship radar helped the British shadow the German warships. However, in the subsequent gunnery exchange, the *Bismarck* sank the battle cruiser *Hood* (only three of the crew of 1,418 survived) [35] and seriously damaged the battleship *Prince of Wales*. A shell from the latter, had, however, hit the *Bismarck*, causing a dangerous oil leak that led the commander to set course for France and repairs.

The *Bismarck* soon faced a massive deployment of British warships, including 5 battleships, 2 battle cruisers, 13 other cruisers and 2 aircraft carriers. The *Bismarck* was eventually crippled by a hit on the rudder by an aircraft-launched torpedo (26 May), a demonstration of the vulnerability of surface ships to air power. Heavily damaged by battleship fire, the *Bismarck* then fell victim to a cruiser-launched torpedo (27 May).[36]

The German submarine assault on British shipping was more serious and sustained. Submarines were less vulnerable than surface ships to blockade, detection and destruction, and could be manufactured more rapidly and in large quantities; although the Germans did not focus their entire naval construction effort on them until the spring of 1943, and too many of their U-boats had only a restricted range and could not therefore operate in the Atlantic. In August 1940, there were only 27 U-boats free for operations. Nevertheless, submarines were more sophisticated than in World War One, the Germans also had the effective Type VIIc, operational from 1940, and they now had bases from which it was easier to threaten British shipping. As a result, the amount of shipping sunk by U-boats rose from the summer of 1940, at a time when British warships were focused on home waters to cover the evacuation of forces from France and to retain control of the English Channel in the face of German invasion preparations. There were also severe Allied ship losses in the winter of 1940–1, as the U-boats attacked Atlantic convoys and developed wolf-pack tactics.

The situation, however, improved in the summer of 1941, as a result of an increased number of escorts and of more aircraft over and ahead of convoys. The American willingness to play a major role in the defence of shipping in the western Atlantic was also important. During the Placentia Bay conference of 9–12 August 1941, Churchill and the American President, Franklin Delano Roosevelt, had agreed to allocate spheres of strategic responsibility. The Americans agreed to be responsible for the western Atlantic, and, from September, became responsible, alongside the Canadians,[37] for escorting in that region. On 4 September, the *Greer*, an American destroyer, was attacked by a U-boat south-west of Iceland, leading Roosevelt to give the navy the authority to fire on German and Italian warships in waters protected by the Americans. The British also benefited from a major advance in the intelligence war, the capture, on 8 May 1941, from a U-boat, of an undamaged Enigma code machine. Their subsequent ability to decipher German naval codes was a major advantage.

Most U-boat 'kills' were made on the surface, which rendered Allied sonar less effective. Aircraft, however, forced U-boats to submerge where their speed was slower and where it was harder to maintain visual contact with targets. Nevertheless, neither the RAF, which was interested in strategic bombing and theatre fighters, nor the navy, which was primarily concerned with hostile surface warships and content to rely on convoys and sonar to limit submarine attempts, had devoted sufficient preparation to air cover against submarines. In addition, land-based aircraft faced an 'Air Gap' across much of the mid-Atlantic, although Iceland's availability as an Allied base from April 1941 increased the range of such air cover. The British had used carrier-based planes against submarines at the start of the war, but the sinking by *U-29* of the carrier *Courageous* on 17 September 1939 ended this practice, and the remaining fleet carriers were needed for operations against Axis surface warships. The demands of the bomber offensive against Germany on available long-range aircraft restricted the numbers available for convoy escort, while it took time to build escort aircraft carriers: the first entered service in late 1941.

The Germans also did not devote enough emphasis to submarine construction. As a result, they had insufficient submarines to achieve their objectives, and those they had lacked air support. In 1940, the Germans lost U-boats more speedily than new ones were being brought into service. Italian submarines operated in the Atlantic from July, but with only limited success. U-boat pressure in the Atlantic was reduced in late 1941 as submarines were moved to Norwegian and Mediterranean waters, in order to attack Allied convoys to the Soviet Union and to deny the Mediterranean to Allied shipping.[38]

Although neither was as damaging as the submarine (70 per cent of Allied shipping destroyed by the Germans during the war), the Germans also sank shipping by the use of mines (6.5 per cent), especially the air-dropped magnetic mine, and aircraft, particularly the long-range, four-engined FW200 Kondor (13.4 per cent), as well as by surface raiders. The conquest of France and Norway provided bases for Kondors, although there was a lack of adequate co-operation between naval and air commands, which, in part, stemmed from Göring's control of air assets.

Concern about German submarines and surface warships ensured that, from March until July 1941, British Bomber Command concentrated on warships in docks, particularly the *Scharnhorst* and *Gneisenau* in Brest, as well as docks and shipyards.

France's surrender and Italy's entry into the war greatly altered the naval situation, especially by challenging the British position in the Mediterranean. The British had planned that, in the event of war with Japan, they would be able to rely on the French to protect their joint interests in the Mediterranean, while much of the British fleet sailed to Singapore. The Fall of France transformed the situation. Anxiety in 1940 about the fate of the French fleet at Mers-el-Kébir near Oran in French North Africa led to a demand that it scuttle, join the British, or sail to a harbour outside possible German control. When this was refused, the fleet was attacked on 3 July 1940. One battleship was sunk and two were damaged. This attack, which led to 1,297 fatalities, weakened support for de Gaulle within France and her empire, and made it easier for the Vichy government to collaborate with the Germans: two days later, the government broke off diplomatic relations with Britain. Other French warships surrendered or allowed themselves to be neutralised with far fewer difficulties.[39]

The ability of Vichy forces to fight back was made clear on 23 September 1940, when they opened fire from Dakar in West Africa on a British-backed amphibious attempt by de Gaulle and his Free French to seize the strategic port in West Africa. British warships took damage from Vichy shore and ship guns and submarine torpedoes, and, on 25 September, the operation was abandoned. Far from being a curiosity on the fringes of the war, the Dakar operation indicated the need for well-informed planning when mounting amphibious operations and the difficulty of suppressing defensive power in the absence of sustained and effective air attack. Under the Paris Protocols of May 1941, Vichy agreed to the establishment of a U-boat base at Dakar.[40]

The Vichy response to the British attack at Mers-el-Kébir, two bombing raids on Gibraltar, was ineffective. The more serious prospect of Spanish entry into the war was not realised. Hitler met Franco, Spain's Fascist dictator, at Hendaye on 23 October 1940, but, despite being offered gains in French Morocco, Spain stayed out of the war. This discouraged Hitler from pursuing the idea of a league of the Axis, Spain and Vichy France, with the last bribed with British colonies. Spain's entry would have led to an attack on Gibraltar, and would have destroyed the British ability to operate in the western Mediterranean, not least as the Germans would have gained airbases in southern Spain. There was also concern in Britain that Spanish entry into the war would enable the Germans to gain submarine bases on Spain's Atlantic coast, making the task of containing the U-boats even more difficult. There was also anxiety about the possibility of the Germans gaining naval bases in the Canary Islands, a Spanish territory.

Concern about the implications for the war against German submarines led to British planning for the invasion of neutral Ireland in order to ensure the use of the ports – Cobh, Castletown Bere and Lough Swilly – that the British had retained the right to use when Ireland gained independence, but which they had handed over in 1938. This concern also led to planning, in early 1941, for landings on the (Portuguese) Azores and Canaries to pre-empt possible German moves. That July, American forces replaced the British as the garrison of Iceland, as part of their attempt to protect the Western Hemisphere, a policy outlined at the Havana conference of July 1940.

There was, indeed, German interest in acquiring bases in the Atlantic. From these, it would be possible to threaten British convoy routes, to increase German influence in South America and to challenge American power. This was an aspect of the interest of the Naval Staff in Germany becoming a power with a global reach provided by a strong surface navy. However, although Hitler was interested in Germany regaining the overseas colonies it had lost in World War One, this was tangential to his central concern with creating a new Europe.

## The situation in 1941

As Roosevelt had successfully fought the 1940 presidential election on a platform of neutrality, there appeared scant prospect of American entry into the war. However, the loss of Crete to German attack and the failure of the attempt, in Operation Battleaxe (15–17 June), to relieve the besieged garrison of Tobruk in Libya were the last defeats for an isolated British Empire. Subsequent defeats occurred when the Empire had powerful allies. The nature of the war was about to change with Hitler's attack on the Soviet Union. His refusal to accept what others might consider objective diplomatic and strategic considerations ensured that the local wars he had won were, from 1941, transformed into a world war. The Japanese shortly after took the same route, when they added war with the USA and the British Empire to their unresolved struggle in China.

Meanwhile, within their conquered territories, both the Germans and the Japanese treated the populations harshly. Large areas (including northern France) remained under direct military command; in others (Denmark, much of Poland) a German civilian authority was instituted; and in others (including Manchuria, Vichy France, Croatia) puppet states were created; although the extent to which puppet states and indigenous civilian authorities were allowed to take decisions varied greatly. In Europe, large numbers of people found their citizenship status transformed, while Nazi regulations were extended. The Germans sought to direct the economies of conquered areas to the benefit of the German war economy. This caused serious disruption, as did the loss of earlier maritime economic links: with colonies, as well as with Britain and the USA. Living standards were hit hard by the regulatory regime introduced by the Germans and by the diversion of resources to support Germany. In addition, there was much harshness at the individual level. Property was seized, people brutalised, and killing continued, particularly in Poland.

The campaigning between the Battle of France in May–June 1940 and the German attack on the Soviet Union the following summer can seem inconsequential and, when word-space is limited, frequently gets scant attention. Campaigns such as the Italian attack on Greece appear of limited importance, while there seems to be an inevitability about German dominance of the Balkans and British victories over Italy. France having been beaten, it is not credible to think that Yugoslavia would have avoided the same fate, and discussion of *Blitzkrieg* concentrates on the campaigns of 1939 and 1940. Those of early 1941 are presented as a prelude to Operation Barbarossa against the Soviet Union, with the major question being whether German success in the latter was hindered by earlier commitments in the Balkans, specifically by the time that they took.

This approach underplays the importance and interest of the earlier campaigns. As far as operations are concerned, they indicated anew the importance of combined-arms capability and tactics, not least in terrain where there were few communication routes. German skill at air–land coordination was particularly important in the Greek campaign. Furthermore, the vulnerability of naval operations to air attack was demonstrated even more clearly than in the Norway campaign. Indeed, it was Mediterranean warfare in early 1941 that indicated the degree to which air power had changed the arithmetic, range and rationale of naval power, as Admiral Cunningham pointed out.[41] Aircraft carriers clearly represented a major change to naval warfare in World War One, but operations within range of land were now vulnerable unless air superiority could be gained. This affected the rationale of naval operations, because the risk of a rapid and serious loss of ships, and thus of the loss of relative naval capability, was now far greater. These factors were to be underlined when the Japanese attacked in the Far East in December 1941, and were to affect the debate over the preparations necessary before the Allies could launch amphibious operations in Europe. The enclosed nature of the Mediterranean, all of which is close to land, accentuated the vulnerability of shipping there to air attack.

The African and Balkan campaigns of 1940–1 also demonstrated the emptiness of Mussolini's claims about Italian power. Instead, Italy brought problems and commitments for Germany, as its defeats left the strategic situation in the eastern Mediterranean uncertain and apparently ripe for British exploitation. This led to a German intervention that cost relatively little in the short term, but that was more troubling in the longer term. The troops, armour and aircraft committed to North Africa in 1942 and, even more, to Tunisia in early 1943 would have been a small, but valuable, addition to German force levels on the Eastern Front, while the numbers of troops committed to garrison duty in Greece and, even more, to anti-insurgency campaigns there and in Yugoslavia were considerable, and a major commitment until 1944, and added greatly to the defensive burden of securing Hitler's conquests.

Had the war ended in 1941 without a German assault on the Soviet Union, then the successive German victories might have been seen by military historians as comparable to Prussia's success under Moltke the Elder against Denmark (1864), Austria (1866) and France (1870–1). The failure to force Britain to a quick peace would have been compared to the similar problem with France in 1870–1: swiftly won victories near the frontiers could not prevent a lengthier commitment. There were of course many differences, not least the naval and air dimensions, but, in essence, in 1864–71, Prussia had used operational skill and tactical capability to offset its weakness for the sort of long-term or 'total' war faced by Napoleon in 1812–14 and by Germany in 1914–18. Greatly helped, like Moltke the Elder, by his ability to attack opponents sequentially, rather than simultaneously, and by their operational deficiencies, Hitler had come close to matching this achievement in 1939–41.

Britain still held out. The Blitz (as the Germans termed the bombing attacks on British cities, especially London, mounted from the autumn of 1940) failed to break civilian morale or destroy the infrastructure. This campaign continued the Battle of Britain, but without any operational focus or the capability to match its destructive purpose. Nevertheless, over 43,000 civilians were killed and there was massive devastation. London was heavily attacked from 7 September, and, although it bore the brunt of the attack, there were also destructive raids on other cities, including Coventry and Southampton. Not least because of the absence of good aerial radar, it was hard to hit German aircraft once they had switched to night attacks in September 1940.[42] Relatively few German planes were shot down, although the winter weather led to many losses. However, by the late spring of 1941, the defence was becoming more effective thanks to the use of radar-directed planes and ground defences. The Blitz came to an end as the Germans transferred their planes for use against the Soviet Union. It had not brought Britain to her knees. Furthermore, the Germans lacked the submarine force necessary to give full effect to their plans for blockade.

Britain could not be overcome, although there was concern that Hitler would attempt an invasion in the spring of 1941. The passage by Congress of the Lend–Lease Act in March 1941, under which Roosevelt was granted a total of $7 billion for military *matériel* that he could sell, lend or trade to any state vital to American security, opened the way for the shipping of American military supplies to Britain. However, the British were unable to mount a serious challenge to the German position, and the Germans hoped that the British people would realise their plight, overthrow Churchill and make peace.

This was a serious misreading of British politics and public opinion. Chamberlain's ill health opened the way for Churchill to become leader of the Conservative Party in October 1940, and he was strong enough politically to send Halifax to Washington. While public unity was not quite as strong as was claimed in wartime propaganda, there was an impressive resolve in the face of Britain's perilous position. There was no equivalent to the political malaise that had weakened France in 1940.

Hitler had grander plans than Bismarck and Moltke the Elder had had for Prussia in the nineteenth century. He sought not to defeat but to conquer and hold, and to remould Europe to the service and image of a new ideology. To that end, he jeopardised the operational successes of 1939–41 by declaring war on, first, the Soviet Union and, then, the USA; but, to Hitler, these successes were of scant value unless they were means to his goal.

Much of the German army was not involved in conflict in the year between the Fall of France and the beginning of Operation Barbarossa. This ensured that casualty levels were low, and that training and the provision of new and improved equipment could take place. The German military in the summer of 1941 was an impressive force, ready and poised for a titanic struggle.

## NOTES

1   J. Erickson, *The Soviet High Command. A Military-Political History 1918–1941* (3rd edn, 2001), p. 499.

2   L. Lincoln, *The Japanese Army in North China, 1937–1941: Problems of Political and Economic Control* (Oxford, 1975); J.H. Boyle, *China and Japan at War, 1937–1945: The Politics of Collaboration* (Stanford, 1972).

3   G. Bunker, *The Peace Conspiracy: Wang Ching-wei and the China War 1937–1941* (Cambridge, Massachusetts, 1972).

4   I. Chang, *The Rape of Nanking: The Forgotten Holocaust of World War II* (1997); K. Honda, *The Nanjing Massacre: A Japanese Journalist Confronts Japan's National Shame* (Armonk, New York, 1999).

5   F. Dorn, *The Sino-Japanese War, 1937–1941: From Marco Polo Bridge to Pearl Harbor* (New York, 1974); Hsi-sheng Ch'i, *Nationalist China at War: Military Defeat and Political Collapse, 1937–1945* (Ann Arbor, 1982).

6   F.N. Bethell, *The War That Hitler Won: The Fall of Poland, September 1939* (New York, 1972); S.J. Zaloga and V. Madej, *The Polish Campaign, 1939* (New York, 1985).

7   M. Gilbert, *The Routledge Atlas of the Holocaust* (3rd edn, 2002), pp. 32–43.

8   N. Smart, *British Strategy and Politics During The Phony War* (Westport, Connecticut, 2003).

9   A.F. Chew, *The White Death: The Epic of the Soviet–Finnish Winter War* (East Lansing, 1971); C. Van Dyke, *The Soviet Invasion of Finland, 1939–40* (1997).

10 D.M. Glantz, *Stumbling Colossus: The Red Army on the Eve of World War* (Lawrence, Kansas, 1998).

11 P.R.O. PREM 3/328/5, pp. 23–6.

12 Pound to Admiral Cunningham, 20 May 1940, BL. Add. 52560 fol. 120.

13 K. Assmann, *The German Campaign in Norway* (1948); T.K. Derry, *The Campaign in Norway* (1952); F. Kersaudy, *Norway 1940* (1990); K. Rommetveit, *Narvik 1940: Five Nation War in the High North* (Oslo, 1991).

14 N. Jordan, 'Strategy and Scapegoatism: Reflections on the French National Catastrophe, 1940', in J. Blatt (ed.), *The French Defeat of 1940: Reassessments* (Oxford, 1998), pp. 13–38, esp. pp. 22–9.

15 M. Melvin, 'The German View', in B. Bond and M.D. Taylor (eds), *The Battle of France and Flanders 1940* (Barnsley, 2001), p. 215.

16 V.F. Bingham, *'Blitzed': The Battle of France, May–June, 1940* (1990).

17 P. Deichmann, *Spearhead for Blitzkrieg: Luftwaffe Operations Support of the Army 1939–45* (1996).

18 M. Cooper, *The German Army, 1933–1945: Its Political and Military Failure* (Lanham, Maryland, 1990); J.P. Harris and E.H. Toase (eds), *Armoured Warfare* (1992).

19 J.A. Gunsburg, 'The Battle of Gembloux, 14–15 May: The "Blitzkrieg" Checked', *Journal of Military History*, 64 (2000), pp. 97–140.

20 H.A. Winters, *Battling the Elements. Weather and Terrain in the Conduct of War* (Baltimore, 1998), p. 23.

21 A. Lentin, *Lloyd George and the Lost Peace. From Versailles to Hitler, 1919–1940* (Basingstoke, 2001), p. 126.

22 R. Overy, *The Battle* (2000), pp. 116–17.

23 P. Addison and J.A. Crang (eds), *The Burning Blue. A New History of the Battle of Britain* (2000).

24 J.L. Granatstein, *Canada's Army. Waging War and Keeping the Peace* (Toronto, 2002), p. 186.

25 Pound to Admiral Cunningham, 24 July 1940, BL. Add. 52560 fol. 152.

26 M. Cervi, *The Hollow Legions: Mussolini's Blunder in Greece, 1940–1941* (1972). On Italian weaknesses, see M. Knox, *Mussolini Unleashed, 1939–1941: Politics and Strategy in Fascist Italy's Last War* (Cambridge, 1982).

27 I.S.O. Playfair *et al.*, *The Mediterranean and Middle East: the Early Successes Against Italy* (1954).

28 A.J. Barker, *Eritrea, 1941* (1966).

29 M. Glover, *An Improvised War: The Abyssinian Campaign of 1940–1941* (1987).

30 R.M. Salerno, *Vital Crossroads. Mediterranean Origins of the Second World War, 1935–1940* (Ithaca, 2002), p. 209.

31 M.A. Bragadin, *The Italian Navy in World War II* (Annapolis, 1957); J.J. Sadkovich, *The Italian Navy in World War II* (Westport, Connecticut, 1994); J. Greene and A. Massignani, *The Naval War in the Mediterranean, 1940–1943* (Rockville, New York, 1999).

32 Fuller pieces written for *Sunday Pictorial* of 27 April 1941, first forbidden, second heavily censored, Rutgers, University Library, Fuller papers, Scrapbooks vol. 6.

33 C. MacDonald, *The Lost Battle: Crete 1941* (1993).

34 Cunningham to Pound, 28 May 1941, BL. Add. 52567 fol. 117.

35 R. Chesneau, *Hood. Life and Death of a Battlecruiser* (2002), p. 161.

36 G. Rhys-Jones, *The Loss of the Bismarck: An Avoidable Disaster* (1999); D.J. Bercuson and H.H. Herwig, *The Destruction of the Bismarck* (Woodstock, New York, 2001).

37 On whom, see M. Milner, *North Atlantic Run: The Royal Canadian Convoys and the Battle for the Convoys* (Toronto, 1985).

38 J. Terraine, *Business in Great Waters: the U-Boat Wars 1916–45* (1989).

39 W. Tute, *The Deadly Stroke* (1973).

40 A. Heckstall-Smith, *The Fleet That Faced Both Ways* (1963).

41 Cunningham to Pound, 28 May 1941, BL. Add. 52567 fols. 117–18.

42 For the problems facing ground-based anti-aircraft fire, see C. Dobinson, *AA Command. Britain's Anti-aircraft Defences of World War II* (2001), pp. 228–33.

# CHAPTER 3

# *The war widens*

## Operation Barbarossa

Hitler's overconfidence and contempt for other political systems reinforced his belief that Germany had to conquer the Soviet Union in order to fulfil her destiny and obtain *Lebensraum* (living space). He was convinced that a clash with Communism was inevitable, and was concerned about Stalin's intentions. All this led him to launch Operation Barbarossa, his attack on the Soviet Union. Although Britain was undefeated, she was no longer able to make any effective resistance to German domination of mainland Europe. Hitler was confident that the Soviet system would collapse rapidly, and he was happy to accept misleading intelligence assessments of the size and mobilisation potential of the Red Army. Nevertheless, appreciable casualties were anticipated by the Germans, who deployed as many troops as they could. Hitler's adventurism and conceit were a reflection of his warped personality, and also the product of a political-ideological system in which conflict and hatred appeared natural, making genocide all too possible. In addition, the Russian military defeat and political collapse in World War One encouraged the Germans to feel that victory could again be had.

It has been suggested by some commentators that the German invasion pre-empted plans for a Soviet attack, a claim initially made by Josef Goebbels, Hitler's Minister of Propaganda, in June 1941, and repeated by Hitler to Mussolini that August. Despite Soviet plans for a major build-up in military capacity, there is little evidence to support this interpretation. Certainly, in so far as the campaigning season of 1941 was concerned, the Soviet deployment was defensive, with an emphasis on counterattacking German advances; and long-term plans focused more on enabling the Soviet Union to defend its interests rather than on an attack on Germany to match Barbarossa.

In July 1940, Hitler gave orders for preparations for an invasion of the Soviet Union, and planning began for an invasion in May 1941 as that autumn seemed too soon. Having initially planned, after the fall of France, to cut the army, Hitler ordered its build-up to a size of 180 divisions by May.

On 18 December 1940, in response to Stalin's demands for gains in Eastern Europe, planning received a fresh impulse. Hitler signed the 'Barbarossa' directive: preparations for attack were to be finished by 15 May. These preparations took precedence over the war with Britain, although there was a link, because Hitler believed that the defeat of the Soviet Union would make Britain ready to settle and to accept German dominance of Europe. He ignored Admiral Raeder's proposal in September 1940 that the Germans concentrate their activities on the Mediterranean in order to wreck British power.

In preparation for the campaign, a new headquarters was built near Rastenburg in East Prussia, the *Wolfsschanze* (Wolf's Lair), from which Hitler was to direct operations. In the event, Hitler was to spend much of the war there until November 1944, when the Soviet advance made it prudent to leave.

On 22 June 1941, 151 German combat divisions, supported by 14 Finnish and 13 Romanian divisions – nearly 3.6 million German and allied troops, supported by 3,350 tanks and 1,950 planes – were launched in a surprise attack. The Germans planned to concentrate their attack between the Pripet Marshes and the Baltic, with much of the armour (two of the four panzer groups) under Army Group Centre, whose commander was Field Marshal von Bock. This was ordered to destroy opposing forces and then move north from Smolensk to help Army Group North under Field Marshal von Leeb capture Leningrad (now St Petersburg). The latter was seen as a prelude to the advance on Moscow: this reflected Hitler's priorities, rather than military advice, which had pressed for a concentration on Moscow. Meanwhile, Army Group South, under Field Marshal von Rundstedt, was to capture Kiev and then encircle Soviet armies in Ukraine, preventing these forces from falling back to defend the interior. In the next phase, forces from Leningrad and Smolensk were to drive on Moscow, while Army Group South advanced to Rostov in order to open the way to the Caucasus. The crucial operations were seen as those by Army Groups North and Centre. Hitler hoped to capture Moscow by late August.

The German plan represented an attempt to seize all objectives simultaneously, a source of potential weakness that reflected the failure to settle the core target of the operation. It was also assumed that the defeat of the Soviet forces near the frontier would lead to the Soviet collapse. It was believed important to prevent Soviet forces retreating into the interior. Hitler did not assume that the Soviet Union could be conquered, but rather that the destruction of most of its army and a German advance to a defensive line from Archangel to the Volga would achieve his goals. Having destroyed the Soviet state, Hitler then intended to overrun North Africa and the Near East. The advance of Army Group South to the Caucasus would prepare the way for the latter.

The Soviet war plan drawn up in March 1939, and revised in the summer of 1940, assumed that the centre of German deployment would be between Warsaw and the Baltic, and that the main attack would be directed north of the Pripet Marshes. However, from late 1940, Soviet planners, encouraged by Stalin and by Marshal Timoshenko, the new Defence Commissar, believed that the Germans would direct their main thrust to the south. Stalin thought that Hitler would seek the grain of Ukraine and the coal of the Donbass in order to provide resources for the German war machine. This emphasis was reaffirmed in the Soviet war plan of 11 March 1941. As a result, forces were concentrated on the South-West Front.

Along a 2,000-kilometre front, the Germans initially made major advances, inflicting heavy casualties and conquering the former Baltic republics, White Russia and Ukraine. Soviet forces were numerous, but poorly prepared and deployed for the German attack, and with inadequate doctrine for defensive operations. The Soviets were not ready for war with Germany, although there had been some planning and defence preparations. Stalin, who, in his attempt to benefit from international developments, specifically war in the West, and to avoid 'provocations', became the real appeaser of Nazi policy, co-operating in the destruction of Poland, did not expect attack in 1941. He ignored repeated warnings from the West and the advice of his own frontline commanders about German preparations. The limited progress made with planned frontier fortifications was an apt indication of a more general failure. More generally, the Soviets had underestimated the pace of German mobilisation and the extent to which the Germans would be able to advance.

Stalin's instructions that units were to hold their positions and not retreat, and his encouragement of counterattacks, ensured that the Soviets were vulnerable to German breakthrough and encirclement tactics, for example east of Bialystok and near Minsk, pockets that led to nearly a third of a million prisoners, and again near Smolensk (310,000 prisoners) and near Kiev (665,000 prisoners). Aside from his heavy responsibility for the unprepared condition of the Soviet military at the outset of the war, and, particularly, for the state of the command, Stalin had not appreciated that the Red Army would suffer from *Blitzkrieg*, and his failure to order retreats in time helped lead to encirclements that hit Soviet numbers hard. The Germans were dazzled by the success of the frontier battles and their deep advances into the Soviet Union, and the speed of their advance impressed observers. After major victories in early October, the Germans had advanced close to Moscow by early December. These were considerable achievements that require attention and analysis as much as the failure of the German campaign. As with the latter, it is necessary to give due weight to both sides; in this case to German effectiveness and Soviet failure.

Yet, there were also serious deficiencies in the German army and campaign, while the Soviet forces had been seriously underestimated. Motivated by ideological and ethnic contempt, overconfident after earlier successes, and certain that their armed forces were better in every respect, the Germans had underestimated Soviet capability, effectiveness and determination. They exaggerated the bad affects of Stalin's purges, although these had, indeed, not only robbed the Soviet forces of effective commanders but also encouraged officers to be overly cautious. However, from an admittedly low base, there had been important improvements in the Soviet military after their debacle in Finland in December 1939. Many were organisational, including the establishment of mechanised corps, although there had not been time to implement and assess these changes before the Germans attacked. Decreeing improvement was not the same as implementing it.

Aside from this problem, the Soviets were faced by a general lack of relevant command and fighting experience, certainly in comparison with the Germans, with the absence of supply and maintenance systems to match the impressive quantity of weapons they had, not least poor logistics and inadequate transport, and with a General Staff that did not match that of the Germans. Thus, the Soviets did not understand as well as the Germans the operational implications of mechanised warfare. In addition, their armour was still being reorganised, and they were also adjusting to the introduction of new tank models.

On the other hand, Hitler misjudged the ruthlessness and ability of Stalin to drive the Russian people into major efforts to build up their military capacity and to commit to furious fighting. Although Soviet casualties in the 1941 campaign were far higher than those of the Germans, the Soviets, nonetheless, inflicted considerable losses. These losses affected German strategy in 1941, and were to reduce the number of troops available for the 1942 offensive. The Germans were also seriously affected by wear and tear among their tanks and other vehicles.

To the surprise of Hitler, some Soviet forces fought well and effectively from the outset, especially the South-West Front, which was strong in armour. However, a misguided emphasis on the value of counterattacks caused heavy Soviet casualties and lessened Soviet defensive strength.[1] Indeed, the potential of well-led Soviet forces had been shown in August 1939 when, led by Zhukov, they had heavily defeated the Japanese in a frontier battle at Khalkhin-Gol/Nomonhan in Mongolia. Fuller wrote in the *Evening Standard* of 2 August 1941 that, unlike the French, the Red Army fought on even when broken into fragments, and he pointed out that 'this unexpected change from field to, what may be called, morcellated siege warfare' hit German logistics.

Instead, the Germans had foolishly anticipated a weaker response and a collapse in fighting quality and morale as they advanced. They had planned and prepared for a single, decisive campaign, and had not thought out adequately the consequences of a longer conflict. In addition, while Soviet resistance could not wrest the initiative from the Germans, it affected German strategy and accentuated the consequences of a prior failure to settle grand strategic choices. This, in part, reflected uncertainties over where best to focus the advance that had existed from the outset of planning. There had also been a tension between the desire to seize particular areas and the intention to provoke a key battle that would wreck Soviet opposition. At the planning stage, both objectives were combined in an advance on Moscow. However, instead of focusing on the advances on the planned axes, towards Leningrad and Moscow, Hitler diverted the panzer divisions of Army Group Centre to effect an encirclement of Soviet forces in Ukraine. He was determined to crush the Soviet South-West Front before advancing in the centre, but was also attracted by the prospect of victory there and by Ukraine's economic resources. This led to a major victory after the panzer pincers met on 15 September, closing the pocket near Kiev, but one that seriously delayed the advance on Moscow.

This was part of a more general pattern of tension between overcoming space and defeating troops, and, more specifically, between advancing east and creating and destroying pockets, a tension linked to the different capacity for rapid advance of armour and of the unmechanised infantry. Thus, instead of refitting after destroying the Red Army's Smolensk pocket, and then renewing the advance against a vulnerable opposition, Army Group Centre had, against military advice, been given the new priorities in Ukraine. The delay in advancing on Moscow enabled the Soviets to prepare their defences, although they were to be surprised when the attack came.

This strategic failure was linked to a serious conceptual problem with German warmaking. The space of the Soviet Union had not been conceptually overcome, as Filippo Anfuso noted when he accompanied Mussolini to the Wolf's Lair on 25 August 1941.[2] Insufficient thought had been devoted to the difference between winning frontier battles and the situation in the Soviet rear areas. Unlike in Poland in 1939, France in 1940 and Yugoslavia in 1941, these rear areas were not threatened by the German attack. German warmaking, with its emphasis on surprise, speed and overwhelming and dynamic force at the chosen point of contact, was designed for an offensive strategy that was most effective against linear defences (as against Poland, France, Yugoslavia and Greece), not against defence in depth that retained the capacity to use reserves.

In essence, the Germans planned for war as they had done since the Prussian offensives of the 1860s. The new land-warfare technology of tank attacks with air support was employed to defeat France in 1940, in a fashion that was not dramatically different to the offensive of 1870 and that attempted in 1914. In each case, the use of technology was framed by strategy, not vice versa.[3] Furthermore, France was weaker in 1940 than she had been in 1914, because Germany was not having to fight a two-front war as she had done then. In 1918, in their last major offensive of World War One, the Germans had been largely engaged on only one front, but, by then, France was supported by powerful Allied forces in an at least partially integrated command system, which was far less the case in 1940. Thus, Hitler's success in dividing his opponents, his political strategy, with its principle of divide and attack, was important to German success in 1939–41, although his failure to settle with Britain was a significant limitation, while in 1941 he threw away the principle of divide and attack when he declared war on the USA.

Furthermore, Hitler's self-evident determination to destroy the Soviet system meant that victory in a short war followed by a dictated peace to produce a Vichy-like solution, let alone the agreement offered Britain in 1940, was not an option. By seeing struggle as a means of national purification, Hitler ensured that the successful earlier stage of the conflict was merely instrumental in moving towards a bleaker process in which, in a prolonged war, the German military, the industrial system, and Hitler's own policymaking were all found wanting. Thus, the military shift from success to failure in 1941 was an aspect of a wider parallel political shift.

The Soviet ability to create defence in depth proved effective once the initial shock and surprise of the German attack had been absorbed. The Soviets responded rapidly in order to rebuild their forces. They had created an effective response system that further ensured that the German timetable for victory was totally derailed. Having lost the border battles, Stalin pushed through a reorganisation of the Red Army, including the creation of Stavka, a strategic high command. Soviet resources were mobilised to an extent the Germans had not anticipated, industries were moved east, and the

Soviet popular response focused on an appeal to patriotism, rather than Communism. In addition, supply lines shortened as the Soviets were pushed east, although it was necessary to adapt to Soviet industry moving east and to the loss of Ukraine. In the last third of 1941, 100 aircraft factories were evacuated east of the Urals. It was not only a propagandist flourish when Zhukov subsequently claimed that '[t]he heroic feat of evacuation and restoration of industrial capacity during the war...meant as much for the country's destiny as the greatest battles of the war'.[4]

Thanks to an effective mobilisation scheme, fresh forces were raised to replace those destroyed by the German advance. Although planning had been accompanied by extensive high-level aerial reconnaissance, German intelligence had grossly underestimated the number of divisions, aircraft and tanks available to Stalin, and had neglected the development of reserve armies, just as there was a failure to appreciate the resilience and productive capacity of the Soviet industrial regions east of Moscow. Once the psychological shock of the initial German successes had been overcome, and effective anti-tank weapons reached the battlefield, then the defence could again cope with the German attack.

Despite having the biggest air force in the world, the Soviets were less impressive in the air, in part because of a lack of good pilots and the extent to which effective new planes had not replaced obsolescent models. The Soviets had no radar and most of their planes lacked radio telephones. Their pilots were poorly trained and their morale was low. The air force had been badly affected by Stalin's purges. The Germans rapidly gained superiority in the air, and used it both to assist ground operations and to destroy ships of the Soviet Baltic and Black Sea fleets. However, they were short of the necessary planes, in part because the losses suffered during the Battle of Britain had not been replaced. In addition, the German bombers lacked the necessary range and bomb capacity to be an effective strategic force on the Eastern Front. Furthermore, as the Germans advanced, the *Luftwaffe* was forced to rely on improvised airfields, and was affected by the general logistical crisis of Barbarossa.

The Red Army was also helped by the nature of the German advance. Although the Germans presented their attack in terms of rapidly advancing armour, most of their troops were slow-moving infantry, dependent on horse-drawn transport. The Germans suffered from a lack of investment in tank production. The armour was insufficient in number, not least because the front of its advance was unprecedentedly wide, and also affected by serious fuel shortages and maintenance problems. Fuller had speculated, in the *Evening Standard* of 19 July 1941, that '[i]f tanks can be supplied by air, then the whole organisation of the mechanised forces will have to be modified', but no such development was possible. The infantry was not able to keep up with the armour, which made it difficult to seal pockets and was also a problem when the tanks encountered anti-tank guns. Fuller had claimed, in the *War Weekly* of 10 November 1939, that, '[b]ecause of the enormous numbers of anti-tank weapons which today will be met with in attacks on narrow and strongly fortified fronts, the tank, originally designed to storm parapets and trenches, has ceased to be an effective siege warfare weapon'. The serious deficiencies in the German army, and the improvised solutions they gave rise to in combat conditions, had not been exposed by earlier opponents, but they became clear in late 1941.

The Germans were helped by allies, but their contribution to the 1941 campaign was limited, not least because of a lack of effective armour. The Finns, who attacked from 30 June, made the most important contribution by providing troops and a base from which, supported by the Germans, pressure could be exerted on Leningrad and the far north. However, they fought less well than they had in the Winter War, in part because they were less adept in attacking Soviets positions than they had been in defending Finland, but also because their morale was not so high. The Soviet defence proved particularly determined in the Karelian Isthmus, and, rather than continuing the offensive, the Finns went onto the defensive in December after they had taken the territory they wanted.

On the opposite flank, the Romanians, whose army had been retrained by the Germans, made less of an impact, although they provided the manpower for a number of tasks, including the lengthy siege of Odessa (10 August–16 October), for which they provided seventeen divisions and where they suffered 90,000 casualties. The outnumbered Soviet garrison was finally evacuated to the Crimea, a step that reflected the strength of the Black Sea Fleet. The long defence of Odessa indicated the potential difficulty of capturing defended cities. Romania had entered the war in order to regain Bessarabia and Northern Bukovina from the Soviet Union, and in order to help overcome Communism.

Hungary declared war on the Soviet Union on 27 June, and sent a small force; a much larger, but still poorly equipped, contingent followed in 1942. Slovakia and Italy also sent units. The Italian commitment to the Eastern Front, 60,000 strong in 1941 and 220,000 strong the following year, gravely weakened the Axis effort in the Mediterranean, not least because it was supported by much of the Italian artillery, as well as large numbers of aircraft and motor transport.

In strong response to Soviet pressure, the British reluctantly declared war on Finland, Hungary and Romania on 5 December. However, the Japanese, who could have made a major contribution to the German campaign with their Manchurian army, preventing the dispatch of Soviet reinforcements from Siberia, were not involved. Probably because he believed that it would be easy to defeat the Soviets without them, Hitler had ordered that the Japanese were not to be informed of the planned attack, a fact that Soviet intelligence was aware of. As a result, in order to protect their rear for expansion in South-East Asia, the Japanese had signed a Neutrality Pact with the Soviets in April 1941, and this was an agreement they did not breach. It is unclear how much this owed to defeat at the hands of the Soviets in 1939, but, in 1941, there were more immediate concerns for Japanese policymakers in the shape of the developing crisis in relations with the USA.

The vastness of the Soviet Union drained the invader of energy. In contrast to the relatively small size of the crucial field of operations in Poland and northern France, the Germans were handicapped by the length of the front and the area they had to advance across, ensuring that they had fewer reserves and were therefore less able to maintain the tempo of advances. The vast distances were exacerbated by the primitive nature of the road network: the overwhelming majority of the roads were unpaved. As Fuller pointed out, in the *Evening Standard* of 2 August, 'Mud is Stalin's ally', not least because mechanised forces were mostly wheeled, depended on roads and could not operate cross-country. Indeed, as early as the first week of July, heavy rain had affected the movements of Army Group Centre. German logistical support could not keep up with the advancing forces, and was affected by growing Soviet guerrilla activity. These problems, and the growing strength of Soviet resistance, were to be exacerbated by the onset of winter.

When the Germans resumed the advance on Moscow, in Operation Typhoon, on 2 October 1941, with about 220 miles to cross to their goal, they broke through the unsuspecting opposing forces and encircled them at Vyazma (10 October) and Briansk (13 October), capturing over 650,000 troops. These losses left Moscow exposed and created a panic there. The German panzers pressed on towards Moscow, leading to the evacuation of much of the government (although not Stalin) to Kuibyshev on the Volga. The Red Army, however, was helped by rain from 10 October, and, far from collapsing, resistance became stronger, in part as troops were brought in from the Far East: the Soviet Union benefited from growing evidence that the Japanese would attack south. On 18 October, nevertheless, the Germans captured Mozhaysk, part of the Moscow defensive system, and there were increasing signs of panic, including looting, in the city. Yet, although the Germans advanced far closer to Moscow in 1941 than they had done in World War One, there was to be no collapse akin to that in 1917. Soviet control was far stronger than that of Tsar Nicholas II, and there had been no equivalent to the cumulative defeats over several years suffered from 1914.

Rain, mud and Soviet resistance slowed the Germans, whose units were suffering from increasing exhaustion. Furthermore, commitments to offensive operations across the lengthy front left the Germans with too few forces near Moscow. Their supplies were also inadequate, and there were particular problems with fuel and with tanks, too many of which had been destroyed or damaged or were no longer fit for service.

The Germans attacked again in mid-November, benefiting from the firmness that frost brought to the ground. The high command planned to push on past Moscow to Yaroslav, and, further south, Voronezh. However, the Germans were stalled in late November, and, rather than committing them, a growingly-confident Stalin maintained reserve forces near Moscow for use in a counterattack he was planning. Increasingly unable to make any real impact, the Germans had to cease attacking towards Moscow in early December. Hitler reluctantly agreed on 5 December to abandon the offensive. The savage fall in temperature hit the operating effectiveness of machines and troops, as well as German morale, and underlined the problems caused by the delay in launching the offensive earlier in the year and the resulting cut in the fine campaigning season. Special winter clothing had not been prepared, as a speedy victory had been anticipated. This neglect badly hit German morale, and was symptomatic of a wider failure of generalship and forethought.

Much of the discussion about Barbarossa focuses on whether, and how, the Germans could have captured Moscow. While useful, much of this discussion appears to be based on an assumption that its capture would have led to Soviet collapse. This is misleading. The Soviets intended to fight on and to hold the line of the Volga east of Moscow. The precedent of Napoleon's failure in 1812 is valuable, but there was the additional element added by the 'total' character of German goals and the brutality of their methods. This made it difficult for much of the Soviet, particularly Russian, people to do anything other than struggle on. Thus, at the wider strategic level, in judging Barbarossa there is a failure to move beyond operational issues.

The Germans were also stalled on the approaches to Leningrad, where Hitler had complemented the blockade of the city with an advance to its east that was stopped by Soviet reinforcements east of Tikhuin. Heavy casualties, exhaustion and the winter robbed the Germans of their ability to sustain operations against firm opposition. Field Marshal Wilhelm von Leeb, the commander of Army Group North, was to respond to Soviet attacks in January 1942 by seeking permission to retreat from the Leningrad area, and resigned when Hitler refused. Leeb's attitude reflected the exposed situation in which German forces in the region had been left at the close of the 1941 offensive.

Further south, the Soviet forces had lost another 106,000 prisoners in a new pocket between the Dnieper and the Sea of Azov in early October 1941, while, to avoid encirclement, they abandoned Kharkov, which the Germans easily captured on 24 October. Nevertheless, the Germans were continuing to encounter resistance, the Soviets were deploying fresh troops, and the mud was further reducing the pace of the advance. When they advanced on Rostov, the crossing place over the Don, the Germans found that the Soviet ability to regroup was far greater than had been appreciated. Rather than relying on a simple system of linear defences, the Soviets created an effective system of belts of defences. Rostov fell on 21 November, after a hard-fought advance, but the Soviets then mounted a well-planned and prepared counterattack which forced Field Marshal Rundstedt to abandon the city and to withdraw to a better defensive line. When Hitler ordered him to stand fast, Rundstedt resigned. Had the Germans stood fast they would have been committed to linear defences in a vulnerable position and would probably have been encircled.

In December 1941, continued German underestimation of the Soviets' numbers and fighting quality was further seen in the success of the Soviet winter counter-offensive, launched on 5–6 December, which took the Germans by surprise. Using fresh troops, helped by better logistics, and benefiting from surprise and effective command, the Soviets initially made significant gains at the expense of exhausted and spread-out units of Army Group Centre, leading the German high command to suffer a crisis. Whatever is meant by *Blitzkrieg* no longer appeared a winning formula: it had failed tactically, operationally and strategically, although German successes the following spring were to indicate the resilience of German warmaking. Fuller was to review the German failure in the *Sunday Pictorial* of 20 August 1944:

> when they turned on Russia they made the enormous blunder of hinging these tactics of velocity onto their theory of the unlimited offensive…. In Poland and France, the conditions favoured the Germans. The one was a flat open country, the other a well-roaded one. In both the depth of the vital area was comparatively shallow…. In two stupendous campaigns [1941 and 1942] they charged into Russia until their momentum was exhausted. But still the vital area was not fully occupied…. In such fighting, unless both sides are exhausted, or a narrow front can be found, you can only do one of two things: advance or retire.

The strength of Soviet resistance in late 1941 also affected German plans and operations elsewhere, not least by depriving their army in

North Africa of adequate reinforcements.[5] The *Luftwaffe* was also now spread more widely.

## Genocide

The German advance into the Soviet Union in 1941 had brought far more people judged unsuitable by Hitler, both Jews and Slavs, under his control, providing both a problem and opportunities for the implementation of Nazi plans. Action Groups (*Einsatzgruppen*), advancing close behind the advancing troops from the opening day of the invasion, killed Jews, political commissars and others deemed 'undesirable', in general with the co-operation of the army. Close to 1 million Jews were killed within six months in the territories conquered in Barbarossa. Most were killed by the Germans, although the Romanians did their part in the area they overran, while in Lithuania and Ukraine the Germans had some local support. The killings were in open country, not in concentration camps. At Babi Yar, outside Kiev, the Germans recorded slaughtering 33,771 Jews in three days.[6]

Terrible as this was, a still more drastic 'Final Solution' was being planned from late 1941. This was the detention of Jews throughout Europe, their deportation to distant camps, mostly in Poland, and their gassing. The policy led to experiments in how best to kill people. At the concentration camp at Auschwitz, Zyklon B (prussic acid) poison-gas crystals were used on Soviet prisoners, instead of the rats it was intended for, from August 1941. From at least 8 December, Jews were killed in gas vans en route to the concentration camp at Chelmno, where eventually over 150,000 Jews were killed. Other camps swiftly followed.

The ferocity of Nazi attitudes was also seen in Hitler's speech to his senior commanders on 30 March 1941, to treat Communism as 'social criminality', as well as more specific injunctions, for example the secret instructions to Colonel-General Küchler, Leeb's successor, to wipe Leningrad off the face of the earth by bombing and artillery fire, and to reject any surrender terms that might be offered. The harsh content and tone of orders of the day by many commanders to their units scarcely encouraged a reasonable treatment of Jews, Communists and prisoners. In the field, the treatment of Soviet prisoners by the army was brutal. Under instructions issued in July 1941, any resistance by prisoners, however passive, was to be immediately ended by force. Most were sentenced to a lingering death, by giving them very low rations, as well as by taking their greatcoats and hats and denying them heating and, often, shelter. Combined with epidemics, this treatment ensured that several million Soviet prisoners died.

German plans for the future of Europe might seem a macabre contrast to this brutality, but, in fact, the killing of those deemed unwanted was central to this schema. The Nazi leadership planned a 'New Order', with Germany central to a European system and the Germans at the top of a racial hierarchy. The economy of Europe was to be made subservient to German interests, with the rest of Europe providing Germany with labour, raw materials and food, and taking German industrial products; industrial plant in occupied areas was taken over. New rail and, in particular, road routes were to provide transport links. Much of the former Soviet Union was designated for occupation, but, to the east, Siberia was to be maintained as a rump state to which undesirables who were appropriate neither for Germanisation nor for extermination were to be forcibly transferred.

## Japan moves to war

In a world away from the Russian snows, a different war had been launched in the Pacific on 7 December. It also was to indicate the difficulty of sustaining a high tempo of advance and of translating military triumphs into an acceptable outcome. The collapse of France and the Netherlands to German attack in 1940, and the weakening position of Britain, already vulnerable in the Far East (of which the Japanese were well informed), created an apparent power vacuum in East and South-East Asia. This encouraged Japanese ambitions southwards into Indo-China and the East Indies, while leading the Americans to feel that only they were in a position to resist Japan.

The unresolved character of the war in China not only embittered Japanese relations with America but also exacerbated resource issues in Japanese military planning, as well as placing a major burden on Japanese finances. Japanese economic weakness was such that her trade deficit was condemning her to the prospect of national bankruptcy in the spring of 1942.

Germany's victory over France in 1940 encouraged Japan to revive relations that had been dimmed when Hitler had concluded his non-aggression pact with Stalin the previous year. On 27 September 1940, in response to pressure from the military, Japan joined Germany and Italy in the Tripartite Pact. The Japanese government and military, although divided, were determined to expand at the expense of others, particularly, from 1940, in South-East Asia, which was, to Japan, the 'southern resources area'. From June 1940, the Japanese navy had begun full mobilisation, although the German failure to invade Britain discouraged ideas of an attack on Britain's colonies that year. Continued Japanese aggression against China and, more particularly, expansion in French Indo-China (Cambodia, Laos and Vietnam) helped to trigger American commercial sanctions, specifically an embargo on oil exports. This was tantamount to an ultimatum, because, without oil, the Japanese armed forces would grind to a halt; so this, in turn, provoked the Japanese to act against the USA, in order to protect their position. They were unwilling to accept limitations on their expansion in the Far East. In 1941, the Japanese increasingly focused on the raw materials to be gained from South-East Asia and the East Indies.

The Americans considered themselves entitled to react forcefully to events on the other side of the Pacific. The passage of the Two-Ocean Naval Expansion Act on 19 July 1940 served notice on the Japanese that the Americans were going to be in a position to dominate the Pacific. Although it did not want war with Japan, the American government was resolved to prevent Japanese expansion, yet unable to make an accurate assessment of Japanese military capability.

French Indo-China came to play a crucial part in the crisis. America registered responses to what she saw as aggressive Japanese steps there. Indo-China was indeed of strategic importance as an axis of Japanese advance to the 'southern resources area'. Japanese gains there also indicated a willingness to exploit the weakness of the colonial powers that the Americans sought to contain. The occupation of crucial positions in northern Indo-China from November 1940, after a brief conflict with Vichy forces, led the Americans to step up limits on trade with Japan. However, in March 1941, the Japanese made the French accept a garrison in Saigon airport. Two months later, the Japanese obliged the French to accept their mediation award to Thailand of lands it claimed from Laos and Cambodia. These had been the cause of a Thai invasion earlier in the year, in which the Thais had been successful on land, but defeated at sea in the battle of Koh-Chang on 17 January, with the loss of two destroyers and one coast-defence ship, while one destroyer had been badly damaged.[7]

The declaration, on 24 July 1941, of a joint Franco-Japanese protectorate over all French Indo-China led to a trade embargo and the freezing of Japanese assets in America. The Americans also demanded that the Japanese withdraw from China and Indo-China. From May 1941, the USA sent supplies to China under Lend–Lease legislation, following up, in July, with the establishment of a Military Mission to China.

In turn, the Japanese built up reserves of raw materials, and, subsequently, decided to launch a war if diplomacy failed to lead to a lifting of the embargo. On 25 June, the army and navy agreed to obtain their goals in South-East Asia so as to be able to respond subsequently to the apparently imminent collapse of the Soviet Union, with which a Neutrality Pact had been signed on 13 April 1941. This Pact had initially been seen as a way to strengthen Japan's position in negotiations with the USA. On 4 September, the Japanese government yielded to military pressure for war at the end of October.

On 17 October 1941, a hard-line ministry under General Hideki Tōjō, hitherto the Army Minister, gained power. Tōjō was resolved not to withdraw from China, but there was a serious division of opinion as to whether to fight America or focus on other goals, either China or South-East Asia, and also, in the event of war with America, as to what targets should be attacked. Admiral Isoroku Yamamoto, the Commander of the Combined Fleet, pressed for a surprise attack on the base of the American Pacific Fleet at Pearl Harbor on the island of Oahu in the Hawaiian archipelago. Other naval commanders were opposed, but Yamamoto's insistence that such an attack was a necessary prelude for covering operations against Malaya, the Philippines and the Dutch East Indies, with their crucial oilfields, won the day. The plan was approved on 3 November.[8]

## Pearl Harbor

On 7 December (8 December on the other side of the International Date Line), the Japanese attacked Pearl Harbor without any prior declaration of war, stealing 'the most basic of freedoms: the freedom to choose war and peace',[9] as well as achieving a degree of surprise that indicated considerable deficiency in American intelligence gathering and assessment, and that has led to a morass of conspiracy theories.[10] The Americans had considered the prospect of a Japanese pre-emptive strike, but thought the Philippines the most probable target, while the Pacific Command in Hawaii focused on the threat from the nearest Japanese territory, the Marshall Islands, and not from the north, the direction from which the Japanese came. The defences on Oahu were manned for sabotage, not air attack.

The Japanese planned to wreck the American Pacific Fleet, but the bombers found battleships, rather than the more crucial aircraft carriers, which were not in harbour; 353 aircraft from six Japanese carriers totally destroyed two American battleships and damaged three more, while nearly 300 American aircraft were destroyed or damaged on the ground. A supporting attack by Japanese submarines accomplished little. The damage to their battleships forced an important shift in American naval planning away from an emphasis on capital ships and, instead, towards carriers. The attack also revealed grave deficiencies in Japanese (as well as American) planning, as well as in the Japanese war machine. Only 45 per cent of naval air requirements had been met by the start of the war, and the last torpedoes employed in the attack were delivered only two days before the fleet sailed, while modification of planes to carry both torpedoes and heavy bombs was also last minute.

Tactically successful, the Japanese had nevertheless failed to destroy Pearl Harbor. Because of the focus on destroying warships, there was no third-wave attack on the fuel and other harbour installations. Had the oil farms (stores) been destroyed, the Pacific Fleet would probably have had to fall back to the base at San Diego. Had the Japanese invaded the island of Oahu, the Americans would have had to do so, but the logistical task facing the Japanese in supporting such an invasion would have been formidable. Furthermore, the course of the war was to reveal that the strategic concepts that underlay the Japanese plan had been gravely flawed. Aside from underrating American economic strength and the resolve of its people, the Japanese had embarked on an attack that was not necessary. Their fleet was larger than the American Pacific and Asiatic Fleets, particularly in carriers, battleships and cruisers, and the American fleets, as a result, were not in a position to have prevented the Japanese from overrunning British and Dutch colonies. From the point of view of the Pacific naval balance, the Americans had too many warships in the Atlantic.[11]

## The fall of the Philippines

The Japanese also attacked British and American positions in the Western Pacific and East Asia. Hong Kong was attacked by a larger Japanese force on 8 December. The 12,000-strong garrison, with limited naval support and only seven outdated aircraft, was too weak for the task, not least because the defensive line in Kowloon on the mainland was too long to hold. The line was breached on the 9th, the defenders retreated to Hong Kong island, and the Japanese were able to make a night-time amphibious landing. Air support enabled them to block interference with their supply routes from British motor torpedo boats. Once on the island, the Japanese wore down their determined, but exhausted opponents. The strong Japanese attack was not inexorable, but the repeated pressure put great strain on the defenders. The remaining positions were forced to surrender on 25 December. The Japanese slaughtered wounded troops in the hospital.

After preliminary landings from 8 December, the main invasion of the Philippines was launched on 22 December, and organised resistance came to an end on 6 May 1942. The Japanese ability to destroy much of the US Far East Air Force on the ground on 8 December provided an important advantage, and reflected a serious lack of planning and rapid response on the American part. Having gained superiority in the air, the Japanese used it to attack American installations, seriously hitting morale and removing a threat to Japanese amphibious landings. Understandable fear of Japanese air power, and concern about the relative ratio of naval power, led the navy, mindful of the wider strategic position, to fail to provide the support requested by the commander of the US Forces in the Far East, General Douglas MacArthur (1880–1964). A convoy of reinforcements turned back, the navy refused to fly in planes, and the submarines were evacuated. This left the defenders in a hopeless position. The overall strategic misjudgement was comparable to that of the British in Malaya.

Superiority in the air and at sea enabled the Japanese to land where they pleased, and their small forces initially made rapid gains against poorly prepared defenders. MacArthur had dispersed his American and Filipino units and supplies to contest Japanese landings on Luzon. This was unsuccessful and deprived MacArthur of an adequate reserve as well as of necessary supplies, once stores had been overrun by the Japanese. The main Japanese force landed in Lingayen Gulf in north-west Luzon, with supporting units landing in south Luzon at Legaspi (12 December) and Lamon Bay (24 December), threatening Manila with a pincer attack.

Some of the poorly trained and inadequately equipped Philippine Army did not fight well (although this was not true of all units), while the designation of defence lines to protect Manila proved no substitute for their vigorous defence. MacArthur had made no adequate provision in the event of a Japanese success.[12] As a result, he decided to fall back to the Bataan peninsula west of Manila Bay, the initial plan that he had overturned in order to defend all of Luzon. Manila itself fell on 2 January 1942.

On Bataan, a more effective defence well supported by artillery was made from lines that the Japanese found it difficult to breach, although MacArthur had failed to prepare adequate logistics. Eventually, fresh troops supported by air and artillery attack drove in the American position. The American–Filipino garrison was malnourished, affected by disease and demoralised by the absence of relief. Bataan surrendered on 9 April, leaving Corregidor, an island in the Bay, as the last position. About 78,000 American and Filipino prisoners were made to walk 65 miles to San Fernando with minimal food and water, and under both a baking sun and the blows and bayonets of the victors. Many died on what was aptly termed the 'Death March'. Under heavy artillery and air attack, and short of food, the 15,000 American and Filipino troops on Corregidor surrendered to a 1,000-strong landing force.

As also elsewhere in response to the unexpected Japanese attack, in the Philippines unprepared Allied forces had been shown to lack a synergy of able commanders and troops able to take the initiative. The Japanese had initially landed only two divisions, whereas there were ten infantry divisions as well as other units among the defenders.[13]

Further east, American islands in the western Pacific were captured. Guam fell on 10 December to an expedition from the Mariana Islands. Wake Island was attacked on 12 December, but the Marine garrison drove off the attack, sinking two destroyers. A failure to relieve the island ensured, however, that, on 23 December, a second attack, supported by carriers from the Pearl Harbor operation, was successful, although only after heavy casualties.[14]

## The conquest of Malaya

The Japanese also mounted a successful invasion of Malaya. The British tried to challenge this with the dispatch of a powerful squadron from Singapore that was intended to contest the landings, but, on 10 December 1941, eighty-five land-based Japanese naval bombers sank the battleship *Prince of Wales* and the battle cruiser *Repulse* off Malaya. These were the first ships of these types sunk at sea solely by air attack, and their loss demonstrated the vulnerability of capital ships without air cover to enemy air attack. It arose primarily from the mistakes of the force Commander, Admiral Sir Tom Phillips. His poorly conceived and executed plan reflected wider problems: a lack of strategic foresight and operational weaknesses, including the problems of air–sea coordination.[15] This blunder was one of a series of serious Allied command lapses that the Japanese exploited, including the loss of most of the American planes in the Philippines on the ground two days earlier.

In Malaya, the British considerably outnumbered the Japanese, but the latter were better prepared, led and trained, had the strategic initiative, fought well, were more mobile, used light tanks, and enjoyed air superiority and control of the sea. Many of the Japanese units had gained battle experience in China. The British, in contrast, were poorly trained and inadequately led. The Japanese landed in northern Malaya (a far from easy opposed landing which led to 15 per cent of the troops becoming casualties) and nearby Thai ports on 8 December, and then rapidly advanced. The destruction of British planes on the ground further accentuated the already marked advantage the Japanese enjoyed in the number and quality of aircraft.

The main axis of Japanese advance was near the west coast. Although some British units fought hard and took heavy casualties, there was a lack of success in battle. More generally, the British alternated unsuitable defensive lines with inappropriate withdrawals. They had relied on the jungle to anchor their positions and limit the opportunities for Japanese advance, but this assumption rested on a lack of knowledge of the terrain combined with a failure to appreciate Japanese capability. Penang fell on 19 December, the capital, Kuala Lumpur, following on 11 January 1942. As the Japanese advanced they gained bases and supplies, particularly airfields, that they could use against the British. The presence of engineers with the advance forces enabled the Japanese to repair the bridges, whose destruction became the major effort of the increasingly exhausted and demoralised defence. The speed of the Japanese advance deprived the British of the opportunity to recover their equipoise and make adequate preparations, and also demoralised them. Numerous British reinforcements were landed in Singapore, but many were not ready for conflict. Their positions outflanked by land and sea, the British fell back on Singapore: Malaya had been fully evacuated by 31 January 1942. Japanese combat effectiveness and skilful command interacted with a British failure to excel in either. Japanese planning was also superior. In large part, this reflected the degree to which the British had concentrated on the immediate threat from Germany.

## The loss of Singapore

Singapore was successfully invaded on the night of 8–9 February 1942. The defence was poorly organised and troop morale was low. The decision to try to defend all of the coastline ensured that there was an inadequate reserve, while at the point of invasion there were insufficient defenders. As in Malaya, the Japanese ability to concentrate on a limited front and exploit success on this axis of advance was crucial. There was also inadequate British air support. The failure to mount an effective counterattack against the main Japanese landing site was a serious error. As the Japanese fought their way across the island, the defenders were threatened by the loss of water supplies, while morale collapsed. Although ordered to fight on and to engage in street fighting in order to tie down and kill Japanese troops, the British commander, Percival, advised by his staff and fellow senior officers, asked for terms on the 15th and surrendered unconditionally with his 62,000 troops that afternoon. The Japanese lost 5,000 dead or wounded in the operation.

Singapore's surrender, later described by Churchill as the 'greatest disaster in British military history', was a major blow to British prestige in Asia and to the military resources of the alliance created by Japanese aggression. It brought to a close a seventy-day campaign in which 130,000 British and Allied troops were taken prisoner.[16] As in the Philippines,[17] the Japanese followed up their victory by harshly treating the surrendered troops, whose lack of fighting spirit and surrender they could not comprehend, and by slaughtering thousands of Chinese civilians: possibly up to 50,000.[18] Many of the prisoners of war were sent to work on the Burma–Thailand railway, where about 12,000 prisoners (from there and other sources) and 90,000 native labourers died as a result of the terrible conditions.

## The conquest of the Dutch East Indies

The Japanese pressed on to attack the Dutch East Indies (now Indonesia) and Burma. Already, in December 1941, the Japanese had struck at north Borneo, capturing Miri in Sarawak with a force sent from Indo-China (15 December), and moving on to Kuching. British North Borneo was to be occupied from Sarawak in January 1942. The attack on the Dutch East Indies began on 11 January with a landing on Tarakan, and, that month, saw Japanese amphibious forces leapfrog forward through the Straits of Makassar and the Molucca Passage, to the west and east of the Celebes, capturing ports there and in Borneo. Another force captured Ambon in the Moluccas, and another advanced from Sarawak to leapfrog down the western coast of Borneo. These gains provided bases from which Japanese attacks on Java, Bali and Timor could be prepared. Aircraft were moved forward into airbases. The poorly equipped Dutch garrisons were too weak to put up much resistance or to provide mutual support. The lack of adequate air power was a particular problem for the Dutch.

In February, a Japanese force that had sailed from Camranh Bay in Vietnam attacked Sumatra. Allied naval forces tried to protect Java, unsuccessfully attacking an invasion fleet in the battle of the Java Sea on 27 February. The battle throws light on the issue of fighting quality. The two fleets were relatively balanced, with 5 cruisers and 10 destroyers in the Allied fleet and 4 and 13 in that of the Japanese. However, the latter was well coordinated, enjoyed superior air support and benefited from better torpedoes. In contrast, the American, Australian, British and Dutch warships lacked an able commander and experience of fighting together.

Heavy Allied losses, then and subsequently, left the Japanese in a dominant position, and, on the night of 28 February–1 March, they landed on Java. With total air superiority the Japanese rapidly advanced. Batavia, the capital of Java, fell on 5 March, and Surbaya, in east Java, three days later. On 8 March, the Dutch East Indies government surrendered.

## The conquest of Burma

Burma fell rapidly, with the mismanaged British defence being exploited by the Japanese, who conquered the country at the cost of fewer than 2,000 dead. As in Malaya, the Japanese proved adroit at outflanking manoeuvres and at exploiting the disorientating consequences for the British of their withdrawals; although the garrison was far weaker than that in Malaya. Yet again, the British troops were untrained for jungle warfare. Serious flaws in planning arose from the contempt for the Japanese of Sir Archibald Wavell, the Commander-in-Chief in India. Confident about the developing situation in Malaya, the Japanese Southern Army invaded from the Kra Peninsula in Thailand on 15 January, while the 55th Division struck across the Thai border towards Moulmein on 30 January. Rangoon fell on 8 March, Mandalay on 1 May, and the Japanese advanced in northern Burma and towards India, capturing Myitkyina on 8 May and Kalewa on 14 May.[19]

Chinese intervention in Burma from March helped the British, but was not sufficient to sway the outcome. Burma was seized in order to provide the Japanese with a buffer against attack from India as well as to cut the Burma Road, opened in 1938, through which the Nationalist Chinese were supplied, and also because it was an important source of oil. The threat to supply routes to China led to speculation that resistance there would collapse. Once Burma had been conquered, the Japanese sought to use it to demonstrate their credentials as liberators of Asia. After Japanese experiments with Burmese civil administration, first by the Burma Independence Army, Burma was awarded independence in August 1943, although very much under Japanese control.

## Japanese warmaking

The Japanese benefited in their conquests from their ability to gain control of the air and, in the East Indies, the sea, from good operational plans, and from the rapid tempo of their advance. The cumulative nature of Japanese advances was important to this rapid tempo. For example, in the Philippines, the Japanese had initially been stalled by the withdrawal of American forces to the Bataan peninsula, but, having captured Hong Kong and Malaya, the Japanese then moved artillery and aircraft to the Philippines. The major bases for their advances in the East Indies were Davao in the Philippines and Camranh Bay.

Aside from Japanese advantages, not least dominating the tempo of war, high morale, the ability to mount effective amphibious operations,[20] and the quality of the navy's lightweight, manoeuvrable and long-range A6M Zero fighter aircraft (which outclassed the American Brewster F-2A Buffalo and the Curtiss P-40), their conquests reflected the poorly prepared and coordinated nature of the opposition. The American, British and Dutch units in the region were insufficient for the vast area they had to cover, they lacked air support, and the ground forces were inadequately trained and equipped, and, some of them, low in morale. Whereas in 1939–40 the Germans had established their superiority in fast-moving mechanised warfare, the Japanese army concentrated on infantry operations, although, in part due to the lightness of their supply 'tail', they were also fast moving. They therefore showed their superiority over Western forces in infantry warfare.

This reflected not only Japanese strengths but also Allied deficiencies, not least in doctrine and training. Infantry units that were essentially colonial gendarmeries and/or all-purpose (rather than specifically tropical warfare) fighting troops proved of limited value. Although they were seriously deficient in mechanised equipment and transport and lacked good anti-aircraft guns, radar and adequate medical facilities, the Japanese weaponry was robust, and they had plentiful artillery, especially howitzers, whose indirect plunging fire was of particular use in the terrain. Typical of the equipment as a whole, the Japanese howitzers, especially the Model 91 (1931) 105 mm and the Model 92 (1932) 70 mm, were lightweight and manoeuvrable, and therefore particularly suitable to being moved forward over difficult terrain. The standard rifle, the Model 99 (1939) 7.7 mm, however, had a magazine capacity of only five rounds, which led to a slower rate of fire than the ten-round British Lee-Enfield Mk III.

## The Indian Ocean

The successes already mentioned did not seem to be the limit of Japanese ambitions. On 19 February 1942, Darwin was bombed, the first in a series of air attacks on northern Australia. These raids were launched from aircraft carriers and from bases on the Celebes. Christmas Island, south of Java and north-west of Australia, was captured by the Japanese on 31 March: the Indian soldiers in the small garrison had already killed their British officers.

A Japanese fleet that included six carriers moved into the Indian Ocean. In April, a Japanese naval raid on Ceylon (Sri Lanka) led to heavy damage to shore installations at Colombo and Trincomalee and the sinking, on 5 and 9 April, of two British heavy cruisers and a carrier inadequately protected from dive-bombers. The Japanese lost no warships in the operation. In addition, a Japanese squadron mounted air raids on ports in east India and attacks on shipping in the Bay of Bengal, while, on land, the Japanese overran Burma.

Had the Japanese been able to establish a permanent naval presence in the Indian Ocean, they would have threatened not only the British position in India, but also that in the Middle East, challenging British oil supplies from the Persian Gulf and routes to Australia. The build-up of Ceylon's garrison to a strength of two divisions by the close of March 1942 was a response. As there was to be no Japanese landing, this force was not tested, and when space is at a premium it is easy to ignore such moves. However, they throw important light on strategic preferences. The troops deployed in Ceylon could not be sent to protect against an advance from Burma, as Wavell wished, and the decision reflected the determination of the Chiefs of Staff to maintain oceanic links. Had the Japanese landed an invasion force on Ceylon, it is difficult to see why they should not have repeated earlier successes: Allied fighting quality was not stronger.

After the sinking of the British warships, the British withdrew their fleet from Ceylon: to East Africa or Bombay. Admiral Somerville was now having to think about the need to protect the Arabian Sea, and thus tanker sailings from the Persian Gulf, as well as the route from both the Gulf and the Red Sea down the coast of East Africa to the Cape of Good Hope.

The crisis ended with most of the Japanese warships being deployed for an attack on Port Moresby. It led, however, to acute concern about the security of Ceylon, and even the whole of India. In response, the British decided to strengthen their position in the Indian Ocean by capturing Madagascar from Vichy French forces, ending Hitler's idea of turning the island into a massive ghetto for Europe's Jews as well as the possibility that it might become a Japanese submarine base. Once Nagumo had withdrawn, the British fleet covered the invasion of Madagascar in May.

The Japanese raid into the Indian Ocean is one of the great counterfactuals (what ifs) of the war. The Allied position there had serious weaknesses, not least in conjunction with Axis advances in North Africa. Britain had the resources of India and the Persian Gulf, but there was a greater vulnerability to Japanese attack than that of the USA in the far larger Pacific. The Japanese were to send submarines into the Mozambique Channel, and there was no equivalent to Madagascar in Latin America, while the entire British position in South Asia would have been challenged had either the Soviet Union or China succumbed to Axis attack.

The British navy had been weakened by its heavy losses in the Mediterranean. With bases, once repaired and developed, in Singapore and Rangoon, the Indian Ocean seemed vulnerable to the

Japanese, and this contributed to the creation of their defensive perimeter. Instead, however, of pursuing their advantage against the secondary enemy, the Japanese sent their carriers into the Pacific theatre against their strongest opponent, first into the Coral Sea and then to Midway. Losses there reduced strategic options for future campaigns in the Indian Ocean. Four of the carriers Nagumo had taken into the Indian Ocean were destroyed at Midway. Conversely, had the Japanese concentrated on the Pacific theatre throughout, and not launched the raid into the Indian Ocean, they might have been in a better position to exploit their initial advantage in the Pacific, not least by destroying the remainder of the American Pacific Fleet.

## Japan versus the USA

Although it was unclear what they would press on to achieve, the Japanese had already, by April 1942, gained control of over 90 million people as well as important resources, including the oil they sought urgently, as well as minerals, rice and rubber. These were the resources designed to support the Japanese war economy and to enable Japan to resist Allied counterattack.

This expansion also encouraged Japan to expand and develop its idea of a Co-Prosperity Sphere. On 21 January 1942, Tōjō, in a statement to the Diet, referred to the benefits to be obtained from co-prosperity in a system in which Japan was the core helping other East Asian peoples find their proper place. This pointed the way towards the creation of the Greater East Asia ministry in November 1942, to the encouragement of pan-Asian thought, and to the granting of titular independence to Burma and the Philippines in August 1943. In the latter, a provisional Council of State, composed of Filipino politicians, had hitherto served as the government in co-operation with the Japanese.[21] That November, the Japanese-backed Provisional Government of Free India, which had been formed by the Indian nationalist Subhas Chandra Bose in October 1943, was given administrative control of the Andaman and Nicobar Islands in the Indian Ocean, which had been occupied by Japan in March 1942.

The pan-Asianism represented by the Co-Prosperity Sphere was of little benefit to Japan. As with Hitler's treatment of conquered territories and allies, there was a serious clash between rhetoric and the reality of Japanese control and economic exploitation. The latter included the setting of exchange rates so as to enable Japan to gain food, raw materials and manufactured goods cheaply. The notion of racial equality did not match the treatment of the Chinese and others. Possibilities for more benign developments were wrecked as much by the logic of Japanese control as by the impact of Japanese failures, and the Japanese gained relatively little willing support.[22] Thailand, which had briefly resisted the Japanese landings on 8 December 1941, ceased to do so the following day, and declared war on Britain and the USA on 25 January 1942. It was rewarded by Japan with territory in Malaya (1942) and Burma (1943), but brought scant benefit to Japan in terms of industrial capacity or military assistance.

Japan's gains had been won at the cost of relatively few fatalities: a total of about 15,000. Seizing and keeping the initiative had enabled them to translate numerical inferiority into a more favourable position at the point of engagement. The Japanese, however, suffered from the lack of a realistic war plan. This, in part, arose from the confusion in Japanese policymaking, with differences between military and civilian populations, and between army and navy, interacting with rifts over strategy. As with Hitler and both Britain and the Soviet Union, a conviction of the weakness of the opposing system led to a failure to judge resolve. The initial Japanese ability to mount successful attacks, to gain great swathes of territory, and to establish an apparent stranglehold on the Far East did not deter the Americans from the long-term effort of driving back and destroying their opponents. The American government and public were not interested in the idea of a compromise peace with the power that had attacked Pearl Harbor. Japan, the weaker power, had gone to war with the one power that could beat her, and in a way most calculated to ensure that she did so. As Hector Bywater had predicted in his novel *The Great Pacific War: A History of the American–Japanese Campaign of 1931–1933* (London and New York, 1925), despite initial Japanese victories, the more powerful state finally won.

There were also serious deficiencies in particular areas of Japanese doctrine, weaponry and military-industrial infrastructure. For example, Japanese air power could not compete in the long term, not least because of coordination failures in its aero-industry. The Japanese also lacked a heavy bomber, while their planes were deficient in armour and self-sealing tanks.[23]

Having declared war on Japan on 8 December, the USA created the most powerful war economy in the world. The War Production Board was established in January 1942, while the Joint Chiefs of Staff were established the following month. Although Fiorello La Guardia, Mayor of New York and the Head of the Office of Civilian Defense, had warned, on 8 December, of likely attacks on the East Coast, creating widespread alarm (and the Japanese were to land on Attu and Kiska in the Aleutian islands the following June), in fact the USA was now the safe powerhouse and centre of the war against the entire Axis.

## The Middle East

A series of Allied operations had ensured that the worlds of German and Japanese conquests would be kept apart. They were at the expense of pro-German neutral powers: Vichy France, Iraq and Persia. German successes in the Balkans, the Mediterranean and North Africa had underlined the importance to Britain of the attitude of the administrators of Vichy colonies. The Free French under Charles de Gaulle had had some successes. In late 1940, de Gaulle won over French Equatorial Africa from Vichy. However, the key colonies remained under Vichy control. Anxiety about the spread of German influence, specifically the establishment of bases for the *Luftwaffe*, spurred the British to act. In May–July 1941, they overthrew the pro-German government in Iraq and conquered Vichy-run Lebanon and Syria.

The conquest of Iraq in April and May indicated the range of environments in which the war was waged prior to Soviet and Japanese entry into the main struggle. It also showed the variety of weaponry employed. On the Tigris, the British used river steamers to open the route to Kut. The range of forces used by the British included aircraft, which made a major impact, and Assyrian and Kurdish levies as well as the Arab Legion. The Iraqis were defeated in a Middle Eastern *Blitzkrieg*, which was a mix of the flying columns and employment of native allies used in the imperial wars of the nineteenth century and the application of more modern weaponry, especially aircraft and armoured cars. With four divisions, Iraqi forces were larger, but, after the Iraqis began the conflict by blockading the British airbase at Habbaniyah, west of Baghdad, on 29–30 April, they lost the initiative.

From 2 May 1941, the British launched air attacks on Iraqi positions near the base, gaining control of the air, and supporting ground action. Other British forces moved into Iraq from Jordan and from the Persian Gulf. The former, a mobile flying column, crossed the desert, linked up with the Habbaniyah garrison. The subsequent advance on Baghdad was more difficult as the marshy ground and dykes of the Euphrates and Tigris valleys and the land in between made for difficult terrain, which was exacerbated by deliberate flooding and the demolition of bridges. Well-entrenched Iraqi positions supported by machine guns and artillery delayed the British advance, but the fall of the government under Rashid Ali, demoralised by British success, led to an armistice and the installation of a favourable ministry. The campaign had shown the importance of engineers, especially in bridging waterways so that motorised forces could cross.

Concern about the *Luftwaffe* using airbases in Syria led the British to decide to intervene there. This would prevent the Germans from opening a new flank from which to attack Egypt and would give the British valuable strategic depth if they were defeated in North Africa.

Attacked on 8 June, the Vichy French forces in Syria and Lebanon put up a fiercer resistance than the Iraqis: they were more numerous than their British attackers, were well trained, had good artillery, tanks and armoured cars, and a determined leadership, and benefited from the terrain. The British found it necessary to blast Vichy defenders out of positions, and also had to face effective counterattacks. However, the initial axes of invasion – from Palestine and Jordan – were supported, from late June, by advances from Iraq. The Vichy forces had already lost Damascus on 21 June. Palmyra fell on 3 July to a force from Iraq that pressed on toward Homs, while in Lebanon, backed by naval support, Allied forces advanced to Beirut. The Vichy commander asked for terms on 10 July, and signed an armistice four days later. Most of the French troops chose to be returned to Vichy France and not to join de Gaulle. He, in turn, was angry about the British role in the conquered territories after the armistice.[24]

On 25 August 1941, British and Soviet troops had entered Persia (Iran), rapidly gaining control of the state and forcing the pro-Axis shah to abdicate in favour of his son. The Allies thus gained control of supply routes across Persia, including those by which the Soviet Union could be supplied, as well as strategic oilfields, and won additional depth in the event of German gains in the Middle East. They remained in occupation of Persia until 1945, and benefited from the increase in its oil production during the war.

## 'Germany First'

Hitler followed up Pearl Harbor by declaring war on the USA on 11 December 1941 (as did Mussolini), in accordance, he said, with German obligations under the Tripartite Treaty (with Italy and Japan), although, strictly, the terms of the treaty did not require it. This was a crucial step that prevented any chance of the USA fighting only Japan. Germany had planned for war with the USA since 1937, but Hitler's motives in 1941 are unclear, although he was angered by American co-operation with the British against German submarine operations in the Atlantic. He claimed that his decision was in response to American 'provocations' in the Atlantic, although there is no sign that there was any informed analysis of the likely trajectory of war between Japan and the USA or of the consequences for Germany of war with America. There appears to have been confidence that the U-boats would weaken the USA and there was a failure to appreciate the impact of American entry in World War One. Hitler may also have hoped that a grateful Japan would attack the Soviet Union.

Hitler's declaration let Roosevelt off the hook, since he agreed with Churchill that Hitler was a greater menace than the Japanese, although not all American opinion shared this view. One of the many counterfactuals that the war readily lends itself to is that of what would have occurred had Germany not declared war. Such counterfactuals are not invalid, not least because many relate to the issues that concerned leaders and planners at the time. Furthermore, the consideration of counterfactuals helps undermine the air of inevitability and determinism that can underlie discussion when the course of events is well known.

Hitler's declaration led to the 'Germany First' strategy, which was to see the bulk of American land and air assets allocated to preparing for an invasion of Europe, although such a strategy had already been outlined in the Rainbow 5 war plan and the Anglo-American–Canadian ABC-1 Plan talks in early 1941, which had envisaged a defensive strategy in the Pacific in the event of war with the three Axis powers. Roosevelt had supported this because of concern that Britain might collapse. This strategy led the American army manoeuvres in 1941 to focus on preparing for European-theatre conflict, and was confirmed by the Washington Conference that began on 22 December 1941. The conference led to the creation of an Anglo-American planning mechanism based on the Combined Chiefs of Staff. It was also agreed both that American forces should be moved to Northern Ireland, to prepare for operations in Europe, and that the Americans should plan an invasion of Morocco. The preparation for the fight-back had begun.

As the Soviet Union, then in a non-aggression pact with Germany, and Japan, which had not been informed of Hitler's forthcoming attack, had signed a non-aggression pact in April 1941, all the conflicts in the world were not linked, but all major powers were, from December 1941, at war. The character of the war had been transformed.

'Germany First' had consequences throughout the world. An emphasis on fighting Germany helped the Soviet Union by diverting German resources to resist American attacks, while a focus on Japan would not have had these consequences. Conversely, an emphasis on the latter might have assisted China, and have ensured that the Japanese were not able to mount offensives there and against India in 1944. However, military assets are not transferable and usable in the simple fashion that such remarks might suggest. There were major problems, particularly, but not solely, logistical, associated with the allocation of units and resources; and the capacity of the Pacific to take, and employ effectively, more troops in 1942 and 1943 was limited.

The question of emphasis did not address the problem of timing. The Japanese successes in early 1942, combined with those of the

Germans against the Soviets that summer, led to American pressure for swifter action than the British envisaged. The latter were concerned about the risks of a premature invasion of France, in large part because they were aware that resources alone could not counteract German fighting quality. Nevertheless, in April 1942, it was agreed that France would be invaded in 1943 and the pace of the movement of American forces to Britain stepped up. Thus, as the Japanese raided the Indian Ocean and planned an advance on Port Moresby in New Guinea, the Allies were already debating how best to destroy the power of the Axis.

## NOTES

1  D.M. Glantz (ed.), *The Initial Phase of the War on the Eastern Front, 22 June–August 1941* (1993).
2  S. Corvaja, *Hitler and Mussolini* (New York, 2001), p. 236.
3  R.A. Doughty, 'Myth of the *Blitzkrieg*', in L.J. Matthews (ed.), *Challenging the United States Symmetrically and Asymmetrically: Can America be Defeated?* (Carlisle Barracks, Pennsylvania, 1998), pp. 57–79.
4  J. Barber and M. Harrison, *The Soviet Home Front 1941–1945: A Social and Economic History of the USSR in World War II* (1991), p. 130; G.K. Zhukov, *The Memoirs of Marshal Zhukov* (New York, 1971), p. 266; R.W. Thurston and B. Bonwetsch (eds), *The People's War: Responses to World War II in the Soviet Union* (Urbana, Illinois, 2000).
5  D.M. Glantz, *Barbarossa. Hitler's Invasion of Russia 1941* (Stroud, 2001); B. Fugate, *Operation Barbarossa: Strategy and Tactics on the Eastern Front, 1941* (Novato, California, 1984); K. Reinhardt, *Moscow, The Turning Point: The Failure of Hitler's Military Strategy in the Winter of 1941–1942* (Providence, Rhode Island, 1992).
6  C.R. Browning, *Ordinary Men: Reserve Police Battalion 101 and the Final Solution in Poland* (New York, 1993).
7  M.J. Whitley, *Destroyers of World War Two. An International Encyclopedia* (2002), p. 227.
8  D.M. Goldstein and K.V. Dillon (eds), *The Pearl Harbor Papers: Inside the Japanese Plans* (1993).
9  W.A. McDougall, *Promised Land, Crusader State. The American Encounter with the World since 1776* (New York, 1997), p. 151.
10  R. Wohlstetter, *Pearl Harbor: Warning and Decision* (Stanford, 1962); H.L. Trefouse, *Pearl Harbor: The Continuing Controversy* (Malabar, Florida, 1982).
11  H.P. Willmott, *Pearl Harbor* (2001); H. Conroy and H. Wray (eds), *Pearl Harbor Revisited: Prologue to the Pacific War* (Honolulu, 1990); R.W. Love (ed.), *Pearl Harbor Revisited* (Basingstoke, 1995).

12  R.B. Meixsel, 'Major General George Grunert, WPO-3, and the Philippine Army, 1940–1941', *Journal of Military History*, 59 (1995), p. 324.

13  L. Morton, *The Fall of the Philippines* (Washington, 1953); J. Toland, *But Not in Shame: The Six Months after Pearl Harbor* (New York, 1961); W. Rutherford, *Fall of the Philippines* (New York, 1971); R.H. Firth, *A Matter of Time. Why the Philippines Fell: The Japanese Invasion, 1941–1942* (2nd edn, Walnut, California, 1981); J.W. Whitman, *Bataan Our Last Ditch: The Bataan Campaign, 1942* (New York, 1990).

14  G.J.W. Urwin, *Facing Fearful Odds: The Siege of Wake Island* (Lincoln, Nebraska, 1997).

15  For a recent study, see C.M. Bell, 'The "Singapore Strategy" and the Deterrence of Japan: Winston Churchill, the Admiralty and the Dispatch of Force Z', *English Historical Review*, 116 (2001), pp. 604–34, esp. p. 633.

16  M. Tsuji, *Singapore 1941–42: The Japanese Version of the Malaya Campaign of World War II* (Oxford, 1988).

17  D. Knox, *Death March: The Survivors of Bataan* (New York, 1981).

18  R. Callahan, *The Worst Disaster: The Fall of Singapore* (1977); A. Warren, *Singapore 1942. Britain's Greatest Defeat* (2002), p. 279.

19  I.L. Grant and K. Tamayama, *Burma 1942: The Japanese Invasion. Both Sides Tell the Story of a Savage Jungle War* (Chichester, 1999).

20  M.J. Grove, 'The Development of Japanese Amphibious Warfare, 1874 to 1942', in G. Till, T. Farrell and M.J. Grove, *Amphibious Operations* (Camberley, 1997), p. 23.

21  D.J. Steinberg, *Philippine Collaboration in World War II* (Ann Arbor, 1967).

22  G.K. Goodman (ed.), *Japanese Cultural Policies in Southeast Asia during World War Two* (Basingstoke, 1991).

23  A.D. Harvey, 'Army Air Force and Navy Air Force: Japanese Aviation and the Opening Phase of the War in the Far East', *War in History*, 6 (1999), pp. 174–204, esp. pp. 177–80.

24  G. Warner, *Iraq and Syria, 1941* (1974); A. Mockler, *Our Enemies the French: Being an Account of the War fought between the French and the British, Syria 1941* (1976); A.B. Gaunson, *The Anglo-French Clash in Lebanon and Syria, 1940–1945* (Basingstoke, 1997).

# CHAPTER FOUR

# *Attacks held, 1942*

In 1942, the Japanese found it impossible to sustain their offensive, the Germans returned to the attack in Russia, ultimately disastrously, and the Allies finally won lasting success in North Africa.

## War in the Pacific

Having conquered the Philippines and the Dutch East Indies, the Japanese planned to press on to fix and strengthen the defensive shield with which they wished to hold the western Pacific against American attacks, although they were now over-extended, especially in light of the continuation of the war in China. Furthermore, their initial successes led to interest in a more extensive perimeter. The Naval General Staff pressed for an attack on Australia or for operations against India and Sri Lanka, but the army was unprepared to commit the troops required, and, instead, favoured a more modest attempt to isolate Australia.

Having seized Rabaul on New Britain on 23 January, the Japanese had decided to press on to seize Port Moresby in New Guinea, New Caledonia, Fiji and Samoa in order to isolate Australia. On 8 March, they landed at Lae and Salamaua in eastern New Guinea, and established bases from which to make further gains on the island. Tulagi, the capital of the Solomon Islands, fell on 3 May. Australia was indeed vulnerable. The Australians had major commitments in the Middle East and had lost troops in Singapore, and there were only seven militia divisions available for home defence. As a result, there were plans to abandon northern Australia and to focus on defending a line north of Brisbane.

However, the Japanese attempt to seize Port Moresby by sea, which would have protected their positions in New Guinea and New Britain, and increased the threat of an attack on Australia, was thwarted as a result of the Battle of the Coral Sea on 7–8 May. This, the first battle entirely between carrier groups in which the ships did not make visual contact, indicated the failure of the Pearl Harbor attack to wreck American naval power. The Americans had intercepted and decoded Japanese messages, and were waiting in the Coral Sea for the Japanese invasion fleet. The Americans suffered serious losses in the battle, particularly the carrier *Lexington*, but the Japanese also suffered, not least with the loss of planes, and they failed to persist with the operation.

The Japanese had not handled the operation or the battle as well as their earlier successes in the war might suggest. They failed to achieve the necessary concentration of force, a characteristic they were also later to show in other naval battles.[1] Coral Sea also demonstrated a serious problem with naval warfare in the period: the difficulty of accurate surveillance. All too often during the war there were to be mistaken estimates of opposing strength, location and direction. Coupled with this, the capability of naval air power in this period should not be exaggerated.

Already, on 17 March, American fighters had arrived at Darwin, providing protection for northern Australia. By the end of June, the Allies were clearly in command of the air in the region. Port Moresby was also protected, and Japanese bases were being attacked. The build-up of air support was important in lessening Australia's vulnerability. The situation was eased by the return of Australian troops from the Middle East and by the arrival of American units, although many were support forces. Christmas Island, to the north-west of Australia, was occupied by American forces.

The battle of the Coral Sea ensured that the Japanese would try to attack Port Moresby overland. Advancing through the jungle of the difficult Owen Stanley Range, they were affected by disease and supply problems and, in September, stopped by successful Australian jungle fighting. A supporting amphibious landing in Milne Bay was defeated by the Australians. Combined with eventual American success at Guadalcanal, this indicated that the Japanese were far from invincible on land. The Japanese were driven back to defensive positions on the north coast of New Guinea.[2]

Rather than focusing on Australia and the south-west Pacific, Admiral Yamamoto preferred a decisive naval battle aimed at destroying American carriers, and, to that end, proposed to seize Midway and other islands that could serve as support bases for an invasion of Hawaii, which, he thought, would lead to the battle. He hoped to lure the American carriers to destruction under the guns of his battleships. A symbolic American air raid on Tokyo on 18 April, mounted from carriers, named, after its commander, the Doolittle raid, led, in May, to a Japanese decision to seize Midway, as well as positions in the Aleutian Islands that appeared to threaten Japan in the northern Pacific.

The continued capacity of the American navy, however, was shown clearly, on 4 June, with the American victory over the Japanese fleet seeking to capture Midway Island and to engage the Americans in a decisive battle. This was a battle in which the ability to locate opposing ships proved crucial. Furthermore, as with combined arms operations on land, the combination of fighter support with carriers (in defence) and bombers (in attack) was important in order to minimise losses. The Americans encountered serious difficulties on both counts. Their strike from the *Hornet* failed because the fighters and dive-bombers were unable to find the carriers, while, lacking fighter support, the torpedo-bombers from the *Hornet* and the *Enterprise* suffered very heavy casualties; with heavily outnumbered fighter support, those from the *Yorktown* suffered comparable losses. However, the result of these attacks was that the Japanese fighters were unable to respond, not least because they were at a low altitude, to the arrival of the American dive-bombers. In only a few minutes, three carriers were wrecked. A fourth, the *Hiryu*, successfully took evasive action. She later launched a wave of planes that inflicted heavy damage on the *Yorktown*, before being caught and crippled by American dive-bombers. The Americans then prudently retired to avoid the approach of the Japanese battleships, which, deprived of their target, retired on 5 June.

The sinking of all four heavy Japanese carriers to American air attack, and the loss of many aircraft and pilots, shifted the naval balance in the Pacific to the Americans. Both the initiative and the arithmetic of carrier power moved against the Japanese. The loss of pilots was particularly serious as the Japanese had stressed the value of training and had produced an élite force of aviators. Once lost, they proved difficult to replace.[3]

The very extent of Japanese conquests strained the capacity of their military to increase, or hold, them, but, in addition, in the Midway operation, the Japanese had been seriously hit by flawed planning and preparation. This contrasted with American preparation, including the more effective repair effort that, after Coral Sea, had returned the damaged American carrier *Yorktown* to service. The Americans also had the ability to intercept and decipher coded Japanese radio messages, enabling them to outthink their opponents: the intelligence failure of Pearl Harbor was more than rectified. Furthermore, the Japanese had underestimated American strength, while their deployment in pursuit of an overly complex plan and their tactical judgement were poor. Yamamoto's inflexible conviction of the value of battleships in any battle with the Americans had served him ill.[4] Defeat at Midway derailed Japanese schemes, thwarting their plan to invade Hawaii, which, had it been successful, would have made it very difficult for the Americans to recapture the western Pacific. The Japanese had lost their offensive capacity, and that at a time when the Germans were still taking the initiative in Russia and North Africa.

In addition, the rallying of much Indian opinion behind Britain, especially the increase of the Indian army to become 1 million strong in 1942, the largest volunteer army in history, helped ensure that the Japanese were held in South Asia. The Quit India movement of that year was a serious crisis for British rule, with a series of rural rebellions, mainly in eastern India. The British responded by arresting senior Congress leaders, after which the movement became more violent, hindering the operation of British authority. However, the Quit India agitation did not encompass all of India and was nationalist rather than pro-Japanese.

The fall of Burma was not followed by that of India. Nevertheless, the first British Arakan offensive, an attempt to make limited gains on the Burmese coast, failed in December 1942. The Japanese proved superior at jungle warfare, the British were handicapped by difficult supply lines, and the poorly conceived campaign was mishandled.

In geopolitical terms, the loss of Japanese offensive capability made thoughts of joint action with the Germans against the British in South-West Asia even more implausible. Germany and Japan were unable to create a military partnership, or to provide mutual economic assistance that in any way matched that of the Allies. Their ineffectual attempts at naval co-operation, which included the dispatch of German technology, indicated that, even where co-operation was possible, it did not achieve much.

For the Germans, the naval opportunities presented by American entry into the war came not from co-operation with Japan, but from the poorly defended nature of American waters. Due, in part, to a reluctance to learn from earlier experience, it took time for convoys to be introduced in these waters, and there were very heavy losses to German submarine attacks in the first half of 1942, although, in May 1942, the situation improved considerably as effective convoying was introduced. This led the U-boats, from July, to focus anew on the mid-Atlantic.

## Germany versus the Soviet Union

In Europe, the major clashes were again on the Eastern Front. The Soviet counter-offensive, launched in December 1941, had revealed the extent to which the Germans were not trained for defence and found it difficult to fight well in that role.[5] However, at the beginning of 1942, the impact of the Soviet winter counter-offensive was lessened, in part because Stalin focused on a wide-front attack, including attacks near Leningrad and an advance south-east of Kharkov in late January, which could not be sustained; while Hitler issued a 'stand or die' order to his forward forces. Commanders, such as Guderian, who advocated withdrawal were ignored, even dismissed. In total, thirty-five generals were removed.

Stalin's wish to translate early successes into an offensive along the entire front that would destroy all the German armies proved singularly inappropriate. He hoped to prevent the Germans from being in a shape to mount a renewed offensive later in 1942, but his policy deprived the Soviet forces in the centre of the reinforcements necessary for them to encircle Army Group Centre, a goal that had seemed possible as the defeat of the German pincers north-west and

113

south of Moscow was exploited. The Germans relied on defensive 'hedgehogs', based on the main communication nodes, and were able to prevent major breakthroughs and to hold on to the Rzhev–Gzhatsk line, from which a new attack could be mounted on Moscow; but stabilising the front placed an enormous strain on German resources. Compared to their gains near Moscow, the Soviets made far smaller inroads at the expense of Army Groups North and South, although there were advances south-east of Leningrad and on the Kerch peninsula. By the end of January 1942, nearly 918,000 German troops had become casualties.

Their heavy loss of manpower in the winter of 1941–2 was a permanent blow to German capability and one that affected the Germans in three ways in 1942. First, these losses, which left many divisions below operational levels, forced the eventual summer offensive to be concentrated on one front. Secondly, troop levels were such that diversionary attacks on any scale could not be mounted elsewhere, although, in late June, a Russian salient south of Leningrad, the Volkhov front, was destroyed, with the loss of the surrounded Second Shock Army. Subsequently, German troops were sent north, after conquering the Crimea, to increase the pressure on Leningrad. The city, however, famously and successfully, held out against both blockade and bombardment.[6] Thirdly, pressure on troop numbers reduced opportunities for training.

The Soviets also suffered greatly from the strain of the winter offensive as well as from the attempt to mount a sequel, which, initially, was optimistically aimed at driving forward towards Kiev. Stalin ignored the General Staff's advice to revert to the defence. Eventually, a poorly planned and executed Soviet attempt to make a breakthrough near Kharkov in May 1942, which would drive the Germans back towards the Dnieper, led, instead, to the encirclement of the attacking forces. The Soviets lost a quarter of a million troops in the Barvenkovo salient. This offensive was a major failure that enabled the Germans subsequently to gain the initiative. The period of Soviet initiative, begun by their winter counter-offensive, had been brought to an end.

The superior ability of the Germans to execute encirclement plans reflected greater command skills and flexibility, but much of the responsibility was Stalin's. He failed to heed intelligence reports and military advice. Stalin, also, was overly keen on attacks whatever the situation, and over-estimated the improvement in the Red Army's effectiveness. There were still serious deficiencies in equipment, organisation and command training. Although, in the T-34 and KV-1, the Soviets now had impressive tanks, the Germans proved more effective in mobile warfare and benefited from superiority in the air. The Soviets, however, put much of the blame on the Anglo-American failure to open a Second Front in Western Europe.[7]

The German capture of the Kerch peninsula in the eastern Crimea on 8–20 May helped clear the southern flank for their summer offensive, and also demonstrated the deficiencies of Soviet forces, including a lack of adequate air–land co-operation and of command skills. These were exploited by the Germans who benefited from effective air support. Heavy Soviet losses here and near Kharkov prepared the way for the main German offensive.

In June 1942, the Germans launched a fresh offensive against Soviet forces. To Hitler, gaining Soviet resources was the best preparation for conflict with the USA, specifically for opposing a Second Front in Western Europe. Unlike in 1941, the Germans were not able to attack along their entire front, while the Red Army was, initially, allowed by Stalin to fall back. Across the entire front (including Finland) there were 3.5 million German and 1 million allied troops, but the Soviet forces were considerably larger: excluding numerous reserves, 5.5 million men were in the field. The Red Army was also developing armoured units at the level of tank armies in response to the German armour, although, as yet, their tank tactics did not match those of the Germans. In particular, the Soviets placed more of an emphasis on supporting infantry. From March 1942, Soviet industrial production began to increase.

Furthermore, poor direction by Hitler led to a division of German resources and, eventually, to an obsession with taking the Volga crossing-point of Stalingrad, rather than keeping the focus on the initial plan for Operation Blue. This had called for the destruction of Soviet forces west of the Don, followed by an advance into the Caucasus in order to capture the Soviet oilfields and then put pressure on Allied interests in the Near and Middle East. Cutting Soviet supply links through Persia (Iran) was seen as important and there were hopes of winning the support of neutral Turkey. The seizure of the oilfields was seen as a preparation for the lengthy struggle that American entry into the war appeared to make inevitable, and Hitler expanded the original objective in order to seize all the oilfields, including Baku. The plan was flawed from the outset, however, because it was supported by insufficient logistical preparations, underestimated Soviet strength, and offered a massive flank in the north open to attack by the Red Army, a problem that concerned Field Marshal Bock. He was dismissed.

Launched on 28 June 1942, the first section of the plan was achieved in July, when, in ideal tank conditions, German forces pushed into the Don bend and the Germans captured Rostov, although poor planning ensured that the armour necessary to help clear the river crossings at the eastern end of the Don bend was in the wrong location, and thus unable to help the attempt to push through to Stalingrad in late July. 'The Russian is finished,' declared Hitler on 20 July, and this confidence ensured that advice to deal with Soviet forces on the German flank was ignored as the Germans advanced. Stalin had anticipated the blow falling on Moscow and had deployed his reserves accordingly. However, this also enabled him to benefit from Moscow's central position in the Soviet rail network and to move troops to either flank as required. A willingness to withdraw troops ensured that the Germans were deprived of an encirclement victory in the bend, and, although the retreat hit morale, Soviet forces gave a good account of themselves in late July and held onto a bridgehead over the Don at Kletskaya that was to be important when they counterattacked later in the year.

To the south, the Germans crossed the Don and easily advanced across the Kuban, supported by other forces that had crossed from Kerch. Stavropol was captured on 5 August, and the most westerly oil fields round Maikop were captured on 9 August. The Germans pressed on into the Caucasus, capturing Mount Elbruz, the highest peak, and Mozdok, and nearing Grozny, but logistical problems mounted as supply lines lengthened, while resistance was also a problem.

## Stalingrad

To the east, in August, German forces advanced from the Don to the Volga, which they reached north of Stalingrad on 23 August.

However, the Red Army was now better able to improvise defensive positions and deploy reserves than it had been the previous summer, and Stalin entrusted the city's defence to commanders who had proved their quality in the counter-offensive the previous winter.

Taking Stalingrad assumed a great and increasing symbolic importance for Hitler, substituting a political goal for operational flexibility. Hitler also hoped that Stalin would commit his forces to hold the city. With an obsession resembling the bloody Franco-German conflict at Verdun in 1916, Hitler concentrated military assets on what, in large part due to German bombing, became a wrecked urban terrain. This made it very difficult for the German attackers. Armour and air attack could achieve little in the ruined terrain, and much of the fighting was at very close range. The Germans could not utilise their skill at mobile warfare. Both sides used massive quantities of artillery. As losses mounted, more and more German forces were sucked into the battle and expended in repeated attempts to seize individual complexes, especially the Tractor, Red October and Barricades factories. Already, in June 1942, the Germans had seen the difficulty of capturing a city when their attack on the Crimean port of Sevastopol had proved far more difficult than had been anticipated. It had taken longer and cost more men. As at Stalingrad, hand-to-hand combat became common. Although it fell, Sevastopol was in a weaker position than Stalingrad as it was isolated by land, as well as being partially blockaded by sea.

The difficulties the Germans encountered at Stalingrad were exacerbated by poor command decisions, including a failure both to drive against the flanks of the Soviet position in the city in an attempt to cut it off from the river and to focus on the same targets throughout and, instead, attacks on a broad front and the switching of targets.

On 14 October, Hitler ordered his forces to take up defensive positions everywhere except at Stalingrad and in parts of the Caucasus. The German offensive had largely run its course before the Soviet counterattack, Operation Uranus. Even had the Germans succeeded at Stalingrad, the victory would have been of limited value. The resource base (both German and captured Soviet) required for further conflict on the Eastern Front and, eventually, against the Western Allies, would have been attenuated, not strengthened, by the struggle. At an operational level, the advances made in 1942 had used up available German reserves.

German concentration on the city itself, and their more general failure to give due heed to Soviet capability, helped clear the way for a skilfully planned and prepared Soviet counterattack that benefited from gaining a local concentration of strength. German military intelligence had again underestimated the size of Soviet reserves, and this affected not only German plans but also their confidence when the Soviet blow fell.

Launched on 19 November, under heavy artillery cover, the Soviet attack centred on Romanian forces holding flank positions. They were swiftly overrun; a defeat that arose from poor German command decisions that had allocated important positions to these units and also left them inadequately supported. The Soviets swiftly exploited their success. The encirclement of the German Sixth Army in and near Stalingrad (about 330,000 men) was complete four days later, in part because of a poorly handled response.

German relief attempts failed in December and were overshadowed by Operation Little Saturn, in which Soviet forces protected their encirclement by driving forward against Axis forces that might otherwise have contributed to Stalingrad's relief. This led to heavy Axis casualties in the Don basin.

Despite Göring's promises, it proved impossible to provide sufficient supplies for Stalingrad by air, although the very attempt to mount a large-scale airlift testified to the advances made by air power, while what was transported helped keep the Sixth Army alive.[8] The pocket was driven in by Soviet attack, and, by 2 February 1943, the remaining Germans had surrendered. In all, about 110,000 troops surrendered.[9]

The campaign was a triumph for Soviet offensive art, and was far more successful than the counter-offensive the previous winter, although the German position was far more exposed than it had been. The Soviets also benefited greatly from the recovery and development of their munitions industry, for example in tank production. The campaign was badly mishandled by the Germans, in large part due to poor direction from Hitler, who failed to respond with the necessary flexibility, and exaggerated the potential impact of his determination to hold out. The deleterious consequences of the strengthening of Hitler's position in the military in the autumn of 1941 were increasingly apparent, as was the consequent decline of that of the General Staff. Also the Sixth Army commander, Paulus,[10] refused to allow a shrinking of the pocket that would have permitted a concentration of German forces.

As a reminder that it was not only the Germans who made foolish command decisions, the successful Stalingrad counter-offensive – Operation Uranus – was matched, in November 1942, by the disastrous Operation Mars on the central front west of Moscow. Planned and directed by Zhukov, Mars failed and was covered up. In subsequent years, Zhukov provided a wholly inaccurate and incomplete account in which he ignored the poor planning and execution of the operation. The premature commitment of the Soviet armour into too small a bridgehead prevented the subsequent forward movement of supporting artillery. As a result, the exploiting forces had to engage a counterattacking enemy without proper artillery support. Furthermore, repeated, costly frontal Soviet attacks quickly led to the combat exhaustion of units. Soviet forces lost about 100,000 killed and about 235,000 wounded, men forgotten in the Soviet portrayal of a continuous and heroic drive to victory from late 1942: 'Operation Mars was analogous to the circumstances Allied military leaders would have faced should Operation Overlord (the Normandy landings) have failed.'[11] The Nazi government, in turn, disseminated a misleading account of the Stalingrad campaign.[12]

Operation Mars was not the sole Soviet offensive failure in the second half of 1942. On 24 August, they had launched Operation Sinyavino, in order to break the siege of Leningrad. Despite heavy losses in repeated attacks, from both Leningrad and relief forces, the Red Army was unable to prevail, and on 26 September the orders were given to retreat to the starting lines. The Germans mounted an effective defence, although they suffered heavy casualties and were unable to advance on Leningrad anew. These failures underline the achievement of Operation Saturn.

## Madagascar

Concern about possible Japanese submarine bases in Vichy-run Madagascar led to its conquest by the British in May–November

1942. Operations there indicated the potential of amphibious attacks when they could operate on a broad front, and the value, to the British, of enjoying carrier-borne air superiority, but also the problem that, once landed, troops could meet more serious opposition. The Madagascar campaign provided valuable experience in mounting amphibious assaults. In May, the port at Diego Suarez was captured and, in September, a full-scale attempt – both overland and with fresh landings – was launched to seize control of the rest of the island. The isolated French put up enough resistance to justify this major effort. Although this operation was peripheral to the main campaigns, it lessened the danger that the Allied world would be fractured by German and Japanese advances.

## North Africa

The success of Operation Torch, the Allied conquest of Vichy-run Morocco and Algeria in November 1942, contrasted with the German failure earlier that year to overcome Malta, Britain's air and naval base in the central Mediterranean. A strong air attack on the island that spring had been damaging but, despite heavy losses of German and Italian aircraft, it had not led to Malta's fall. Plans for an invasion were seen to be unviable and the airborne troops earmarked for the operation were anyway transferred to Rommel when he was checked at El Alamein.

Leaving Malta as a threat to precarious logistical links, Rommel had advanced into Cyrenaica (eastern Libya), defeating the British at Gazala and capturing nearby Tobruk on 20–1 June 1942. Rommel proved an adroit commander, able to outthink his opponents and better able to direct the battle, although the margin of advantage was very narrow and luck played an important role. The Axis army was also superior in fighting quality, and more skilled in tank warfare, not least at coordination between armour and artillery cover. Rommel also benefited from control of the air. The Allies lost 33,000 prisoners. An Allied over-reliance on defensive boxes had proved harmful. They enabled Rommel to direct the flow of the battle and, once heavily attacked, could not be held.[13]

In terms of weaponry, the British lacked an effective anti-tank gun, while the Crusader tank was mechanically poor. The Select

Committee on National Expenditure had uncovered serious problems in tank production and its chairman responded to Tobruk by moving a censure motion in the House of Commons on 1 July. Churchill easily survived this mishandled attack, but it reflected widespread political concern about military failure and his leadership.

As Rommel pressed on to the Egyptian border and then towards Cairo and the Suez Canal, the entire Mediterranean was threatened with Axis control. The British Eighth Army, weakened by recent defeat, fell back, though losing over 7,000 prisoners when units were encircled at Mersa Matruh on 27–8 June. The retreat continued. Combined with failure in Malaysia and Burma, this leads to serious questions about British operational effectiveness, command skills and fighting quality at this juncture.

In July 1942, however, Rommel came up against the British near El Alamein, about 60 miles west of Alexandria, and he failed to defeat them that month and in early September. British operational command and tactics had now improved and the British had the advantage of shorter lines of communications. The British benefited in July from Auchinleck's readiness to engage in mobile warfare, making effective strokes in combination with the holding of defensive positions. Heavy losses were inflicted in July, and the dynamic of Rommel's success was broken. Indeed, this helped lead to a scholarly controversy over British generalship, specifically over whether Auchinleck, rather than General Bernard Montgomery, was the commander responsible for thwarting the Germans, not least because his plans were the basis for those used after he had been dismissed as Commander-in-Chief, Middle East, by an impatient Churchill.[14]

A British attack in late July was checked. In turn, the Germans renewed their advance on 31 August, in the battle of Alam Halfa, only to be blocked and to retreat. The British benefited from intelligence information about German plans and from good air support. The 8th Army, now under Montgomery, then built up their strength in order to outnumber the Axis forces in the planned counterattack.[15] This was also an aspect of a more general qualitative transition in the British army, as it came to be better prepared to take the offensive against the Germans.

On 23 October–4 November 1942, Rommel was defeated in the final battle of El Alamein. The British faced positions well defended by minefields and anti-tank guns and supported by armour. Skilful generalship, the availability of deciphered intelligence on German moves, greater numbers of men, artillery and tanks, effective use of artillery, air superiority and support, and attacks on Rommel's vital petrol supplies from Italy,[16] broke the German–Italian army, destroying most of the German tanks and most of the Italian units. The Axis line was eventually broken on 4 November, leading Rommel to order a general withdrawal. Montgomery had read the terrain ably and his sequential blows eventually succeeded, not least by forcing Rommel to commit his forces, thus facilitating the decisive British blow; although initial progress had been slow and Montgomery's ability to read the battlefield should not be exaggerated. The shift in tank warfare was shown on 2 November when a German counterattack led to heavy German losses.

Thanks to the victory, Churchill was able to survive the growing political crisis of the autumn, which had seen widespread criticism, intrigues by Sir Stafford Cripps, the Lord Privy Seal, who wanted to replace him, and a public call for his resignation from the Labour MP Aneurin Bevan. After El Alamein, Churchill was able to demote Cripps, and his political position was far less vulnerable. The victory also provided an important psychological boost in Britain, although, had Montgomery failed to break through and rested on the defensive, the Torch landings would anyway have unravelled the German position in North Africa.

Cautiously pursued by Montgomery, who was no master of manoeuvre and who failed to encircle the retreating Axis forces on 5 and 6 November, Rommel fell back across Libya to the Mareth Line in southern Tunisia. Unlike on earlier occasions, the British were to advance not only into Egypt and across Cyrenaica, where Benghazi fell on 20 November, but also to drive forward through the German position near El Agheila across Tripolitania, where a second line was overcome at Wadi Zemzem. Tripoli, the capital of Libya, was captured on 23 January 1943, a success that earlier Allied advances into Libya had not matched.[17]

French North Africa was successfully invaded by Anglo-American amphibious forces in Operation Torch on 8 November 1942. The Americans were determined to be seen to act on land in the European theatre (however indirectly) as soon as possible.[18] Thanks in large part to a careful cultivation of the French military leaders in North Africa, resistance by far more numerous Vichy forces was rapidly overcome, although some units, particularly of the navy, resisted firmly. Negotiations after a general ceasefire ordered on 10 November led the French forces to join the Allies, and they were to make a major contribution to Allied success in Tunisia the following spring. The Vichy forces in Dakar also joined the Allies.[19]

The Allied aim was to squeeze the Axis forces in North Africa from the west and east, as well as to acquire experience in amphibious operations. The ability to mount the amphibious attacks was a result of the limited success of the German submarines both as a strategic and as an operational tool. Thanks to successful Allied disinformation, Axis submarines were positioned to prevent a reported attack on Dakar. The Americans landing at Casablanca had sailed directly from Norfolk, Virginia. Given the difficulties experienced in coping with the confusions of a landing and in speedily exploiting the situation, particularly in the Casablanca operation, it was just as well that opposition there was light. The landings at Oran and Algiers were better executed, although the entire operation was affected by the limited time available for preparation and much of the staff work and logistical support was inadequate.[20] Despite Allied concerns, Spain, which controlled a portion of Morocco, did not intervene. Nor did the Italian surface fleet, which was seriously short of oil.

Against no opposition, Axis forces rapidly occupied Vichy-run Tunisia from 9 November, moving from Italy by air and sea and denying the Allies their anticipated rapid success in North Africa. American and British parachute units were dropped near Bône and Tebessa in eastern Algiera on 12–16 November, but the Axis proved better able to exploit the new situation created by the landings. The refusal of American commanders to include eastern Algeria and Tunisia among the landing zones is readily understandable in light of the risk of Axis air attack, but had unfortunate consequences. As a reminder of the number of largely forgotten campaigns that the war encompassed, in December 1942 and January 1943, Free French forces based in Chad overran the Italian-held Fezzan region of southern Libya before advancing to the Mediterranean at Tripoli.

The operations in North Africa demonstrated the importance of logistics. In battle, the Germans were tactically adroit, and in campaign they matched this operationally. However, the fundamentals necessary for success were lacking. North Africa was peripheral to the main area of German commitment, whereas it had far greater importance for Britain, and the American adoption of the 'Germany First' policy led to the Torch operation. In North Africa, British Empire forces were able to make a major contribution. Although this was lessened by the impact of Japanese entry into the war, Britain's imperial position, and the success of overcoming Axis, pro-Axis and potentially pro-Axis forces in Italian East Africa, Syria, Iraq, Persia and Madagascar, gave the British strategic depth. This ensured a favourable supply situation, with the flow of *matériel* from the Indian Ocean as well as, for aircraft, from West Africa via French Equatorial Africa and Sudan. Aside from an ability to direct resources to the region, the British benefited from a superior infrastructure in moving them when there: the Germans were faced with limited capacity in the Libyan ports and poor overland routes thereafter. The British, in contrast, especially when on the defensive, and therefore able to use shorter routes, benefited from a better transport infrastructure.

## Western Europe

Allied forces made no lasting impact on German positions in Western Europe in 1942, although the threat of invasion was emphasised by commando attacks, by the successful combined-services attack on the dry dock at St Nazaire on 28 March and by the raid on Dieppe on 19 August. The latter assault on a well-fortified position led to heavy Allied, mainly Canadian, casualties, to accurate machine-gun, artillery and mortar fire, and underlined the problems of amphibious landings. It also showed that attacking a port destroyed it; hence the need to bring port facilities with the invasion in 1944. In the Dieppe raid, the RAF lost 106 planes to the *Luftwaffe's* 48, indicating a serious problem that had to be overcome were an invasion to be mounted. It was also clear that an invasion would require more intelligence and a greater prior bombardment from air and sea. The Dieppe raid lacked the latter because the RAF was committed to the bombing campaign on Germany, and, in addition, it had been hoped to benefit from the element of surprise.

The Germans used a large amount of resources preparing to resist attack. Indeed, there were more German troops and their allies defending Western Europe in late 1942 than there were British forces in Britain. This was an important Western contribution, although far less than that of the Soviet Union. Furthermore, the Germans kept few élite units in Western Europe.

On 11 November 1942, in response to Operation Torch, the Germans occupied Vichy France, with Italian support. There was no resistance. Vichy's most strategically important capability, the warships in Toulon, were scuttled by the French on 27 November as the Germans pushed into the naval base, which had remained outside their control by prior agreement: 3 battleships, 7 cruisers, 32 destroyers and 16 submarines were among the warships scuttled. Most of Vichy France became a German-occupied zone, although the Italian-occupied zone was greatly expanded.

In order to make a direct impact on the Germans in Western Europe, the Allies stepped up their bombing of Germany and occupied Europe. Lübeck, many of whose buildings were wooden, was badly damaged in a firestorm on 28 March 1942. On the night of 30 May, the British launched over 1,000 bombers at Cologne. Although the raid did not achieve all its objectives, in terms of destruction of industry and morale, it indicated the ability of the Allies to make a major attack on a German city, and was seen as a way to persuade the British public that the Germans could be hit hard. However, for attacks to be sustained, it would be necessary to have a major build-up in air power, in terms of not only the number of planes but also their quality. As a sign of what was to come, most of the casualties in Cologne were civilian. The British air force was supplemented by the Americans from July 1942. The Cologne attack was an exception. Most of the raids were fairly small scale, but they were important to the development of an effective ground-support system to support a bombing offensive, as well as in the gaining of operational experience. The Germans, in turn, continued to bomb British cities, especially in the Baedeker raids.

Meanwhile, the Nazis had expanded their war on the Jews. The Wannsee meeting of 20 January 1942 determined to give force to what was intended as a 'Final Solution', in which all European Jews, including those not hitherto under German control, were to be deported to death camps and slaughtered. A series of camps were opened including Treblinka, Sobibor and Belzec in Poland, Maly Trostinets near Minsk, and Jungerhof near Riga, while the camp at Auschwitz near Cracow in Poland was extended and was to be the site where the largest number of Jews were killed.[21] Aside from Jews, large numbers of gypsies were also killed in the death camps,[22] as were others deemed unacceptable.

## 1942 reviewed

On the respective fronts, Midway, Stalingrad and El Alamein were clear turning points in the flow of the war, although it had been the German failure before Moscow in December 1941 that had been the real turning point in the war on the Eastern Front. The statement that German failure at Stalingrad marked 'the final conclusion of a process of diminishing options of victory in the east'[23] is more generally applicable to defeats on other Axis fronts.

In April and July 1942, George Marshall, the American Chief of Staff, had pressed for an invasion of France that year. The success of Operation Torch cannot conceal the risks of such a scheme, not least in terms of Atlantic and Channel weather, lack of shipping, and German opposition, including U-boats in the Atlantic. There was still a need to win the Battle of the Atlantic and to gain air dominance, as well as to plan operations and train, equip and move forces.

There was also the need to confront an ever more zealous opponent. The difficulties that faced the Germans before the Soviet counterattack led a furious Hitler to sack General Franz Halder, the Chief of the Army's General Staff, on 9 September 1942, and this was followed by a transformation of much of the officer corps as established ways of appointing and promoting officers, including notions of class and honour, and staff-officer training, were replaced by an emphasis on ideology and fighting fervour: 'Führer-selection through battle.'[24]

Churchill announced on 10 November 1942 that recent successes signified not 'the beginning of the end', but 'the end of the beginning'. The Allies could now move over to the offensive, not as a series of counterattacks, but as part of a planned attempt to undo Axis conquests and then to take the war to the Axis states themselves.

## NOTES

1 B.A. Millot, *The Battle of Coral Sea* (1974); J.B. Lundstrom, *The First South Pacific Campaign: Pacific Fleet Strategy December 1941–June 1942* (Annapolis, 1976); D.A. Thomas, *Japan's War at Sea: Pearl Harbor to the Coral Sea* (1978).

2 R. Paull, *Retreat from Kokoda* (1958); P. Brune, *Those Ragged Bloody Heroes: From the Kokoda Trail to Gona Beach, 1942* (Sydney, 1991).

3 I. Hata and Y. Izawa, *Japanese Naval Aces and Fighter Units in World War II* (Annapolis, 1989); J.B. Lundstrom, *The First Team: Pacific Naval Air Combat from Pearl Harbor to Midway* (Annapolis, 1984).

4 H.P. Willmott, *The Barrier and the Javelin: Japanese and Allied Pacific Strategies, February to June 1942* (Annapolis, Maryland, 1983).

5 T.A. Wray, *Standing Fast: German Defensive Doctrine on the Eastern Front During World War II: Prewar to March 1943* (Fort Leavenworth, Kansas, 1987).

6 L. Goure, *The Siege of Leningrad* (Stanford, California, 1962).

7 D.M. Glantz, *Kharkov 1942: Anatomy of a Military Disaster Through Soviet Eyes* (Rockville, New York, 1998).

8 J.S.A. Hayward, *Stopped at Stalingrad: The Luftwaffe and Hitler's Defeat in the East, 1942–1943* (Lawrence, Kansas, 1998).

9 G. Jukes, *Stalingrad: The Turning Point* (1968); L. Rotundo (ed.), *Battle for Stalingrad: The 1943 Soviet General Staff Study* (1989); A. Beevor, *Stalingrad* (1998).

10 On whom, see W. Goerlitz, *Paulus and Stalingrad* (1963).

11 D.M. Glantz, *Zhukov's Greatest Disaster: The Red Army's Epic Disaster in Operation Mars, 1942* (Lawrence, Kansas, 1999), pp. 319–20.

12 J.W. Baird, 'The Myth of Stalingrad', *Journal of Contemporary History*, 4 (1969), pp. 187–204.

13 S.W. Mitcham, *Rommel's Greatest Victory: The Desert Fox and the Fall of Tobruk, 1942* (Novato, California, 1998).

14 C. Barnett, *The Desert Generals* (1960); R. Parkinson, *The Auk: Auchinleck, Victor at Alamein* (St Albans, 1977); J. Strawson, *El Alamein: Desert Victory* (1981).

15 M. Carver, *Dilemmas of the Desert War* (1986).

16 A.J. Levine, *The War Against Rommel's Supply Lines, 1942–1943* (Westport, Connecticut, 1999).

17 S.W. Mitcham, *Rommel's Desert War: The Life and Death of the Afrika Korps* (New York, 1992).

18 M. Howard, *The Mediterranean Strategy in the Second World War* (1968); K. Sainsbury, *The North African Landings 1942: A Strategic Decision* (1976).

19 A.L. Funk, *The Politics of Torch: The Allied Landings and the Algiers Putsch, 1942* (Lawrence, Kansas, 1974).

20 G.F. Howe, *Northwest Africa: Seizing the Initiative in the West* (Washington, 1957).

21 O. Bartov, *Murder in Our Midst: The Holocaust, Industrial Killing, and Representation* (Oxford, 1996).

22 B. Alt and S. Folts, *Weeping Violins: The Gypsy Tragedy in Europe* (Kirksville, Missouri, 1996); K. Fings, H. Heuss and F. Sparing, *From 'Race Science' to the Camps. The Gypsies during the Second World War* (Hatfield, 1997).

23 B. Wegner, 'The Historical Topos of the Second Campaign against the Soviet Union', in H. Boog *et al.*, *Germany and the Second World War. VI. The Global War. Widening of the Conflict into a World War and the Shift of the Initiative 1941–1943* (Oxford, 2001), p. 1,214.

24 M. Knox, '1 October 1942: Adolf Hitler, Wehrmacht Officer Policy, and Social Revolution', *Historical Journal*, 43 (2000), esp. pp. 821–3.

# CHAPTER FIVE

# Mounting Allied pressure, 1943

By 1943, the war had taken on the character of attrition, on land, at sea and in the air. The high tempo of campaigning used up troops and material, but the availability of massive resources enabled the Allies to attack on a number of fronts at once, and to return to the attack despite casualties and wear and tear. The Allies also benefited from the extent to which the Germans had used up important military assets during their ambitious offensives in Russia and North Africa in 1942, while the Japanese had done the same at Midway.

Allied insistence on an unconditional surrender, a policy announced by Roosevelt at the press conference after the Casablanca conference of 14–24 January 1943, and the fanatical nature of Hitler's regime combined to ensure that it would be a fight to the finish, and thus contributed to the prolongation of the war. Unconditional surrender was a response to the character of the Nazi regime. It also underlined the flawed political analysis of the German military leadership. Their willingness to accept Hitler not only morally corrupted them, as the military came to collaborate in Hitler's genocidal policies, but also led them into a conflict in which, from 1941, limited war and political compromise ceased to be options. As a consequence, the operational ability of the German military was linked to a task that risked, and in the end caused, not only their defeat but also their dissolution, along with the total conquest of Germany. Yet, it would be wrong to suggest that, except for Hitler, the German military would have made appropriate strategic decisions. There were serious flaws in the German high command, although these were seriously exacerbated by Hitler's ideas and management.[1]

## Conflict in Russia

Again, the most important fighting in the European theatre in 1943 was on the Eastern Front. German defeat at Stalingrad had led to very heavy casualties and to the loss of a mass of *matériel*. These losses were not only the Sixth Army but were also heavy amongst the units that had tried to relieve it. The southern portion of their Eastern Front was left short of men and equipment, and the initiative was totally lost. The German units that had advanced into the northern Caucasus were now threatened with encirclement.

There had also been a major shift in psychological advantage. The loss of an entire army and the failure to relieve it were serious blows that contrasted markedly with the situation during the Soviet counter-offensive the previous winter. The strength and fighting quality of the German army relative to that of the Soviets appeared to have deteriorated. The prominence of the struggle for Stalingrad in German propaganda the previous year ensured that the blow fell all the heavier. At the command level, Hitler suffered a major loss of confidence and there were serious doubts about the quality of decisions.

Parallel to this, there was a welcome boost for Soviet confidence and morale. This affected both military commanders and the wider public. German failure also led to a marked increase in partisan activity behind the lines, both because of higher morale but also because the prudence of collaboration with the Germans was now seriously in question.

The Red Army exploited the success of the Stalingrad counter-offensive, although Stalin's hopes of trapping German forces north of the Caucasus and of the rapid reconquest of Ukraine proved wildly over-optimistic. Although there was usually much more movement than on the Eastern Front in World War One, the Front in World War Two also took on the character of a prolonged struggle of attrition.

On 13 January 1943, the Soviets launched a new offensive, seeking both to advance on Kharkov, moving into Ukraine, and also to seize Rostov, cutting off German retreat from the Caucasus. These plans expanded in new offensives launched on 29 January and 2

February. The latter called for an advance from Kharkov both to the Dnieper and north-west to attack the flank of Army Group Centre. The Soviets were swiftly successful, capturing Voronezh (26 January), Kursk (8 February) and Kharkov (16 February), and advancing close to Dnepropetrovsk on the Dnieper (18 February). The Soviets were most successful against the over-extended Second Hungarian Army south of Voronezh, which was destroyed with the loss of over 100,000 men. The Soviets were better equipped and the Hungarians lacked anti-tank guns powerful enough to stop the Soviet tanks.[2]

However, Field Marshal Erich von Manstein, the commander of the reconstituted Army Group South, proved skilful at mobile defence and stabilising the front. The Germans counterattacked from 20 February, benefiting from the extent to which the Soviet forces had been exhausted by the offensive, not least with wear and tear to their tanks, and from their ability to defeat their opponents in the air, albeit at the cost of many planes. The Germans were able to inflict heavy casualties, destroying most of the Soviet 3rd Tank Army. The Soviets lacked nearby reserves to maintain the offensive. The Germans recaptured Kharkov on 15 March 1943 and Belgorod on 18 March, before ending the advance on 21 March. This was the last German offensive victory in the east.

The Germans had thus returned the front to the situation it was in prior to the launch of Operation Blue. Given their failure at Stalingrad, this was unexpected, but it reflected Stalin's mishandling of the Soviet offensive, Manstein's command skills, the continued fighting skill and morale of most of the German forces in the region, and the availability of air support. The Soviets, nevertheless, in addition to destroying the forces deployed in the Stalingrad operation, had reversed German gains from the previous year, and the German counterattack still left the Soviets in control of Kursk and Rostov. The Soviets had closed the approaches to the Caucasus, safeguarding their oil supplies, while the campaign had left them with a salient centred on Kursk. This offered opportunities for exploitation in a subsequent offensive as it threatened the flanks of German salients to north and south, thus challenging both the centre and the south of the German front. At the same time, the Soviet offensive had indicated the incremental nature of success. It was only possible for advancing forces to achieve so much before exhaustion, losses and supply difficulties had an impact and led to, first, the slackening and, then, the stopping of the offensive. Until 1945, there was to be no one-campaign end to the war. This gave the conflict an attritional character and led to an emphasis on resources.

The net effect of nearly a year's conflict was a major exhaustion of German resources without equivalent gains, while Soviet effectiveness and resilience had both increased. The Soviets were also benefiting from the build-up of munitions production from areas far distant from German attack.

Soviet successes were not restricted to the southern front. In January 1943, the siege of Leningrad had been broken. Although this did not have the strategic importance of the Stalingrad campaign, it was a powerful sign of Soviet success and a symbol that resilience under pressure would be rewarded. The Soviet offensive against Army Group Centre in late February achieved little, in part because of the thaw that also affected operations elsewhere, but also because the Germans retired to a shorter line, and were thus able to beat off attacks. The shortening of lines increased their defensive strength and the availability of reserves. This, however, signalled a recognition of their inability to fight their way through to Moscow.

In July 1943, the Germans launched their last major offensive of the war on a principal theatre of the Eastern Front, an attempt to break through the flanks of the Soviet Kursk salient and to achieve an encirclement triumph to match the Soviet success at Stalingrad. Still engaging in strategic wishful thinking, Hitler saw this as a battle of annihilation in which superior will would prevail and ensure the destruction of Soviet offensive forces. More mundanely, the elimination of this salient would rob the Soviets of a position from which they could attack neighbouring German salients in the flank. Had Operation Citadel succeeded, the Germans were considering a further advance to the north-east, designed to outflank Moscow from the south and east, and thus avoiding the direct approach from Army Group Centre against strong Soviet defences. However, such a follow-up offensive would have faced serious resource problems, not least the replacement of destroyed or damaged tanks and other mechanised vehicles, and the availability of fuel.

To prepare for the offensive, Hitler focused munitions production on his armour. He was not temperamentally ready to accept the idea of staying on the defensive and conserving resources while trying to make success cost his opponents dear. Such a policy seemed politically unacceptable. It would test the morale of the German population, undermine the cohesion of the Axis coalition, and, at best, produce defensive successes and buy time, rather than winning victory. Hitler hoped that the latter would undermine the Allied coalition, by lessening Western confidence in the likelihood of Soviet victory and increasing Soviet demands for a Second Front in France.

To mount an offensive, the Germans were able to draw on the benefits of greatly increased production of tanks, aircraft and artillery, and of the introduction of new types of each, including the Tiger and Panther tanks, Ferdinand self-propelled guns and the Focke-Wulf 190A fighter. Manpower losses over the previous year had been replaced, and in 1943 the Germans had their largest number of troops under arms, with about 6.55 million men in the army and 0.45 million in the Waffen-SS, compared to a joint strength of 3.76 million in 1939, 4.49 million in 1940, 5.4 million in 1941 and 5.94 million in 1942. The Germans benefited greatly from the absence of a Second Front, such that two-thirds of their army were deployed on the Eastern Front: there were now more German troops there than at the start of Barbarossa.

The Red Army was ready for such a challenge. Forewarned by accurate intelligence information, a product of the intelligence war that the Germans were losing, the Soviets had prepared a dense defensive system of six belts, appropriately designed to resist tank attack, including extensive anti-tank defences, field fortifications and minefields. This provided a defence in depth and artillery-support system that inflicted heavy casualties when the Germans attacked on 5 July. They had about 2,400 tanks and self-proclaimed guns, 1,800 planes, and 700,000 troops against 3,400, 2,100 and 1.3 million, respectively, on the Soviet side.

Once the German armour had been weakened, as it fought its way through the defences, the Red Army was better able to commit its tank reserves, which it did with some success, from 6 July, against the northern German pincer and, decisively, on 12 July, against the southern. In the latter, at Prokhorovka, what has traditionally been seen as the largest tank battle of the war, with about 1,200–1,500 tanks (three-quarters Soviet) involved, was, in fact, a number of separate engagements, in which it is unclear how many tanks were involved. The Germans had Panther and Tiger tanks, but the standard Soviet T-34 had been upgraded, and was used effectively at close range, where it matched up well with the new German armour. The Soviets suffered greater losses (about 5 to 3 ratio in tanks), but their force was not destroyed. As Soviet production of aircraft and tanks was far greater than that of Germany, battles such as that of Kursk aided the shift in the situation in their favour; the Soviets could better afford to take losses, while German losses that day made it difficult to maintain the offensive. The Soviet threat to the rear of the northern pincer, in an offensive launched on 12 July, combined with Hitler's wish to move troops to respond to the Allied invasion of Sicily on 10 July, further undermined the German effort. On 13 July, Hitler cancelled the operation, which had greatly weakened his forces in the east. The battle also showed how the struggle in the air had moved against the *Luftwaffe*. Large numbers of Soviet fighters prevented it from gaining control of the skies, and, although German ground-attack planes inflicted much damage on Soviet forces, the same was true of their opponents. Although attacking on a far more concentrated front than in 1942, let alone 1941, the Germans had advanced less than 40 miles.[3]

Having stopped the Germans, the Soviets were now in a position to counterattack. Their own forces had not been so exhausted in the defensive struggle that they could not move over to the offensive. This reflected the presence of large reserve forces, a particular strength of the Soviet military, and also an organisational system that was better able to meet the demands of an offensive than had been the case in the more improvised circumstances at the beginning of the year. The Germans were heavily outnumbered, while the Soviets were increasingly effective in attack.

The Soviet counter-offensive, which finished on 27 August, regained all the lost territory and went on to make bigger gains: the German Orel and Kharkov salients to the north and south of the Kursk salient, Kharkov falling on 21–2 August. The Germans proved less effective in defence than the Soviets. They did not have a prepared defensive system to match that of the Soviets, in particular effective artillery support. In addition, German tank losses in the

Kursk offensive lessened the availability of the mobile reserves necessary to resist offensives successfully.

The success of the Soviet offensive deserves attention, for too much of the discussion about the Eastern Front in 1943 has been devoted to Operation Citadel. This both fails to put the German defeat in the context of a wider Soviet success, and also enables an analysis of the operation's failure to serve as an explanation of Germany's wider difficulties. This is misleading, because Operation Citadel was a failure of the Germans on the offensive, but the wider Soviet success represented a failure of the Germans on the defensive.

Linked to this is the extent to which German generals writing after the war, especially Manstein, attributed German strategic and operational mistakes and weaknesses to Hitler. This neglected serious deficiencies in the German military. For example, after the war, Manstein criticised Hitler for his preference for holding positions rather than turning to mobile defence, but the latter posed serious logistical challenges, especially for fuel supplies. Tactical and operational choices have to be considered against such a background, although Hitler was scarcely willing to subordinate issues of strategy and operations to such practical matters.

Before the struggle round Kursk had finished, the Red Army had already launched an offensive further south, advancing on a broad front. Soviet forces drove the Germans from the Donets, and, by the end of December 1943, had recovered Ukraine east of the Dnieper and Kiev, and created two large bridgeheads across the river. These lessened the defensive value of the Dnieper to the Germans and were to be used as the base for a fresh Soviet offensive the following year. The commitment of German troops and armour on the Orel–Kursk front lessened the resources available to resist the Soviets in Ukraine. Although Hitler had called for an 'East Wall' anchored on the Dnieper, this remained an empty boast. Furthermore, Hitler's delay in giving Army Group South permission to retreat to the Dnieper, as Manstein had requested in July, led to it suffering heavy casualties in open terrain in which it lacked prepared defences. Similarly, the response to Soviet advances further south was mishandled, enabling the Soviets to cut off the German forces in the Crimea. Repeatedly, the Germans had held individual Soviet advances only to be placed under fresh pressure by breakthroughs from a new direction. It was this that led to the loss, first, of the Dnieper line and, then, of Kiev. This Soviet flexibility reflected not only resources but also operational skill.

Further north, the Soviets recaptured Smolensk on the central front, although there was little movement on the northern front near Leningrad, other than in January when the Soviets broke the blockade. Neither side focused its efforts on operations near Leningrad.

The campaign of 1943 reflected the shift in the relationship between the German and Soviet armies, in particular the growing relative numerical weaknesses in the tank and air strength of the former, improvements in Soviet armour and aircraft,[4] and the enhanced operational capability of the Soviet army. This was inspired by Soviet theories of deep operations advanced in the 1930s, but now refined in the cauldron of war. Rather than seek encirclements, the Soviets deployed their forces along broad fronts, launching a number of frontal assaults designed to smash opposing forces and to maintain continued pressure. The Soviets denied the Germans the ability to recover from attacks, lessened their ability to move units to badly threatened positions, and searched out the weakest points in their positions. This lessened the value of German defensive 'hedge-hogs'. While they had an operational importance on narrow-front campaigns, narrowing the advance and challenging its flanks and rear, these 'hedgehogs' were less significant in resisting broad-front attacks, particularly when they could not rely on air support or armoured counter-offensives. The loss of air support also ensured that it would not be possible to reinforce encircled positions by air. Thus, the Germans could not respond as the British could to Japanese attack on the Indian frontier in 1944. Instead, their positions were vulnerable, as British defensive 'boxes' had been in North Africa to the *Afrika Korps* in 1941–2.

The strategic advantage had passed to the Red Army as its strength, confidence and operational capability increased. This shift was important to the dynamics of the Allied coalition. The Soviet Union was now clearly going to play a major role in the future of, at least, Eastern Europe. Furthermore, the failure of the Kursk offensive and the success of the subsequent Soviet advances meant that the Germans were less able to spare troops for the Italian campaign (where the Allies were held but not driven back), and, even more, that the mobile reserve necessary to oppose successfully a Second Front in France was being destroyed in the Soviet Union. German tank and other losses on the Eastern Front in late 1943 and early 1944 were heavy, and, although the campaigns after Kursk commonly receive little attention in general histories of the war, they were important in the degradation of the German army, even more so because the bulk of the German army was deployed on the Front, while the Western allies were inflicting little damage on the German army in this period. The course of campaigning would have been less serious for Germany had the political situation been different. However, the failure to obtain peace with any one of their opponents put the Germans in a difficult position to secure victory, or, at least, avoid defeat, on any of its fronts.

## War with Japan

In 1943, the Japanese also suffered heavy blows at crucial points of their perimeter, although, in the Pacific, in China and on the Burma front, both sides rebuilt their forces and there was far less fighting than in 1944. Furthermore, the bulk of the Japanese army remained committed to China and Manchuria. In the former, guerrilla opposition (largely by the Communists) remained a problem, but, in January 1943, the Nanjing-based puppet government of Japanese-occupied Central China declared war on the Allies, and its army, which may have been 900,000 strong, took over much of the task of local control.

Nevertheless, the threat to their position led to major Japanese defensive efforts on the Pacific perimeter. They were more vulnerable there than in Burma, where the failure of their first Arakan offensive indicated that the British had mastered neither jungle operations and tactics nor the regional supply situation. Arakan, on the coast of Burma, provided an axis of advance for British troops from India, as well, hopefully, as an opportunity for weakening Japanese forces that might attack India, but it proved difficult to translate moves on the map into the field, and the Japanese remained more adept at mobile jungle warfare, challenging British advances in Arakan by outflanking them. Further east, Orde Wingate's campaign with his Chindit force behind Japanese lines in Burma was more promising, but did not lead to any long-term weakening of the Japanese position. The campaign also showed that, although the British could operate in the jungle, not least by using aerial supply, it was difficult to counteract the impact of disease and exhaustion.

The Japanese were less successful in the Pacific. They lost both Guadalcanal in the Solomon Islands and their position in eastern New Guinea. The fate of Guadalcanal, which the Japanese had seized on 7 July 1942 and on which the Americans had landed on 7 August, had been settled by American naval success in the naval battle of Guadalcanal of 12–16 November 1942, which compromised the ability of the Japanese to support their force on the island. The fighting quality of the well-led American marines, in difficult terrain and against a formidable opponent, was crucial on the island itself, ensuring that repeated attacks on the American positions failed. In January 1943, the Americans launched an offensive against the Japanese, and the latter evacuated their troops from Guadalcanal the following month.[5]

The naval campaign indicated not only the impact of carrier aircraft,[6] but also the important role of surface ships other than carriers. On 14 November 1942, off Guadalcanal, the radar-controlled fire of the battleship *Washington* pulverised the battleship *Kirishima*. Destroyer torpedo attacks could also be very effective, as when used by the Japanese, with their Long Lance torpedoes, off Guadalcanal on 13 and 30 November. In the night-time surface actions, carriers could play little role, but losses of carriers earlier in the campaign also encouraged reliance on surface shipping. Japanese submarines were also responsible for American losses.

Midway had shown the power of carriers, but also their vulnerability. They were a first-strike weapon, and required a doctrine similar to that developed in the Cold War for nuclear confrontation. This vulnerability led to a continued stress on battleships and cruisers, both of which were also very important for shore bombardment in support of amphibious operations. Air power in the Pacific was seen as a preliminary to the latter, rather than as a war-winning tool in its own right. Battleships and other surface warships were also seen as a valuable support for carriers against air attack, providing a powerful anti-aircraft screen. The Japanese, in contrast, continued to assume that battleship firepower would play a key role in a decisive naval battle, and this led them to underrate the need to retain carrier strength.

Due to their losses in 1942, the Japanese had lost their lead in carrier strength, and, by the spring of 1943, only one fleet carrier was prepared for conflict. The others listed were damaged or light carriers. Three more were due for completion that year, but the Americans were planning or building far more. There was a similar disparity as far as cruisers, destroyers and submarines were concerned. The marked difference in the industrial capability and effective war mobilisation of the two powers was readily apparent, and this was to be accentuated by naval action. Whereas the Japanese navy could not strike at the American economy, the inroads of American submarines affected the movement of raw materials to Japan and, therefore, its industrial capability.

The difference between the two economies was also seen in the construction of merchant shipping, in which the Americans opened up a massive lead. The American advance in the Pacific would have been impossible without the ability to ship large quantities of supplies and to develop the associated infrastructure, such as harbours and oil-storage facilities. In many respects, this was a war of engineers, and the American aptitude for creating effective infrastructure was applied to great effect in the Pacific.

In the Guadalcanal campaign, the Americans developed a degree of co-operation between land, sea and air forces that was to serve them well in subsequent operations. They also inflicted important losses on the Japanese. At sea, there was an equal loss of warships, but the build-up of American naval resources ensured that they were better able to take such losses. On land, the Japanese had lost nearly 24,000 men (the American army and marines lost 1,752 killed); but, more seriously, they had lost over 600 airmen. Many were well-trained pilots and they could not be replaced. The same was true of the air war over New Guinea. This contributed to an increasingly apparent aspect of the Pacific war, a decline in the quality of Japanese air power that reflected an inability to ensure good training for pilots.

The Japanese defeat in the Guadalcanal campaign was also very important to American morale. The island had strategic importance, but it took on a significance to contemporaries that exceeded both this and the size of the Japanese garrison. It was important to demonstrate that the Japanese could be beaten not only in carrier actions, but also in the difficult fighting environment of the Pacific islands, while, for Pacific campaigns to succeed, it was necessary to show that air and sea support could be provided to amphibious forces, both when landing and subsequently. In addition, Coral Island and Midway had been defensive successes, but, at Guadalcanal, the attack had clearly been taken to the Japanese and, despite much effort, they had been unable to hold the position.

Also, the time taken to defeat the Japanese on the island, and the large number of islands they continued to hold, ensured that it would be necessary to focus American efforts carefully, a policy that required the identification of key targets. Thanks to a growingly apparent American superiority in the air and at sea, the Japanese would be less able to mount ripostes and any bypassed bases would be isolated. Thus, the Pacific war was to become one that was far from linear.

In eastern New Guinea, American and Australian forces finally prevailed in particularly arduous fighting conditions: the jungle, the mountainous terrain, the heat, the malaria and the rain combined to cause heavy casualties. Amphibious and overland attacks led to the capture of Salamaua and Lae in September 1943. The Allies had benefited from intelligence gained by interceptions, as well as from gaining control of the air, to which this intelligence and the absence of radar to help protect Japanese airfields greatly contributed. Combined with Guadalcanal, this success ensured that Australasia was protected and prepared the way for further Allied attacks. The Japanese still had substantial forces in New Guinea, and there was fighting there until the end of the war, but successive positions were taken, in part thanks to amphibious operations.[7]

Heavy Japanese losses of aircraft and crew over Guadalcanal helped the Americans seize the initiative in 1943, as they began a process of island-hopping in the Solomon Islands in June with an attack on New Georgia. Carriers played a major role, but so also did the creation and securing of airfields. They were important not only for their attack role, but also as part of the far-flung American command and control and supply systems. The value of air power had been dramatically displayed on 3–4 March 1943, when a convoy carrying troops to reinforce New Guinea was attacked by American and Australian planes with the loss of over 3,600 Japanese troops and four destroyers.

The Americans were not only effective thanks to their land-based aircraft and carriers. Covering the landing on Bougainville in the Solomons on 1 November 1943, a force of American cruisers and destroyers beat off an attack that night by a similar Japanese squadron, with losses to the latter in the first battle fought entirely by radar. Radar also helped carriers defend themselves against air attack. It was an important aspect of the application of science.

The Solomons advance culminated with the capture of Admiralty Island at the end of February 1944. The Japanese base in Rabaul was now isolated, while, on Bougainville, Japanese forces that had been beaten away from the defensive perimeter round the Allied bridge-head were left. Maps of American advances tend to ignore the Japanese positions that remained, but, nevertheless, they lacked strategic relevance. The notion of a broad-front advance meant less at sea than on land (where vulnerability on the flank was far more of an issue), but American policy depended on an ability to neutralise as well as outfight Japanese units. In 1943, they were able to demonstrate this ability.

The consequences of this were also seen at the northern tip of the Japanese advance, in the western Aleutians. After the Americans had gained air and naval dominance and beaten the Japanese on Attu in May 1943, the Japanese garrison on Kiska became of little consequence. The Americans did, however, invade it that August, only to discover that the Japanese had already evacuated the island at the end of July. Thereafter, Japanese concern about an American approach, via the northern Pacific, to Hokkaido, the northern of the 'home islands' that make up Japan, led to the stationing of significant forces in the region, although the Americans did not take this approach. It was logistically difficult and there was a lack of intermediate bases that could be seized: the Soviet Union was neutral. The Japanese presence in the western Aleutians and Hokkaido failed to prevent the development of the route from Alaska to the Soviet Far East as the most significant source of Western *matériel* for the Soviet military.

There was also a lack of much action on what had become another peripheral front, the naval war in the Indian Ocean. The Japanese concentration on the Pacific ensured that there were no raids into the Indian Ocean, and no British warship was lost there in 1943. Conversely, the British fleet there was run down to support operations in the Mediterranean and, whereas the British had had two carriers to cover the attack on Madagascar in May 1942, from January 1943 there were none until October, when an escort carrier arrived.

The Americans benefited in the Pacific from better aircraft. Whereas the Japanese had not introduced new classes of planes, the Americans had done so, enabling them to challenge the Zero, which had made such an impact in the initial Japanese advances. Now the Americans had the Corsair, the Lightning and the Hellcat, each of which outperformed the Zero. The Lightning was a twin-engined plane, while the Corsair and the Hellcat had powerful Pratt and Whitney air-cooled radial engines. In addition, their specifications included better protection, which enabled them to take more punishment than Japanese planes. The Japanese had designed the Zero with insufficient protection, in part because its light weight increased range and manoeuvrability, but also because the safety of their pilots was a low priority. When combined with the growing disparity in quality between pilots, a matter of numbers, training and flying experience, it was clear that the Japanese could not compensate for growing numerical inferiority in the air. Masters in aerial combat, American fighters were able to provide cover for their bombers, which were, anyway, better able than their counterparts in Europe to deal with opposition without heavy losses. With far more territory to cover, the Japanese lacked a fighter defence system to match that of the Germans.

In the Central Pacific, the Americans opened up a new axis of advance in 1943. They captured key atolls (especially Makin and Tarawa) in the Gilbert Islands in November, although only after difficult assaults on well-prepared and highly motivated defenders: Tarawa cost 3,000 American dead and wounded.[8]

The Japanese willingness to fight on even in hopeless circumstances, a product of effective indoctrination as well as great bravery, ensured that there were very few prisoners and also led the Americans to seek to take few. This has led to some discussion of the war as a racist struggle, but, although American society was one in which racism played a major role, there are few signs of a policy of indoctrination of troops against the Japanese. Instead, it was the fervent determination of the Japanese to fight on in hopeless circumstances, the difficulty, had they wished to do so, of surrendering given the nature of the battlefield, as well as episodes in which they pretended to surrender and then killed their supposed captors, that helped to ensure that the Americans did not anticipate appreciable numbers of prisoners. Although there was some killing of those trying to surrender, this was not common, and there was no equivalent to the systematic killing of SS troops by the Soviets, let alone the brutal treatment of Soviet prisoners by the Germans and of Allied prisoners by the Japanese.

American successes in the Gilberts helped prepare the way for operations against the Marshall Islands in early 1944. This route revived the pre-war Plan Orange, and represented the shortest route for an advance on the Philippines. The army wanted a southern drive, the navy a central Pacific drive, but the real story was that the Americans had enough resources to do both. The choice of strategy was important alongside the availability of resources, because, however weak the Japanese might be becoming at sea and in the air, there were a large number of Japanese island bases and it was necessary to plan an effective strategy that did not involve the loss of too many men or too much time in attacking most of them. The Americans gained cumulative experience in successful amphibious operations and in their coordination with naval and air support.[9] They developed and used a variety of effective specialised landing craft, including tracked landing vehicles. However, the difficulties that were to be faced by the Americans on Omaha Beach in the D-Day landings in Normandy in 1944 showed that the lessons learned in the Pacific were not universally applicable: some that were, however, were not applied in Europe, but there was also the issue of the dynamic nature of German defensive ideas and constructions.

## Battle of the Atlantic

In 1943, the Allies also won the Battle of the Atlantic. The previous year, 1,664 merchantmen had been sunk by submarines and U-boat losses were less than new launchings. For the first time, there were enough U-boats to organise comprehensive patrol lines across North

Atlantic convoy routes, although, after the summer of 1942, the effectiveness of individual submarine patrols, in terms of tonnage sank, fell. This reflected the increase of convoying and the greater strength of convoy escorts. The majority of merchantmen sunk that year were sailing independently.[10]

New emphasis was given to the submarine war when, in January 1943, Admiral Karl Dönitz, the head of the U-boat service, replaced Grand Admiral Erich Raeder as commander of the navy, as a result of Hitler's anger with the failure of the surface ships to destroy a British convoy on 31 December 1942 in the Battle of the Barents Sea. In 1943, the Allies responded to the U-boats with improved resources, tactics and strategy: they introduced more powerful depth-charges and better sonar detection equipment, and increased the use of ship-borne radar. Enhanced anti-submarine weaponry, especially effective ahead-throwing systems, was important to the Allied success, as were signals intelligence (the ability to intercept and decipher German naval codes) and effective anti-submarine tactics by both convoy escorts and aircraft. Accumulated experience increased Allied operational effectiveness. However, it is salutary to be reminded that technology frequently did not operate as anticipated. Admiral Sir John Power complained in 1943 about communications between British warships:

> It was painfully obvious immediately that V/S [visual signals] and W/T [wireless telegraphy] communications within the squadron were quite hopeless. The E-G [escort group] frigates owned up that they never used anything but R/T [radio telephone], and, as the three destroyers could not use R/T, we had to start off at scratch teaching elementary signal procedure.[11]

In 1942–3, a fierce debate had raged in London, with the Admiralty demanding more air cover from the RAF. Using long-range aircraft for anti-submarine patrols was, however, opposed by Sir Arthur Harris of the RAF, who pressed for a concentration on bombing Germany. This reflected the doctrine and institutional culture of the RAF,[12] which was similarly disinclined to support anti-shipping operations in European waters.[13] The RAF's capacity to navigate accurately over water was poor and they had equipped themselves with a totally inadequate series of anti-submarine weapons. More seriously, the RAF did not understand the philosophy behind convoys and did not appreciate the need to address the issue of commerce protection seriously, not least in order to ensure the supplies of aluminium and aviation fuel upon which their bomber offensive depended. This was an extremely dangerous attitude as the Germans were sinking large numbers of ships, reaching a wartime peak of tonnage sunk in November 1942. Allied shipping was particularly vulnerable then because destroyers and frigates that had escorted convoys were allocated to Operation Torch. This indicates the danger to Atlantic supply links had an attempt been made to invade France in 1942 or 1943.

In the event, air power, in the shape of long-range aircraft, was important to the Allied victory in the Atlantic: land-based VLR Liberators were the key to closing the mid-Atlantic air gap in the May 1943, and thus to denying submarines their safest hunting ground. Furthermore, anti-submarine air tactics became more effective, not only because of improved synchronisation with convoy movements, but also due to a series of incremental steps, such as better radar (and improved use of it), better searchlights, improved fuses for depth-charges, the use of white paint that made it harder to spot aircraft, and improved maintenance. Much of this stemmed from the application of the findings of Coastal Command's Operational Research Station.[14] Aircraft operating against submarines were under naval operational control, an important aid to effectiveness. The greater availability of escort carriers was also important.[15] Similarly, with convoy escorts there were incremental steps not only in numbers, detection equipment and weaponry, but also in experience of operating together and thanks to the development of effective formations and tactics.

The building of far more merchant shipping from 1942, particularly by the Americans, was also very important to Allied victory, as was the availability of more escort vessels and their improved armaments. In May 1943, 41 U-boats were lost, and, on 24 May, Dönitz ordered a halt to attacks on convoys in the North Atlantic and the withdrawal of submarines to areas where there was less Allied air power.[16] That year, the ratio of ships sunk to U-boats destroyed was 2:1, a rate of German success well down on the 14:1 of 1940–2.

May 1943 was not the end of the Battle of the Atlantic, and should only be seen as a turning point for the Allies if the need to continue to overcome the submarine challenge is also stressed. In the battle of technological innovation, the Germans made important moves. When they introduced the T5 acoustic homing torpedo in the late summer of 1943, they were, at once, able to sink three escorts and to launch a renewed attack on Allied shipping. This was successfully counteracted by Allied air power, the application of which benefited from intercepted signals information. Deciphered information (codenamed ULTRA) had provided an ability to plot U-boat positions from August 1941, but, in February 1942, a new, more complex key was introduced, and this was not broken until December 1942.[17]

The determined attempt by the Germans to regain the initiative in late 1943 was unsuccessful, and they suffered heavy losses, including thirty-seven boats in July. The German failure in the second half of the year confirmed and underlined their defeat that May, and, although the loss per month never met May's figure, the aggregate total was far higher. The success of stronger convoy defences had been apparent from late 1941, and was now combined in a more effective overall anti-submarine strategy. The mid-Atlantic air gap was lessened in October 1943 when Portugal agreed to permit the British use of airbases on the Azores. This closed what the Germans called the 'Black Pit' to its west.[18] In November, the U-boats were withdrawn from the Atlantic. There was an important shift in the relative quality of personnel. German U-boat losses cost the Germans the crew, while the Allies built up a bank of experience.

In early 1944, the Germans fitted *Schnorchel* devices to their submarines. These allowed them to charge their batteries while submerged, as well as enabling the underwater starting and running of diesel engines, thus reducing their vulnerability to Allied air power. The U-boats were becoming true submarines as opposed to just submersibles. However, this did not significantly increase attack capability *vis-à-vis* escorts. The improvement in Allied escort capability outweighed submarine advances, and the Germans sank relatively few ships in 1944–5. Furthermore, the production of new types of submarine, especially the high-speed Type XXI 'Electro', was badly affected by Allied bombing.

The strategic failure of the U-boat offensive was clarified by Allied, especially American, shipbuilding. In the first quarter of 1943, the Allies built more ships than the U-boats sank, and, by the end of the third quarter, they had built more than had been sunk since the start of the war.[19] The British played the leading role in defeating the U-boats, but the Americans and Canadians also took important parts, both at sea and in the air.[20]

The Allied success in the Battle of the Atlantic was crucial to the provision of imports to feed and fuel Britain, as well as to the build-up of military resources there: only three Allied merchantmen convoyed across the Atlantic in the first three months of 1944 were sunk. This was the background to the Second Front sought by the Allies, and it underlined the strategic quandary faced by the Germans, with an intractable conflict on the Eastern Front likely to be joined by fresh commitments in France. The sensible response – a compromise peace with the Soviet Union or the Western Allies – was not possible, although the Germans did make attempts to probe the possibility of the former. This helped explain the Allies' adoption of the policy of Unconditional Surrender: it was designed to fix the alliance.

Air power also helped limit the role of German surface warships. Their vulnerability led the Germans to withdraw their major warships from Brest in February 1942; although the British were seriously humiliated when these ships successfully sailed up the Channel and through the Straits of Dover and the British attempt to intercept them failed. Norway was an important base for operations against British convoys taking supplies to the Soviet Union, but the serious inroads of German aeroplanes and, in particular, submarines were not matched by surface ships. Instead, the German warships fell victim – the *Scharnhorst*, in the Battle of the North Cape on 26 December 1943, to a British fleet escorting a convoy, and the *Tirpitz*, which had sailed to Trondheim in Norway in January 1942, to British planes on 12 November 1944.

## Submarines in the Pacific

In the Pacific, the USA was increasingly using submarines to attack Japanese trade, and thus stymied Japanese plans to increase munitions production: Japanese industry was dependent on the import of raw materials from the Japanese empire. Despite problems with their torpedoes until mid-1943, which, for example, affected operations off the Philippines in the winter of 1941–2, effective long-range American submarines made major inroads on Japanese trade, particularly from late 1943. The Americans benefited from the quality of their submarines, including good surface speed and range, from the ability to decipher Japanese signals, and from a clear determination to attack. Unrestricted submarine warfare had been ordered after Pearl Harbor. The Japanese did not inflict enough casualties to cause a deterioration in American submarine leadership.[21]

In contrast, although they had large, long-range submarines, which were used to maintain links with Germany, the Japanese did not launch a submarine war against America's lines of communication in the eastern Pacific, and did not mass them for use in offensives elsewhere. The prestige of their submarines had suffered from their failure to make a major impact in the Pearl Harbor operation, and this affected subsequent consideration of them as a strategic and operational tool. Instead, Japanese submarines were more commonly used as part of the battle fleet, stalking American warships.[22] This failure to attack their communication links made it easier for the Americans to deploy resources against Japan.

As a result, there was a clear contrast with the war with Germany. An invasion of France was not feasible until after the Battle of the Atlantic had been won, but there were no such constraints affecting the forward movement of forces in the Pacific. Looked at differently, the Battle of the Pacific was a carrier conflict, that of the Atlantic a submarine war. In both, the ability to apply air power was crucial. Surface warships also played an important role, but less so in the Atlantic, not least as a result of the German focus on commerce raiding, the sinking of the *Bismarck* and the withdrawal of major warships from Brest.

## War in the air

While Japan remained out of the range of regular and heavy American air attack, particularly once the Chinese airbases initially used had been overrun by the Japanese, Germany was under heavy air attack by 1943. At the Casablanca Conference that January, the British and Americans agreed on the Combined Bomber Offensive, with the Americans attacking by daylight and the British by night. This was seen as a way to show Stalin that the Western Allies were doing their utmost to weaken Germany and thus to aid Soviet operations. Until the opening of the Second Front, this was the most effective way to hit at Germany. Strategic bombing was made more feasible by four-engined bombers, such as the British Lancaster, as well as by heavier bombs and thanks to developments in navigational aids and training.

The availability of large numbers of bombers reflected Allied industrial capability: American production rose to 29,365 in 1943.[23] The Allies considerably out-built their opponents in the air. Numbers, however, were not the sole issue. The Allies also developed the ability to organise production so that it could be retooled quickly for improved marks and to ensure the production of a range of planes with different capabilities.[24]

The Americans focused on precision bombing to hit industrial targets, particularly ball-bearing factories. This reflected the unsuitability of their B-17 bomber for night flying and their criticism of the value of British area bombing. The British wished to destroy industrial targets, but the Butt report on night raids in June–July 1941 showed that they were not doing so. Accuracy was difficult with night-time freefall bombing (there were no guided bombs), and, instead, the British focused on area bombing. This could lead to heavy civilian casualties, which were seen by the protagonists of the policy, particularly Harris, as likely to wreck German morale. About 40,000 people were killed in the British raid on Hamburg on 28 July 1943 as the result of a firestorm created by incendiary bombs. The impact was horrifying: those killed were either suffocated or burnt to death. This raid badly affected German morale, leading to the partial evacuation of cities, including Hamburg and Berlin.

Precision bombing was not, however, an easy alternative. Heavily armed bomber formations lacking fighter escorts proved far less effective both in defending themselves and in destroying targets than had been anticipated in inter-war bombing doctrine. This conviction of the value of the bomber was partly responsible for a failure to push the development of long-range fighters sufficiently early. Prior to the introduction of long-range fighters, bombers were very vulnerable to interceptors, and cripplingly heavy casualty rates occurred in some raids, especially those of the American 8th Army Air Force against the ball-bearing factory at Schweinfurt in August and October 1943. The majority of the bombers were lost to German fighters, with anti-aircraft fire and accidents occurring for the rest. The Germans had developed a complex and wide-ranging system of radar warning, with long-range, early-warning radars, as well as short-range radars that also guided night fighters that had their own radars towards the bombers.[25]

The needs of air defence ensured that *Luftwaffe* strength was increasingly concentrated in Germany, to the detriment of air support for ground combat on the Eastern Front and around the Mediterranean, although much of the *Luftwaffe* was employed on the former throughout the war.[26] The protection of Germany from air attack reflected the concern about the prestige of the regime and the morale of the populace that bombing gave rise to. The availability of more air power on the Eastern Front would have been operationally useful, but, given Soviet resources, it would not have had strategic effect. The contribution of the Allied air offensive to Soviet campaigning was valuable but not decisive.

A long-term emphasis on bombers, as well as the consequences of heavy aeroplane losses from 1940, especially in the Battles of France and Britain in 1940, in the Mediterranean and on the Eastern Front, and a failure to increase aircraft production sufficiently until 1943, meant that the German fighter arm was weak. In response to the Allied bombers, German fighter-bombers and medium bombers – the Me-110, the Ju-88Gb and the Do-217J – were adapted to act as night fighters. The Hamburg raid was followed by the development of new night-fighting methods that were not dependent on radar. Radar-defence systems could be wrecked by the British use of 'window': strips of aluminium foil that appeared like bombers on the radar screens. In response, the Germans relied on radar guidance to the general area of British air activity, which 'window' contributed to, and visual sightings thereafter. This caused British losses to mount from the late summer of 1943. Furthermore, that autumn, German radar was adapted so as to be able to circumvent the impact of 'window'. British night attacks on Berlin from 18

November 1943 until 31 March 1944, which Harris had promised would undermine German morale, led, instead, to the loss of 492 bombers, a rate of losses that could not be sustained. In the British raid on Nuremberg of 30–1 March 1944, 106 out of the 782 bombers were lost, with only limited damage to the city and few German fighters shot down. This led to the end of the bomber-stream technique of approaching the target.[27] Bombing, however, had a heavy impact on Italy. By 1943, Anglo-American bombing had wrecked 60 per cent of Italy's industrial capacity and badly affected Italian morale.

## War in North Africa

Italy was the Axis victim of that year's campaigning. This reflected the collapse of the Axis position in important parts of the Mediterranean. After heavy fighting from February, the Germans (and their Italian allies) had surrendered in Tunisia on 13 May 1943.

The western and eastern Allied forces in North Africa (those moving forward from the Torch beaches and from El Alamein) had joined up in pushing the Axis army back on the Mediterranean. The Allies faced the difficulty of coordinating advances of disparate forces from two different directions – Algeria and Egypt. The British advance through Libya was particularly deliberate, or, to its critics, slow. This was a facet of Montgomery's character, but also reflected his concern about the possibility of a German riposte. In addition, Allied air and surface attacks and mining in the Mediterranean built on earlier efforts to cut supply routes to Libya in 1940–2, and, in 1943, succeeded in crippling the flow of supplies to German forces in Tunisia. The earlier German failure to capture Malta, or to wreck its use as a base, left the Germans in a weak strategic position in the central Mediterranean, as Malta again proved its value for the inter-diction of transport links. The British were also greatly helped by an ability, through the ULTRA system, to intercept and decipher German signals traffic.[28]

Ignoring Rommel's advice to withdraw from Tunisia, the German forces there were reinforced by Hitler, who feared the impact on Mussolini of withdrawal. Hitler was ready to send larger forces to protect Tunisia than he had to conquer Egypt the previous year. This merely ensured a larger German defeat, although it also made the Allied task more difficult. The fighting in Tunisia indicated the value of Allied numerical superiority and, in particular, air support, but also that superior German generalship and fighting quality could mount effective ripostes, particularly in the offensive that led to the Battle of the Kasserine Pass in mid-February. The Germans had sought to exploit their central position by attacking the Allies advancing from Algeria and Egypt separately, and benefited from the difficulty of matching the Allied advance with an adequate build-up of support. The Allies were helped by the movement forward of their supply points, both ports and airfields, following the advance on land, but this took time to have an impact. Allied anti-submarine operations helped secure supply routes.

It is interesting to consider the subsequent controversy (see pp. 179–81) about Allied strategy in 1944 after the breakout from Normandy in light of the difficulties encountered in Tunisia in 1943. Initially, the Americans did not fight well in Tunisia against the seasoned German veterans, and they suffered from ineffective leadership: poor communication, lack of co-operation, and command rivalries. All of these reflected a lack of combat-readiness that owed much to an absence of experience in engaging in battle. For all troops, this proved an issue at some stage during the war, but those who began fighting after other powers faced a particular disadvantage.

The campaign also illustrated the resilience of the Germans on the defensive, with their ability to mount defensive–offensive operations. However, there were important flaws in the planning and execution of their offensive, and initial advantages were not sustained. In addition, the Americans eventually rallied,[29] and, in some respects, the operation prefigured the fate of the more serious German counter-offensive in 1944 in the Battle of the Bulge (see pp. 178–9).

The second German strike in Tunisia was launched against Montgomery's Eighth Army, but it was rapidly thwarted by the strength of the British position, in particular in anti-tank weaponry. Once the German assaults had been blocked, their position was weakened by the length of their defensive perimeter. This reduced the number of reserves, and thus ensured that the Germans were not able adequately to respond to Allied breakthroughs when they finally occurred. The Allies also benefited from superiority in the air, particularly in the final attack on 6 May, which cleared the approach to Tunis, although air support was not as effective as it was to become in 1944. Tunis and Bizerta fell next day, and the now isolated Axis units had all surrendered by 13 May; 238,000 Axis troops became prisoners, and their total casualties were greater than those at Stalingrad.[30] The availability of some of those forces on the Eastern Front would have made a valuable contribution to German strength there.

## Italy invaded

Victory in Tunisia was followed by an attack on Italy, although it proved impossible to repeat the success won in Tunisia. Allied forces landed in Sicily on 10 July 1943. Amphibious power and air support allowed the Allies to seize the initiative. They helped ensure a wide-ranging attack on Sicily that included a use of airborne troops; although many of the gliders landed in the sea due to strong winds. In total, 180,000 Allied troops were involved, ensuring that this was the second largest amphibious operation of the war in Europe (D-Day was the first). Although the invasion had been preceded by a thorough air assault during June, which had gained the Allies control of the air, there was concern at the degree of air support provided for land and sea operations. The German defenders of the island fought well, taking advantage of the terrain, which limited the use of armour. The same was not true of all of the Italians, among whom morale varied greatly. The Americans proved far more effective than they had done in Tunisia, and were more successful than the Eighth Army in gaining and using mobility. The fall of Sicily, completed on 16–17 August, provided a valuable base from which mainland Italy could be attacked, although the ability of the Axis to retreat without encirclement and then to evacuate about 102,000 troops – much of their army – seriously compromised the value of the operation. Most of the 162,000 troops captured were Italians.

The failure to ensure encirclement or to prevent evacuation was a major blow, as Sicily was the only large island on which German forces were to resist attack, and the Allies possessed superiority in the air and at sea. To a considerable extent, this reflected poor planning and execution, particularly by the Army Group Commander, General

Sir Harold Alexander, who failed to appreciate the fighting quality of the American Seventh Army under General George Patton.[31]

The invasion of Sicily precipitated a growing crisis of confidence in Mussolini among the Fascist leadership, as well as among other Italian leaders, particularly the king. Mussolini was arrested on 25 July and a government formed by Marshal Badoglio. This was backed by the army, and excluded the Fascists. Badoglio sought to reach an agreement with the Allies, but, meanwhile, the Germans built up their forces in Italy. An armistice for the Italians was signed on 3 September and announced on the 8th. However, the rapid German response, which indicated their already strong concerns about Italian stability, the response capability of the German system, and good staff work, eventually left them in control in central and northern Italy. The new Italian government was unable to organise effective opposition to the Germans. Army commanders were left without orders, although most of the fleet sailed to join the British. On 9 September, German planes, using radio-controlled glider bombs, inflicted serious damage, but most of the warships escaped.

The German response ended the brief opportunity for manoeuvre that the Anglo-Americans had enjoyed in the initial stages of the war in Italy, while German forces were dispersed throughout the peninsula. Allied forces invaded Calabria from Sicily on 3 September, meeting no resistance, while Taranto was seized by an amphibious force on 9 September, and the main invasion force was landed the same day in the Gulf of Salerno, south of Naples. However, the German response to the over-extended Salerno landing proved more rapid than had been anticipated, and the shallow bridgehead was only consolidated and expanded with considerable difficulty. The German counter-offensive of 12–15 September nearly succeeded, but, having failed, the Germans then withdrew on the 16th.[32] On 27 September, Naples rose against the Germans, who retaliated harshly before the Allies reached the city on 1 October. The Allies were left in control of southern Italy, but the Germans created a strong line across the peninsula, making plentiful use of the mountainous terrain to create effective defensive positions, from which they were to fight ably.

The new Italian government declared war on Germany in October. Although that made little difference to the course of the conflict, it eased Allied occupation issues. In a daring airborne operation, the Germans, on 11 September, had rescued Mussolini from captivity. They put him in charge of a puppet state in northern Italy, the Italian Social Republic, or Salò Republic, but he was now of limited importance; an apt example of the way in which the war cast a harsh light on power and pretensions.

The invasion of Italy altered the strategic situation in the Mediterranean. The Balkans and southern France both now appeared vulnerable to Allied attack, and this increased Allied differences over planning. However, because Italy proved a more intractable task than had been anticipated, the resources that might have been freed for such options were not released. That September, the Germans were able to withdraw from strategically irrelevant Sardinia and Corsica, both of which were occupied by the Allies.

In contrast, concern about a possible invasion of Greece, deliberately encouraged by Allied deception, led the Germans to reinforce their forces there in June and July. The invasion did not come, but the strength of the German position helped ensure that the British were unsuccessful in the Aegean when they tried to exploit the Italian surrender. This attempt reflected Churchill's longstanding interest in the region and his hope to bring Turkey into the war. The Americans sensibly advised against the plan. A swift German response, and the failure of the British to secure air superiority, led to a serious failure in the Dodecanese Islands campaign, with the loss of garrisons on Cos (3–4 October) and Leros (12–16 November). This failure indicated the continued importance of air power, and formed a striking contrast with American successes in the Pacific: there, island targets were isolated before attack. Turkey did not enter the war until 1 March 1945.

Victory in Tunisia and Sicily and the invasion of Italy transformed the situation in the Mediterranean. This made a major contribution to the flexibility of Allied supply links, greatly shortening the route from the North Atlantic to the Middle East: it was no longer necessary to face the choice of risking Axis interception or sailing round South Africa. The surrender of much of the Italian navy enabled the British to withdraw warships from the Mediterranean, both to support the invasion of France and for operations against Japan. Once the Allies were established in southern Italy, they began bombing attacks on both northern Italy and the Balkans, and this, indeed, had been one of the goals of the invasion. The Romanian oilfields at Ploesti were the major target in the latter, and were frequently bombed from August 1943, although losses – 350 bombers by August 1944 – were heavy.

## Differences over strategy

The Americans had been reluctant to support an invasion of Sicily and Italy, because they feared that it would detract resources from the invasion of France and the war with Japan and be a strategic irrelevance. American policymakers were opposed to what they saw as the Mediterranean obsession of British policy. The latter commitment reflected British strategic concerns in the region, but these were the product not simply of geopolitical interests but also of the legacy of conflict in the Mediterranean with the Axis since 1940: the British had military resources in the region, as well as commitments, and the former could not be readily reallocated. The British preference for an indirect approach, weakening the Axis by incremental steps as the preparation for an invasion of France, was also important. It was an aspect of British strategic culture and also a response to the specific military circumstances of 1942–3. The British were concerned that a direct attack across the Channel would expose untested forces to the battle-hardened Germans. Their experience in 1940–1 had made them wary of such a step until the Germans had been weakened, and fresh defeats at Axis hands in Asia and, initially, North Africa in 1942 had further hit Britain's military reputation.

In contrast, the Americans argued that Italy was a strategic irrelevance that would dissipate military strength, and sought a direct approach, particularly an engagement with the major German forces in Western Europe and an advance into Germany. German weaknesses in 1943 suggest that this might have been an option that year. Many key units were allocated to the Kursk offensive, the Germans lacked the build-up in munitions production that 1943 was to bring, and their defensive positions in France were incomplete. The Soviets mentioned their suspicion of their allies' failure to open a Second Front to the Germans when probing the possibility of a separate peace. These probings led to a peace offer in September 1943, but

Hitler was not interested in pursuing it. Nevertheless, the possibility of such a development indicated the potential impact of strategic decisions on geopolitical alignments.

However, the British were correct to draw attention to deficiencies in Allied preparedness. As yet, there was only limited experience in (and equipment for) amphibious operations, while it was unclear at the beginning of 1943 how far it would be possible to vanquish the U-boat threat. Aside from the need to build up forces for an invasion, there was also the requirement of assured air and sea superiority. The success of the Torch landings in 1942 was only a limited indicator of capability, as opposition to them had been weak. Operations in the Mediterranean in 1943 provided valuable experience in planning and execution, not least in air support, airborne attacks and the use of landing craft. The landings of 1943, like Anzio in 1944, also provided warnings about the difficulty of invading France, not least in terms of the German response. In 1943, the latter would have been a more serious problem in France than it was to be in 1944, as the Allies did not yet have sufficient air dominance to seek to isolate the area of operations. Operations in North Africa and Italy had also been important in improving military capability on land. The British learned how to respond to German armour, and came to place a renewed stress on artillery. The Americans benefited greatly from their first experience of fighting the Germans in World War Two.

As it was not feasible to invade France in 1943, the Americans finally agreed to the attack on Sicily. It was the fall of Mussolini that helped lead to the commitment of major forces to mainland Italy. These were very much Anglo-American operations. The independent role the British had taken in Egypt under Montgomery was not to be repeated against the Germans. Britain and her empire continued to make a major contribution to the Allied war effort, but her position was now overshadowed.[33] Even in Burma, there was a need for the British to consider American-supported Chinese interests.

## 1943 reviewed

Most of the German and Japanese empires had still not been recovered at the close of 1943, and most of their armed forces had not yet been destroyed, particularly in the case of their armies. The concentration of the Allies on Germany, total in the case of the Soviet Union, and great in that of Britain, Canada and the American army and air force (much of the American navy was also devoted to anti-submarine duty in the Atlantic), ensured that Japan had not yet faced a sustained large-scale attack, although Japanese naval aviation had already been greatly weakened by the Americans. Much of the Japanese army had not taken part in large-scale combat operations in 1943. These units were theoretically available for transfer to combat zones, either for defensive purposes or to mount new attacks. Both Germany and Japan continued to benefit in defending their empires from interior lines, although they were unable to retain their peripheries and faced serious resource issues, not least over fuel supplies.

They also continued to exploit the areas they had conquered and to brutalise conquered peoples. The cruel treatment of the Jews was increasingly focused on their deportation, from the ghettos that had been created by the Germans, to camps, including death camps where gas was used, as well as slave labour camps, most of whose inmates died as a result of malnutrition and disease or were killed. In July–October 1942, over 300,000 Jews had been deported from Warsaw alone, mostly to the nearby death camp at Treblinka. After armed resistance by the Warsaw Jews in January 1943, the Germans, on 19 April, launched a campaign to destroy the ghetto. Although in a hopeless situation, outnumbered and with few arms, the Jews, fighting from bunkers and underground positions, fought on until 16 May.

Despite the large areas that remained under Axis control at the end of 1943, the Allies had made major steps in preparing for funda-mental blows against the Axis. The development of the American military economy was particularly important. The Americans mobilised their resources far more speedily and extensively than they had done in World War One. By 1943–4, the USA was producing abut 40 per cent of the world's total output of munitions, thanks, in part, to an increase in the country's overall productive capacity by about 50 per cent between 1939 and 1944. This helped ensure a determination to direct Allied policy. 1944 was to be the decisive year of conflict.

## NOTES

1 G.P. Megargee, *Inside Hitler's High Command* (Lawrence, Kansas, 2000).

2 D.M. Glantz (ed.), *From the Don to the Dnepr: Soviet Offensive Operations – December 1942–August 1943* (1990).

3 W.S. Dunn, *Kursk: Hitler's Gamble, 1943* (Westport, Connecticut, 1997); D.M. Glantz and J.M. House, *The Battle of Kursk* (Lawrence, Kansas, 1999).

4 V. Hardesty, *Red Phoenix: The Rise of Soviet Air Power, 1941–1945* (Washington, 1982).

5 S.B. Griffith, *The Battle for Guadalcanal* (Philadelphia, 1963); R. Leckie, *Challenge for the Pacific: Guadalcanal – the Turning Point of the War* (1966).

6 J.B. Lundstrom, *The First Team and the Guadalcanal Campaign: Naval Fighter Combat from August to November 1942* (Annapolis, 1994).

7 D. Dexter, *The New Guinea Offensives* (Canberra, 1961).

8 J.H. Alexander, *Utmost Savagery: The Three Days of Tarawa* (Annapolis, 1995); M.B. Graham, *Mantle of Heroism: Tarawa and the Struggle for the Gilberts, November 1943* (Novato, California, 1993). For an eyewitness view, see R.L. Sherrod, *Tarawa: The Story of a Battle* (New York, 1944).

9 J.A. Isely and P.A. Crowl, *The U.S. Marines and Amphibious War: Its Theory, and Its Practice in the Pacific* (Princeton, 1951).

10 C. Blair, *Hitler's U-boat War: The Hunters, 1939–1942* (New York, 1996).

11 BL. Add. 56097 fol. 145.

12 J. Buckley, *The RAF and Trade Defence 1919–1945: Constant Endeavour* (Keele, 1995); C. Goulter, 'Sir Arthur Harris: Different Perspectives', in G. Sheffield and G. Till (eds), *Challenges of High Command in the Twentieth Century* (Camberley, 1999), pp. 78–80.

13 C. Goulter, *A Forgotten Offensive: Royal Air Force Coastal Command's Anti-Shipping Campaign, 1940–1945* (1995).

14 C.H. Waddington, *O.R. in World War 2: Operational Research Against the U-Boat* (1973); A. Price, *Aircraft versus Submarine: The Evolution of Anti-submarine Aircraft, 1912 to 1980* (2nd edn, 1980).

15 K. Poolman, *Allied Escort Carriers of World War Two in Action* (1988).

16 F. Barley and D. Waters, *The Defeat of the Enemy Attack on Shipping* (2nd edn, Aldershot, 1997).

17 W.J.R. Gardner, *Decoding History: The Battle of the Atlantic and Ultra* (Basingstoke, 1999).

18 D. Syrett, *The Defeat of the German U-Boats: The Battle of the Atlantic* (Columbia, South Carolina, 1994).

19 S. Howarth and D. Law (eds), *The Battle of the Atlantic 1939–1945* (1994). For a case study, see J. Rohwer, *The Critical Convoy Battles of March 1943: The Battle for HX229/SC122* (1977).

20 M. Milner, *The U-Boat Hunters: The Royal Canadian Navy and the Offensive against Germany's Submarines, 1943–1945* (Toronto, 1994); R. Sarty, *Canada and the Battle of the Atlantic* (Montreal, 1998).

21 W.J. Holmes, *Undersea Victory: The Influence of Submarine Operations on the War in the Pacific* (New York, 1966); C. Blair, *Silent Victory: The US*

*Submarine War Against Japan* (New York, 1963); M. Parillo, *The Japanese Merchant Marine in World War Two* (Annapolis, 1993); J. Prados, *Combined Fleet Decoded: The Secret History of American Intelligence and the Japanese Navy in World War II* (New York, 1995).

22  C. Boyd and A. Yoshida, *The Japanese Submarine Force and World War II* (Annapolis, 1995).

23  J.B. Rae, *Climb to Greatness: The American Aircraft Industry 1920–60* (1968).

24  A. Furse, *Wilfrid Freeman: The Genius Behind Allied Survival and Air Supremacy 1939 to 1945* (Staplehurst, 2000), pp. 281, 289.

25  G. Aders, *History of the German Night Fighter Force, 1917–1945* (1979).

26  R.R. Muller, *The German Air War in Russia* (Baltimore, 1992).

27  C. Webster and N. Frankland, *The Strategic Air Offensive Against Germany, 1939–1945* (4 vols, 1961); C.C. Crane, *Bombs, Cities and Civilians: American Airpower Strategy in World War II* (Lawrence, Kansas, 1993); N. Longmate, *The Bombers: The RAF Offensive against Germany 1939–45* (1998).

28  R. Bennett, *Ultra and Mediterranean Strategy* (1989).

29  M. Blumenson, *Rommel's Last Victory: The Battle of Kasserine Pass* (1968).

30  K. Macksey, *Crucible of Power: The Fight for Tunisia, 1942–1943* (1969).

31  C. D'Este, *Bitter Victory: The Battle for Sicily, 1943* (1988).

32  E. Morris, *Salerno: A Military Fiasco* (1983).

33  M. Howard, *The Mediterranean Strategy in the Second World War* (1968).

# CHAPTER SIX

# *Defeating the Axis, 1944*

In 1944, far harder blows were delivered at the Axis. They failed to regain the initiative, continued to lose territory and were increasingly outfought. The major losses of territory and manpower were those of the Germans on the Eastern Front, although there were also important Allied gains elsewhere, as well as the opening of the long-awaited Second Front.

## Soviet advance

On the Eastern Front, benefiting from an even greater numerical superiority than in 1943, the Soviets pushed the Germans back across Russia, White Russia (Belorussia) and Ukraine in an impressive series of offensives, and also opened up the Balkans. Whereas, in 1943, the course of the conflict had led to Hitler's loss of his Italian alliance, in 1944 his entire alliance structure in Europe collapsed and only marginal forces, instead of national armies, continued to fight alongside the Germans.

In their campaigning, the Red Army proved adept at developing good co-operation between armour, artillery and infantry, and at making the latter two mobile, successfully executing a strategy of encirclement, as in January–February around Korsun-Shevchenkovski, in the right-bank Dnieper/Ukraine campaign of early 1944. In addition, advancing Soviet forces proved able to split opposing armies. In the right-bank Dnieper/Ukraine campaign, which was launched on 2–4 December 1943, the Soviets benefited from the large bridgeheads west of the Dnieper that they had gained earlier in the year and they were not exhausted by that recent campaigning.

161

The Germans were outnumbered, particularly in artillery and aircraft, although not so much as to make the verdict obvious. They suffered, however, from the consequences of 'no retreat' orders which robbed them of mobility. The campaign was less well handled by German commanders than that of early 1943, although the different verdict also reflected an increase in Soviet operational effectiveness and tactical skill: as a consequence, German counterattacks were less successful than hitherto. The Soviets used their reserves well to maintain the pace of the advance and to thwart counterattacks. As the Soviets had the initiative, they were able not only to choose when and where to attack, but also to leave German and allied units, such as those in the Crimea in early 1944, unable to play a role until the moment of destruction. This accentuated Soviet numerical superiority and operational effectiveness.

The Soviets achieved what has been seen as their own *Blitzkrieg*, especially in the breakthrough attacks in Ukraine in March and April 1944, which drove the Germans back across the Bug, Dniester and Prut rivers, spring mud bringing them no respite. The Soviets repeated their success in attacks in June–September 1944, which overran White Russia and took the Red Army close to Warsaw, destroying much of the German Army Group Centre in a series of successful encirclement attacks that amounted to the most large-scale German defeat in the field during the war. Operation Bagration, the attack launched on Army Group Centre on 23 June, benefited from superiority in resources, including 2.4 million troops compared to 700,000 Germans. It was also a triumph for operational skill. The Germans were outgeneralled and outfought, with the Soviets using effective deception to disguise their plans, persuading the Germans that the attack would come in the northern Ukraine, as well as showing more fighting skill and mobility than in the 1942 and early 1943 offensives. Many of the German units were committed to fortress positions at Vitebsk, Orsha, Mogilev and Bobruysk which, in accordance with Hitler's instructions, were instructed to fight to the last. This doctrine lessened Hitler's need to make difficult command decisions, but exposed the Germans to encirclement and robbed them of the possibilities presented by mobility, although striking Soviet superiority in tanks and aircraft lessened their options.[1] Hoping to defeat the Second Front, the Germans had concentrated their reinforcements in France and Italy, although Soviet successes in March 1944 forced a reallocation of units intended for the West.

Having lost heavily in the first phase of Bagration, which ended on 5 July, the Germans were pushed back to the Vistula and to East Prussia in the second phase; although, in this phase, they managed to show more flexibility and command skill. Lublin was captured by Soviets on 23 July, Lvov on 27 July. A bridgehead over the river Vistula was gained at the end of July and held against counterattacks in the following months. By this stage, the Soviet advance was facing serious problems of exhaustion as well as growing logistical difficulties. The German resistance had also stiffened.

Nevertheless, the Soviet failure to come to the relief of the Polish insurgents – the Home Army – who rose against the Germans in Warsaw on 1 August and were crushed, surrendering on 1 October after over 15,000 insurgents and 200,000 civilians had been killed, has been a source of great controversy. It is clear that Stalin's drive for a Communist Poland was helped by the serious weakening of the non-Communist resistance, and a determination to impose a Communist new order was also seen in the areas of Poland liberated by Soviet forces. The Polish Home Army was seeking to free Warsaw for the Western-backed, London-based Polish government-in-exile. Stalin refused not only to provide assistance but also to permit the use of bases for Western air support.[2]

In 1944, the need for the Germans to defend the entire front against a series of Soviet attacks left them with few resources for staging counter-offensives. The Soviets also proved superior at operational art, enabling them to stage successful offensives focusing on manoeuvre warfare. This counteracted German tactical proficiency, which itself was undergoing strain, both because of Soviet improvements and because the effectiveness of the German army declined as veterans were replaced by poorly trained new recruits, whose composition reflected the extent to which Hitler was having to scrape the barrel. The pressure of Allied attacks in Italy and, even more from June 1944, France had an impact on the German ability to reinforce the Eastern Front.

Both sides employed air power principally in ground support, but the Soviets had far more planes and their tactical and operational effectiveness had improved. They were therefore better able to drive the *Luftwaffe* from the battlefield. The Soviets also benefited from the continued improvement in their armour to match new German tank types. The T–34/85 was more heavily gunned than its predecessors. The Soviets enjoyed a major advantage in artillery and this proved particularly helpful in helping open breaches in German lines. Alongside guns, the Soviet artillery made extensive use of Katyusha rockets. These were a mobile weapon, although, like more conventional artillery, they faced the problem of a supply of sufficient projectiles.

Whereas, after Stalingrad, Soviet advances had largely been achieved without the encirclement and destruction of opposing forces, from June 1944 there was to be much more success in pushing encirclements through to destruction, in large part because Soviet forces had acquired the means and doctrine to fulfil these goals.[3] In contrast, there was no such encirclement and annihilation in the Philippines or Italy, or in France (with the partial exception of the Falaise pocket).

The Red Army showed that a war of fronts did not preclude one of a frequent movement of these fronts. Furthermore, this was not simply an advance on one axis. Indeed, the scale of the Soviet achievement can be grasped by considering their advances on their flanks. These were not strategically crucial operations, but they indicated the inability of the Germans to protect their alliance system as well as their empire. To the north, where the Germans had been pushed back from Novgorod and near Leningrad in January, most of the Baltic States were cleared in a subsequent offensive in late 1944. After a successful Soviet advance to the Baltic, which was reached on 10 August, the Germans were driven into a pocket in Courland (western Latvia), but Hitler, characteristically, refused to evacuate the troops from it, and the Germans remained there until the end of the war, unable to influence the course of the conflict elsewhere. Tallinn, the capital of Estonia, fell to the Soviets on 22 September and Riga on 15 October, while Finland, which had been hit hard in a Soviet offensive in June, signed an armistice on 2 September 1944. The concentration of available German surface warships in the Baltic helped the Germans retain naval superiority there, enabling them to supply the Courland pocket, but this could not sway the course of the war on land.[4]

Stalin was keen to regain the Baltic republics in order to re-establish the Soviet position there. The advance of Soviet forces everywhere was followed by the slaughter, mistreatment or imprisonment of civilians deemed unacceptable. This was particularly marked in the Baltic republics, where the Soviets reintroduced the tyrannical control and 'social cleansing' they had enforced in 1940: the peasantry were forcibly collectivised. There was also widespread slaughter in Ukraine and White Russia, while, once Soviet forces entered East Prussia, German civilians were killed in considerable numbers.[5]

Finland's abandonment of Hitler reflected the strength of the Soviet position. The Finns made important territorial concessions, but avoided the occupation and Communist takeover that were to happen to other German allies that had fought the Soviet Union. Soviet forces were now better able to press the German units based in northern Norway which had advanced towards Murmansk in 1941 but failed to capture the port. The Soviet advance against them was now supported by Finnish forces keen to clear northern Finland of German forces.

On the other flank, Sevastopol surrendered on 9 May 1944, at the end of a rapid conquest of the isolated German and allied Romanian forces in the Crimea that had taken just over a month. Soviet propaganda trumpeted their ability to capture Sevastopol more speedily than the Germans had done in 1942. Hitler had ignored Romanian requests for withdrawal from the Crimea, and had proved all too receptive to reassurances that first the Crimea and then Sevastopol could be held.

The defeat of the German army in Moldavia that August led to the surrender of Romania on 23 August, and this was followed by the Romanian attack on German and Hungarian forces. Invaded by Soviet forces in September, Bulgaria declared war on Germany on 5 September, before it made peace with the Soviet Union, ensuring that, for a few hours, it was at war with all the major powers, bar Japan. The Red Army went on in October to invade Slovakia and to overrun much of eastern Hungary; although a pro-German coup by Hungarian Fascists on 15 October, supported by German special forces, blocked the attempt of the Hungarian government under Admiral Horthy to settle with the Soviets. These were not the sole checks suffered by the Soviets. It proved difficult for them to make major gains in Slovakia, while a German armoured counterattack near Debrecen in Hungary in late October inflicted heavy casualties. Nevertheless, the Soviet advance in Hungary continued and, by 26 December, Budapest was surrounded. The city, however, did not completely fall until 13 February 1945, showing that Stalingrad was not the only city that could be bitterly defended. As with Stalingrad, a German attempt to relieve a surrounded force failed. Mounted in January 1945, it was not helped by Hitler's refusal to countenance a breakout by the garrison.

The collapse of the German position in the northern Balkans exposed their garrisons in Greece, Yugoslavia and Albania, leading to their evacuation, for example of Belgrade on 19 October. Although harassed by partisans, particularly in Yugoslavia, the Germans were able to evacuate most of their troops, committing atrocities as they withdrew. Their departure left former supporters in an exposed position, and many also retreated. Others were caught up in the developing conflict to seize power in these countries: Communist partisans made determined efforts to do so in all three countries. In Yugoslavia, they were greatly helped by the intervention of Soviet forces, which ensured that Tito, rather than Mihailović, would dominate Serbia. The latter's Cetniks were attacked in September by the Soviets, the Bulgarians and Tito's partisans.

The German withdrawal from the Balkans freed units from garrison duty to help form a new front against the Soviets. Nevertheless, the length of the German front line at the close of 1944 was still such as to put a major burden on German resources. Furthermore, the Soviets were now supported by large Romanian and Bulgarian forces. These played a major role in operations in Romania, Yugoslavia, Czechoslovakia and, in particular, Hungary. The Romanians suffered 160,000 casualties in these campaigns.

## War in Italy

Further west, the Allies had to stage a series of hard-fought offensives to surmount successive defensive lines in Italy. The Po Valley was not occupied until April 1945. The Germans were helped by the narrowness of the front, the mountainous terrain and the winter weather, as well as by skilled leadership and the density of their forces on the east–west defensive lines they successively adopted, especially the Gustav (Winter) Line in the winter of 1943–4,[6] and the Gothic Line in the autumn of 1944. However, German counter-offensives, against the bridgeheads of Allied amphibious landings at Salerno in September 1943 and at Anzio in February 1944, could be stopped with the help of sea and air bombardment. General Alexander wrote about Anzio that 'given reasonable weather we should be able to break up any large concentration counter-attack by switching on the whole of the Mediterranean Air Force, as we did at Salerno', while naval bombardment protected the flanks.[7]

It was more difficult to translate this superiority into success in offensive land operations. The pace of advance was slower than in France or Eastern Europe, because, in Italy, the defensive density was higher, the front was narrow and the terrain more difficult. This not only helped the Germans on the ground but also limited the effectiveness of Allied air attacks.[8] There was also concern about Allied strategy and generalship, including the failure to exploit the Salerno and Anzio landings sufficiently rapidly.

Aside from command flaws at Anzio, however, there is the question of whether the entire operation was misconceived. In particular, limitations in the availability of troops and landing craft, and a strategic context that was different to those in which the Sicily and Salerno operations had been launched, made the landing vulnerable. The idea that it would be possible to outflank the Germans on the Gustav Line and cause them readily to abandon their position, thus opening the way for an Allied advance on Rome, both from the Line and from Anzio, was optimistic.[9]

There were subsequent concerns about the ability to exploit the eventual advance after the Gustav Line had been broken in May 1944. The pursuit of the Germans was insufficiently close. In August 1944, Field Marshal Sir Alan Brooke, Chief of the British Imperial General Staff, wrote about Alexander's strategy:

> I am rather disappointed that Alex did not make a more definite attempt to smash Kesselring's forces up whilst they are south of the Apennines. He has planned a battle on the Apennine position and seems to be deliberately driving the Germans back onto that position instead of breaking them

up in the more favourable country. I cannot feel that this policy of small pushes all along the line and driving the Boche like partridges can be right. I should have liked to see one concentrated attack, with sufficient depth to it, put in at a suitable spot with a view to breaking through and smashing up German divisions by swinging with right and left. However it is a bit late for that now...very hard to get old Alex to grasp the real requirements of any strategic situation.[10]

The Germans were able to withdraw to the prepared Gothic Line. Rome had fallen to the Allies on 5 June, Pisa on 23 July and Florence on 4 August, but subsequent progress when the Allies reached the Gothic Line, which took advantage of the difficult terrain in the northern Apennines, was very limited, not least because the serious difficulties of assaulting the German defences were accentuated by the impact of the autumn rains. Furthermore, the detachment of six divisions to support the landings in southern France weakened the Allied forces in Italy, as, more generally, did the dispatch of reinforcements to northern France rather than Italy. The attacks on the Gothic Line in September and October led to heavy Allied casualties and, combined with the weather, to a stop in operations in October, although the Line had been breached east of the Apennines.[11]

Allied forces in Italy in 1944 took appreciable casualties without either strategic results or an attritional wearing down of Axis strength, although Anzio led to the commitment of German reserves that might otherwise have been sent elsewhere. Allied bases in Italy helped support partisan activity in Yugoslavia, and were used in the bombing of targets in southern Europe, but in neither case with crucial consequences.

From the outset, there was criticism of the decision to fight in Italy. In *Newsweek*, on 13 March 1944, Fuller wrote, 'the strategy is execrable. We should never have embarked on this Italian adventure because it was unstrategic from the start'. Claiming that the topography helped the defence, Fuller stated that forces should have been conserved for the Second Front in France. Churchill, in contrast, was anxious to use the Mediterranean as a staging point for amphibious operations into the Balkans. To the Americans, this was a distraction from defeating the Germans in France, and also a logistical nightmare. To Churchill, however, the Balkans presented an opportunity not only to harry the Germans, but also to pre-empt Soviet advances. This reflected his suspicion of the Soviet Union, but also his strong sense that the war was a stage in the history of the twentieth century, a formative stage but one that would be succeeded by challenges and rivalries that had only been partly suspended during the conflict.

## France invaded

In France, American, British and Canadian forces had landed in Normandy on 6 June 1944 as Operation Neptune (the landings) paved the way for Operation Overlord (the invasion). Under the overall command of General Dwight Eisenhower, the Allies benefited from well-organised and effective naval support for the invasion and from absolute air superiority. Combined with the efforts of the French resistance, this air superiority helped to isolate the battlefield. A successful deception exercise, Operation Fortitude, ensured that the Normandy landing was a surprise.

The Germans, instead, had concentrated more of their defences and forces in the Calais region, which offered a shorter sea crossing and a shorter route to Germany. Normandy, in contrast, was easier to reach from the invasion ports on the south coast of England, particularly Plymouth, Portland and Portsmouth. The Germans lacked adequate naval and air forces to contest an invasion, and much of their army in France was of indifferent quality and short of transport and training, and, in many cases, equipment. The commanders were divided about where the attack was likely to fall and about how best to respond to it, particularly over whether to move their ten panzer divisions close to the coast, so that the Allies could be attacked before they could consolidate their position or massed as a strategic reserve. The eventual decision was for the panzer divisions, whose impact greatly worried Allied planners, to remain inland, but their ability to act as a strategic reserve was lessened by the decision not to mass them and by Allied air power. This decision reflected the tensions and uncertainties of the German command structure.

Air power also helped ensure that the Allies were able to secure the flanks of their landing by the use of parachutists and glider-borne troops. These were particularly important to the landing on Utah Beach at the eastern base of the Cotentin peninsula, as the Germans were unable to bring up reserves to support the coastal defences. The disorganised nature of the airdrop, which matched that of the Sicily operation the previous year, further handicapped the defence as there were no coordinated targets to counterattack. The Americans took very few casualties on Utah, in large part because the crucial fighting had already taken place inland.

On the next beach, Omaha, the situation was less happy. The Americans were poorly prepared in the face of a good defence, not least because of poor planning and confusion in the landing, including the launching of assault craft and Duplex Drive (amphibious) Sherman tanks too far offshore, as well as a refusal to use the specialised tanks developed by the British to attack coastal defences, for example Crab flail tanks for use against minefields. The Americans sustained about 3,000 casualties, both in landing and on the beach, from positions on the cliffs that had not been suppressed by air attack or naval bombardment. Air power could not deliver the promised quantities of ordnance on target on time. Eventually the Americans were able to move inland, but, at the end of D-Day, the bridgehead was shallow and the troops in the sector were fortunate that the Germans had no armour to mount an response. This owed much to a failure in German command that reflected rigidities stemming from Hitler's interventions.

Specialised tanks proved effective in the British sector: Gold, Juno and Sword beaches. The Canadian and British forces that landed on these beaches also benefited from careful planning and preparation, from the seizure of crucial covering positions by airborne troops, and from German hesitation about how best to respond. At the cost of 2,500 troops killed, the Allies were back in France: 132,000 troops had been landed, while the airborne force was 23,000 strong.[12]

Over 11,000 sorties flown by Allied air forces that day had a major impact, as did the largely British naval armada that both provided heavy supporting fire and also prevented disruption by German warships. There was no equivalent to the challenge posed by the Japanese fleet to the American landings in the Philippines, but attacks by destroyers, torpedo boats and submarines based in French

Atlantic ports were a threat to the landing fleet and subsequent supply shipping that had to be guarded against.

Fuller pointed out that Overlord also marked a major advance in amphibious operations as there was no need to capture a port in order to land, reinforce and support the invasion force. He wrote in the *Sunday Pictorial* of 1 October 1944:

> had our sea power remained what it had been, solely a weapon to command the sea, the garrison Germany established in France almost certainly would have proved sufficient. It was a change in the conception of naval power which sealed the doom of that great fortress. Hitherto in all overseas invasions the invading forces had been fitted to ships. Now ships were fitted to the invading forces...how to land the invading forces in battle order...this difficulty has been overcome by building various types of special landing boats and pre-fabricated landing stages.

To Fuller, this matched the tank in putting the defence at a discount. The Dieppe operation had shown that attacking a port destroyed it; thus the need to bring two prefabricated harbours composed of floating piers with the invasion.[13] In 1944, the Germans still, mistakenly, anticipated that the Allies would focus on seizing ports. The laying of oil pipelines under the Channel was also an impressive engineering achievement that contributed to the infrastructure of the invasion. The invasion benefited from the experience gained in North African and Italian landings in 1942–3, although the scale of the operation and the severity of the resistance were both more acute in Normandy.

It proved difficult for the Allies to break out of Normandy, and they both faced a hard battle and fell behind the anticipated phase lines for their advance. Hitler was initially confident that the invasion could be repelled, although, due to the success of Allied deception, he remained anxious about a subsequent additional landing near Calais. The Germans had sixty-two divisions in the West. Despite air attacks, especially on bridges, the Germans were able to reinforce their units in Normandy, although the delays forced on them both ensured that the Allies gained time to deepen their bridgehead and obliged the Germans to respond in an ad-hoc fashion to Allied advances, using their tanks as a defence force, rather than driving in the bridgehead. When the German armour was eventually used in bulk, on 29–30 June, it was stopped by Allied air attack.

In trying to break out, the Allied tanks failed to achieve what the Americans and British (and Germans) had expected from tanks. This was more than a matter of difficult terrain: the numerous hedges and sunken lanes of the *bocage* that provided excellent cover for opposing tanks and for anti-tank guns. There were also serious operational limitations for tank warfare, not least vulnerability to anti-tank guns, which had become more powerful since 1940, and the problems of communications with infantry. The German tanks proved better. The M4 Sherman tank used by the Allies was too lightly armoured, and was undergunned compared to the Panther and Tiger, although it was better than the Mark IV, which remained the most numerous type of German tank.

The Germans also benefited from their fighting quality and experience, although they faced many difficulties, not least poor command decisions. The British took heavy casualties in successive attempts to advance near Caen, which they had failed to take on the first day of the invasion. The failure of Operation Goodwood (18–20 July) led to the loss of 500 tanks. These problems led to questions about the effectiveness of the British armour, as well as about British fighting quality and Montgomery's generalship. Many of the units involved had little combat experience and displayed a formality and rigidity in tactics that left them vulnerable. Lieutenant-General Richard O'Connor, the Commander of the British Eighth Corps, which included part of the British armour, noted that British armoured divisions had varied in their fighting quality, adding: 'The enemy, particularly the SS divisions, have fought fantastically.'[14] However, these attacks did help divert German troops from the American front further west, which was to be the crucial breakthrough zone. Montgomery claimed that this had been his plan throughout, although it has been suggested that he had initially planned for a breakthrough on both flanks of the Allied front: the American flank and that of the British Second Army.

The Germans were unable to challenge Allied command of the air over the combat zone and over the nearby communication routes. The effectiveness of Allied ground-support air power owed much to the longer-term process of gaining a degree of air superiority over the *Luftwaffe*. This was also true in Italy. There had also been improvement in air–land co-operation as a result of developments in doctrine and organisation.[15]

In the Normandy campaign, Allied planes were used in ground-support both against specific targets and for 'carpet-bombing', as in advance of American troops in Operation Cobra,[16] although they could not prevent heavy casualties in ground fighting. In 'Some Notes on the Use of Air Power in Support of Land Operations and Direct Air Support', Montgomery argued in December 1944 that

> Present operations in western Europe in all stages have been combined Army/Air operations...the overall contribution of the Air Forces to the successes gained has been immense.... The greatest asset of air power is its flexibility....A retreating enemy offers the most favourable targets to air attack....The moral effect of air action is very great and is out of proportion to the material damage inflicted.... It is necessary to win the air battle before embarking on the land battle.... Experience in battle shows that the degree and effectiveness of the air support which a military formation receives is related in a striking manner to:
> a) The interest it takes in air matters.
> b) The knowledge and proficiency it possesses in air support procedure and the part the Army has to play...
> Technical developments in the air weapon continue apace and their possibilities are bounded only by the imagination. It follows that land operations are likely to be influenced more and more by air action.[17]

Greatly helped by ground-support aircraft and by the extent to which for most of the campaign most of the German armour was committed to oppose the British, the Allies finally succeeded in breaking out from Normandy at the close of July. In Operation Cobra, launched with a heavy bombardment on 25 July, the Americans broke through German positions on the Cotentin peninsula, capturing Avranches on 30 July. A breach had been made, but, better still, by turning the German flank there was now the opportunity to roll up their entire position and turn operational success to strategic advantage. The Germans were unable to establish a new line, and Hitler's 'stand and hold' policy was meaningless.[18]

Advancing through the breach, American units moved into Brittany, while others turned south towards the Loire and yet others east towards the Seine. Rennes fell on 3 August and Le Mans on 8 August. A German panzer counterattack through Mortain, launched, on 7 August, in pursuit of Hitler's hope of wrecking the Second Front and, more particularly, pinching the neck of the breakthrough, was thwarted by strong American resistance and by Allied ground-attack aircraft: these were more important than American tanks.

Combined with the advance of all Allied forces from their positions, this provided an opportunity to encircle the Germans in Normandy. They were driven into a pocket between Falaise and Argentan, but a gap existed to the east between Trun and Chambois, and the Germans began to retreat through it late on 16 August. Many escaped, although up to about 60,000 were killed or captured and losses of equipment were heavy. The Allied failure to close the gap quickly, for which General Omar Bradley, the head of the Twelfth US Army Group, was principally responsible,[19] was a major blunder which possibly cost victory in the West in 1944.

Hitler had hoped to create a line on the Seine, but rapid Allied advances thwarted this. Chartres and Dreux fell to the Americans on 16 August, Orléans the following day, and on 20 August they established a bridgehead across the Seine. Other Allied units liberated Paris on 25 August: the Free French played a major role, an important salute to French pride. The Germans put up only light resistance in the city which, combined with the Allied decision not to bomb it, helped ensure that Paris was one of the best preserved of the many cities of Europe after the war. The breakout from Normandy was followed by a deep exploitation that matched earlier operations in North Africa, as well as the Soviet advance in 1944, but contrasted with Allied operations in Italy. Rather than stopping on the Seine as planned, Eisenhower decided to advance on the German border.

In Operation Dragoon, the Allies also landed successfully in the south of France on 15 August. This was very much an American operation and had been pushed hard by Roosevelt, the American

Joint Chiefs of Staff and Eisenhower, all of whom were opposed to Britain's Mediterranean strategy, with its commitment to Italy and its interest in an attack from there into Austria. Most of the initial landing units were American, although much of the follow-up-force was French. Due primarily to the weakness of the defending force, but also to the strength of Allied naval and air support, the landing did not lead to any major battle comparable to that in Normandy: resistance both on the beaches and inland, where an Anglo-American parachute force landed, was light. Casualties were few.

Instead, the operation speeded the German withdrawal from most of France. Advancing rapidly, the Allies took Avignon on 25 August, Toulon on 26 August, Lyons on 3 September and Dijon eight days later, although the Germans were able to withdraw their forces from southern and south-western France.

The failure to cut them off helped ensure a greater density of German troops when the Allies advanced towards the German frontier, although it was difficult for amphibious forces to transform themselves rapidly for fast-moving advances. In particular, it took time to bring ashore large numbers of vehicles and to prepare for large-scale tank conflict. German operations were stained by the slaughter on 10 June of 642 people, most of the population of the village of Oradour, a response, possibly, to the threat of partisan activity that reflected the cruelty and total contempt for civilians seen more generally whenever the Germans felt their authority threatened. This underlines the extent to which German brutality was not only directed against Jews and Slavs.

The withdrawal of the Germans from France was followed by a popular fury directed against collaborators, many of whom were killed. There was also a harsh gender dimension, with women who had had sex with Germans being publicly stigmatised, for example with their hair cut off. This fury was in part politically directed, but it also reflected the popular enmities that had built up under occupation, enmities that, in France and elsewhere, were also to play a role in the texture of post-war politics, particularly at the level of individual communities.

The Allied advances from Normandy and southern France led to a speedy clearance of most of France and Belgium, although without inflicting casualties on the Germans comparable to those suffered at the hands of the Soviets, in part due to the failure of encirclement plans. The Allies advanced quickly across the battlefields of World War One. Verdun fell on 31 August and Mons on 2 September. The rapid seizure of ports, such as Cherbourg on 27 June and, more belatedly, Le Havre on 12 September, helped ease logistical problems. The capture of Marseilles with its port undamaged on 28 August provided an important logistical support to Allied operations in eastern France. Isolated German positions held out, including not only the ports of Lorient and St Nazaire but also the Channel Isles. However, the Allies focused on the broad front of advance, rather than on gaining these positions.

Fuller felt that the war had been transformed militarily, such that the Germans were now dependent on their opponents' resolve. He informed the readers of *Newsweek* on 10 July:

> Though the German High Command is faced with forces beyond its means to check, it doesn't necessarily follow that it is checkmated because utilization of these forces depends upon the circumstances in which they are placed...the Russians, being more war-worn than their Allies, are more likely to welcome speedy termination of the war...the Americans and the British also seek its speedy termination so that they may still be fresh when they in turn fall on Japan...if the war can be prolonged throughout next winter, by spring or summer of next year political circumstances may have so changed that the Allied powers will be willing to bring the war in the west to an end on terms more favourable to Germany than those of unconditional surrender.... Time is the crucial factor not only strategically but also tactically; tactically for the Russians in order rapidly to beat their enemy; strategically for the Germans in order slowly to sell ground at high cost.

This view seriously underrated the resolve of the Allies to defeat Germany, but helps remind us of the uncertainties of contemporaries and of the need to relate military developments to political objectives throughout the war.

The speedy liberation of France and Belgium created serious re-supply problems as Allied forces advanced greater distances from the ports. As Fuller pointed out in the *Sunday Pictorial* of 10 September, 'at the moment, supply and not fighting power is the key factor of our advance'. Thanks, in part, to Allied resources and the proximity of supply sources in Britain, as well as the dense network of transport routes in France and Belgium, the logistical situation was less serious than that for the Red Army, and the effects were less dire, but it seriously affected operations. In particular, the French rail system had been effectively dislocated by Allied bombing, while the delay in clearing the approaches to the port of Antwerp in the Scheldt estuary prevented use of its facilities, which had been captured on 4 September.

More seriously, tough resistance was encountered, unexpectedly so, as the German border was approached. Despite the strains of retreat, small-unit cohesion was retained by the Germans, while their supply lines shortened as they retreated. The fighting quality the Germans showed in successfully resisting the Allied attack on Arnhem in September, which was designed to create a bridgehead across the lower Rhine, and in the Scheldt estuary in October–November, as well as in opposing the American advance near Aachen and in Lorraine that autumn, indicated the extent to which defeat in Normandy had not destroyed the German war effort in the West, and suggested that there would be no sudden collapse once Germany was invaded. Hopes that the war would end in 1944 proved premature. The strength of the resistance accentuated the debate over Allied strategy and operational choices.

It is too easy, if space is at a premium, to jump from the Normandy breakout to the Battle of the Bulge at the close of the year, with British writers generally also stressing the Arnhem operation. That is to underrate the importance of the German success in restricting the Allied advance, as well as of the Allied ability to continue to make gains, albeit in a far more incremental manner than during the heady days of rapid advances. There was a parallel with the Soviet offensive into Poland in 1944; but, as in that case, it is necessary to place due weight on the consequences of logistical factors, exhaustion and the need to regroup on the part of the Allies, as well as German resistance. The latter benefited from the strength of defensive positions when the Allies surrendered mobility in order to clear particular areas, such as the Huertgen Forest near Aachen. These led to attritional struggles that caused heavy casualties.[20]

Although the German achievement in recovering from defeat in Normandy and in stopping the Allied advance was impressive, it would be mistaken, as some earlier commentators did, to underrate Allied fighting quality. A comparison of American and German performance indicates that the preference of the former for fire-power support from air and artillery did not preclude a willingness to close with the Germans and a high level of effectiveness in the resulting combat.[21] British military effectiveness had also improved since the early years of the war. The army had been transformed into a stronger fighting force with better weapons, tactics and command, including an effective use of artillery and anti-tank guns.[22] Canadian units also made an important contribution to Allied effectiveness.[23]

In December 1944, the Germans mounted a counter-offensive in the Ardennes, which led to the Battle of the Bulge. This offensive was aimed at repeating the success of 1940 by gaining the initiative, pushing apart the Americans and the British and, finally, capturing Antwerp and its supplies: the port had been opened on 28 November. In part because of an Allied failure to appreciate ULTRA information about German military movements, the Germans gained complete surprise when they attacked on 16 December. They benefited from the exhausted and unprepared nature of the opposing American troops, some of whom had been campaigning for months. The uncharitable Montgomery blamed German success on inade-quate Allied generalship over the previous three months. The strength and novelty of the massed German armour was also a factor: this was the first occasion on which American troops were 'subject to a major enemy armoured offensive'.[24]

Initial German successes could not, however, be sustained, in part because of the swiftness with which the Americans deployed rein-forcements and compensated for earlier weaknesses in the area. Benefiting from their post-invasion build-up, the Americans committed more troops than they had in Normandy. Ground-support air attacks helped the Allies regain the initiative, although they had to wait for the weather to improve; Hitler had deliberately launched the attack when bad weather promised protection. These air attacks proved particularly important against German tanks. The Germans also suffered from supply problems, particularly of fuel, as well as from the narrowness of the front, the terrain and the eventual strength of the American resistance, particularly at Bastogne, where an encircled force fought well, refused to surrender, and thus thwarted the pace of the German advance.[25] Other American units halted the foremost German formations, as did British forces.[26]

It is valuable to contrast the 1940 and 1944 offensives in order to throw light on shifts in German military capability. The decision to attack when the weather was bad was an obvious contrast: in 1940, the Germans had wanted good weather in order to ensure air support, as well as to use parachutists and glider-borne troops in Belgium and the Netherlands. The German attack on a narrow front could not be supported by advances elsewhere, as had been the case in 1940; in 1944, the Germans lacked the necessary forces, in large part due to their commitments on the Eastern Front and in Italy. Although, as in 1940, the Germans attacked on a weak portion of the front in 1944, the Americans (unlike the French) responded swiftly and were able to deploy troops in support more swiftly than the Germans could advance. In part, this reflected the tenacity of the defence, but the forces defending the Meuse crossings in 1940 had also fought hard. The differing response once the breach occurred was more significant, and throws light on the deficiencies of Allied generalship in 1940; although the German advance that year had been speeded by the good weather. In tactical, operational and strategic terms, the Allied response in 1944 was better than in 1940, while there was no equivalent to the political collapse of France in 1940.

## Debates over strategy

The failure of their own plan speeded up the German defeat. Heavy losses of tanks and aircraft could not be replaced and, as with their attack on the Western Front in 1918, the Germans had lost yet more of the veterans they could not afford to lose. Nevertheless, the important indication of Germany's continued ability to launch attacks provided by the Battle of the Bulge (there were smaller-scale parallels in Hungary in October 1944 and February 1945) needs to be included in the assessment of the long-running controversy as to whether the Allies followed the best strategy in the West in 1944. This is often reduced to a debate over the virtues of the broad-front approach advocated by Eisenhower and the narrow-front attempt for a rapid advance beyond the Rhine advocated by Montgomery. This clash was linked to Montgomery's unsuccessful pressure for the appointment, under Eisenhower, of a deputy entrusted with command over ground forces.[27] The idea of a narrow-front advance presupposed a war of manoeuvre in which the initiative and tempo were dictated by the Allies. The German Bulge offensive indicated the riskiness of this approach. An advance across the Rhine in 1944 would have been vulnerable to counterattack, as the Germans had been building up a significant armoured force in northern Germany from September. An Allied advance would also have been dependent on a precarious supply route.

At the same time, the preference for a broad front helped the Germans withdraw without heavy casualties after Falaise, while Eisenhower's caution greatly lessened the chance of cutting off German forces. This was a serious Allied failure, as it ensured that more troops, especially experienced units, were available to the German defence as the retreat ceased. Eisenhower has also been crit-icised for the amount of troops sent west into Brittany, as this lessened the force initially available for the advance towards Germany. His broad-front approach would have been more successful in maintaining the pace of the Allied advance had the American army had more combat divisions.

There has also been extensive criticism, particularly, but not only, by some American commentators and scholars, such as Stephen Ambrose, of Montgomery's generalship and of British fighting quality.[28] The British preference for the indirect approach and reluc-tance to risk heavy casualties[29] is not always appreciated; nor, indeed, are the heavy losses that were suffered, particularly in clearing the Scheldt approaches, especially in the capture of Walcheren, given sufficient attention. The serious issue of assessing capability and generalship has not greatly been helped by the tone of some of the discussion, although it originates in criticisms and disputes between some of the generals in 1944.

To British observers, it appears that some American commenta-tors are overly keen to ascribe faults to others and the responsibility for beating the Germans largely to themselves. This can be seen throughout the discussion of the Normandy operation, such that the presentation of D-Day is largely in American terms. This is particularly true of popular works, as well as in the film *Saving Private Ryan* (1998). This is understandable in terms of the audience, but also contributes to the serious lack of knowledge about the wider struggle, seen for example among the large number of Americans who think that the war began in 1941, when the USA went to war.

To mention this in a discussion of the merits of strategic options in 1944 may seem far-fetched, but is a reminder of the wider resonance of differences of opinion. In this context, it is worth underlining that the generals who can be adopted as national standard-bearers, and who were built up to that end by wartime propaganda, for example Patton, Montgomery and, in the Pacific, MacArthur, were regarded with considerable disfavour by many of their compatriots. Major-General William Penney, Director of Intelligence, HQ, Supreme Allied Commander, SE Asia 1944–5, who visited Manila in April 1945, reported:

> Theatre commanders are extremely independent and resentful of interference. This as a matter of fact extends through all U.S. formations…feuding between U.S. Army and Navy, including Marines, is openly expressed. In the General's Mess at Manila I was astounded to listen to the scornful references to operations on Okinawa and other land battles fought under Naval or Marine command.[30]

Given the resilience of the German military, hopes of victory in 1944 were exaggerated. From that perspective, Eisenhower's broad-front approach[31] and Montgomery's methodical warmaking were both sensible options.

Whether or not Hitler had chosen to launch the Bulge offensive, the impact on German military manpower of continuous fighting in France, Italy and on the Eastern Front in the second half of 1944 had been heavy. The number of experienced troops had been greatly depleted, and there was no time to train fresh levies. This led to a serious compromising of fighting ability that matched the strains on command structures posed by the burdens of a multi-front war and the erratic leadership of Hitler. German resources had to be spread out across long front lines. On 7 December, Eisenhower 'emphasised the heavy rate of attrition they were forcing on the enemy, a rate very much greater than our own. He pointed out that the enemy could not afford losses on such a scale'.[32] Indeed, although thirty divisions were launched in the Ardennes counter-offensive only nine days later, the German army was weaker than it had been in the summer.

## War with Germany at sea

The same was true at sea and in the air. The submarine war continued to go the Allies' way, although merchantmen were still sunk. The build-up and supply in, and from, Britain of the massive American and Canadian forces that landed in Normandy and subsequently were a reflection of the failure of the German submarines to achieve strategic results. After the Allied breakout from Normandy, the Germans evacuated their submarine bases in west France and concentrated their force in Norway. From there, the U-boats focused on British waters, but they were no longer able to sink large numbers of merchantmen, and, instead, suffered serious losses, both as a result of air attacks, not least on their bases, and at sea, although there sinkings were due more to convoy escorts and their use of forward-firing weaponry. However, the submarine threat remained potent, as U-boat construction maintained overall numbers. This obliged the Allies to continue to devote considerable naval resources to escort duty and anti-submarine warfare. Given Allied, particularly American, shipbuilding capability and the resulting size of the Allied navies, this did not, however, limit or prevent other uses of Allied naval power, particularly the movement of British warships to the Indian Ocean and the Pacific.

## The air attack on Germany

Air attacks on the economic capability and civilian morale of opponents were stepped up in 1944. The Germans, who had launched the first such attacks of World War Two, bombing undefended Warsaw in 1939, offered a further refinement in 1944 with the beginning of rocket attacks. Ground-to-ground V-1s, launched at Britain from 13 June, were followed, from 8 September 1944, by V-2s, which travelled at up to 3,000 mph, could be fired from a considerable distance, and could not be destroyed by anti-aircraft fire as the V-1s could be. Their explosive payload was small and they could not be aimed accurately, but this was scant consolation to those killed and maimed. Large numbers of rockets were aimed at London, although other targets, particularly Antwerp once it had been captured by the Allies, were also hit. The damage inflicted by rockets led the British to devote particular effort to air raids on production facilities, as well as to capturing the launching pads in the advance from Normandy.

The use of missiles reflected the inability of the Germans to sustain air attacks, as well as Hitler's fascination with new technology and the idea that it could bring a paradigm leap forward in military capability. Missiles, in fact, lacked the multipurpose capacity of aircraft.[33] The manufacture of missiles was also symptomatic of the nature of the German war economy, with the use of harshly treated foreign slave labour leading to high death rates among the malnourished and brutalised workers. The V-2s were constructed in the underground Nordhausen factory in the Harz Mountains. The workers were transferred from Mittelbau KL, a concentration camp. An average of 100 died daily during the building of the factory.

The Final Solution continued to be brutally pursued by the Nazi regime. By April 1944, there were twenty concentration camps. At Birkenau, which was part of the Auschwitz complex, at least 6,000 people were being killed daily. However, the advance of Soviet forces led, from the autumn, to the movement of slave labourers from Poland to Germany.

The Allied air attack on Germany was stepped up in 1944. The introduction of long-range fighters, especially the American P-38s (twin-engine Lightnings), P-47s (Thunderbolts, which used drop fuel tanks) and P-51 (Mustangs, which also used drop fuel tanks), provided necessary escorts for the bombers, and also enabled Allied fighters to seek out German fighters and thus to win the air war above Germany. This contrasted with the *Luftwaffe*'s failed offensive on Britain in 1940–1: the Germans had lost the air war over Britain and had been unable to accompany serious devastation with the destruction or degradation of the British air force.

The Mustang's superiority to German interceptors was demonstrated in late February and March 1944, when major American raids in clear weather on German sites producing aircraft and oil led to large-scale battles with German interceptors. Many American bombers were shot down, but the *Luftwaffe* also lost large numbers of planes and pilots as a result of the American policy of attrition, while there had also been heavy *Luftwaffe* losses over combat zones. Pilots were very difficult to replace, in large part because German training programmes had not been increased in 1940–2, as was necessary given the scale of the war. This helped to ensure that, irrespective of aircraft construction figures, the Germans would be far weaker in the air. German aircraft construction was itself hit hard. In 'Big Week', an Anglo-American bombing offensive in late February, in which about 6,100 bombers were escorted by long-range fighters, German aircraft production was put back by two months.

Towards the end, the Germans could not afford the fuel for training, while a lack of training time was also a consequence of the shortage of pilots. The net effect was a lack of trained pilots comparable in quality to those of the Allies. By the time of the Normandy landings, the Germans had lost the air war, and their units treated aircraft as probably hostile.[34] The contrast between the *Luftwaffe*'s ability to threaten the British retreat from Dunkirk in 1940 and its failure to disrupt the Normandy landings was striking.

In 1944, the Allied emphasis was not on precision attack, which had proved difficult to execute, but on area bombing, with its attendant goals of disrupting the war economy and destroying urban life. This was clearly the policy of the RAF, and, although the US Army Air Forces (USAAF) never officially switched to area bombing over Europe, their winter months' campaigns often became area-bombing operations in practice. By increasing the target area, area bombing also made the task of the defence more difficult.

The effectiveness, as well as the morality, of bombing has been the subject of considerable debate, and was so at the time. British Bomber Command ignored intelligence reports that stressed the limited value of the area bombing of German cities. This obstinacy reduced the value of air attack and possibly led to a misuse of resources better devoted to ground or naval support. In January 1944, a group of scholars, asked by the USAAF to determine whether strategic bombing could force Germany out of the war by that spring, reported:

Although the blockade and bombing have deranged Germany's economic structure, [the] German military economy has not been crippled at any vital point.... Although bombing has made a vital contribution to the ultimate defeat of Germany and although complete defeat cannot be achieved without an acceleration and intensification of bombing, it is improbable that bombing alone can bring about a German collapse by spring of 1944.[35]

These themes were also taken up for the public. Fuller, who was in favour of a negotiated peace, argued in *Newsweek* on 2 October 1944 that the bombing of Germany had not ended the war and had not cracked the morale and will of the German forces, and wrote of the 'ineffectiveness of the Douhet theory'. A fortnight later, he added that bombing had failed to paralyse the German high command.

Moral issues were raised by George Bell, Bishop of Chichester and others, and have been pressed much more vigorously since.[36] The most frequently cited instance is that of 'Dresden', a reference to the heavy casualties caused by the Anglo-American bombing of Dresden on 13–14 February 1945, towards the close of the war, which is sometimes mentioned as an Allied atrocity. However, the general consensus at the time was that the bombing campaign was a deserved return for earlier German air attacks (as well as current missile attacks), and also was likely to disrupt the German war effort and hit morale. As far as the latter was concerned, the hopes of inter-war air power enthusiasts were not fully realised. During the war, most military leaders did not argue that bombing alone could win. Instead, it was generally accepted that bombing should be part of an integrated strategy. Nevertheless, it was claimed that area bombing would cause heavy casualties, which would terrorise the civilian population and hopefully put pressure on their governments.

The extent to which civilian morale was broken is controversial, but it is possible that the impact of bombing on civilians has been underestimated by the habitual conclusion that the bombing did not end the war. There was more to German resilience than Hitler's determination, and the inability to stop bombing encouraged a sense that defeat was likely, indeed was already occurring. A recent study of Nuremberg has suggested that bombing was responsible for a serious decline in civilian morale from 1943, a process of social dissolution and a matching crisis of confidence in the Nazi Party.[37] Whether that justified heavy civilian casualties and also a high level of losses among Allied aircrews is a question that has modern resonance given current sensitivity about civilian casualties, but, by 1944, total war was being pushed as precisely that.

As a result, the concerns of contemporary military planners can best be addressed in instrumental terms: with reference to the effectiveness of air attack and to possible alternative use of the resources devoted to it. The latter issue has attracted attention, as indeed has the question whether the German rocket programme represented an unwise allocation of resources that would have been better devoted to air power. On the Allied side, there were alternative uses of air power, including different possible targets for heavy bombers. As, however, there were serious institutional restrictions to any reallocation of resources and economic difficulties confronting the retooling of manufacturing, the feedback process of judging policy could not be expected to work even had information flows been accurate and speedy – as is rarely the case in war.

Bombing was also advocated for the damage it could do to particular targets, an approach that accords with modern doctrine. Despite the limited precision of bombing by high-flying aeroplanes dropping freefall bombs, strategic bombing was crucial to the disruption of German communications and logistics, largely because it was eventually on such a massive scale, and because they could not be attacked by any other means. Attacks on communications seriously affected the rest of the German economy, limiting the transfer of resources and the process of integration. The reliance of European industry on rail was far greater than today, and that increased its vulnerability to attack, because rail systems lack the flexibility of their road counterparts, being less dense and therefore less able to switch routes. Bridges and marshalling yards proved particular targets for attack. For similar reasons, the communication system was prone to partisan attack in occupied areas.

In addition, the oil industry and aircraft production were savagely hit by Allied air attack. Such bombing directly benefited the Allied war effort. It acted as a brake on Germany's expanding production of weaponry, which had important consequences for operational strength. For example, thanks to bombing, the construction of a new, faster class of submarine – type XXI – was delayed, so that it did not become operational until April 1945, too late to challenge Allied command of the sea; although even had it become operational earlier, it would not have been in sufficient numbers to determine the struggle.[38]

Furthermore, the Germans diverted massive resources to anti-aircraft defence forces, for example the 88 mm anti-aircraft gun, which was also very effective against Allied tanks, as well as much of the *Luftwaffe* itself. These guns and planes might otherwise have made a major contribution on the Eastern and, later, the Western Front.

This is a counterfactual that it is impossible to prove, not least because it assumes a ready response on the part of German decision-makers, but it is not less pertinent for that. Many of the military assets employed by the Germans in air defence were readily transfer-able – they were not fixed defences – and, for that reason, their commitment to air defence and non-availability for transfer, whether permanently or as a form of strategic asset, was important.

The Allied air assault also played a role in the wider strategic equa-tion. For example, once the Allies had invaded southern France, the holding of northern Italy was of dubious value to the Germans as it committed troops to an extensive perimeter, rather than the shorter line that would have been gained from relying on the Alps, a line that would also have taken advantage of Swiss neutrality. However, aside from Hitler's disinclination to countenance retreat, and his particular wish not to abandon Mussolini, there was also a concern that an Allied presence in Lombardy would facilitate the aerial assault on Germany by permitting a major advance of Allied airbases.

The impact of the Second Front on the air war provided a salu-tary lesson. Part of the German air-defence system was lost as the Allies advanced in 1944, and the lack of depth of defence that resulted from the advance compromised the rest. Furthermore, Allied bombers and escort fighters were now based in reconquered areas and able to support the heavy bombers based in eastern England. As a result, the bombing offensive on Germany that was launched from the autumn of 1944, as air support for the Second Front became less necessary, was more damaging than hitherto.

More generally, the Allied air attack intensified economic disruption within Germany and speeded up defeat. It affected not only Germany but also her allies. For example, heavy bombing attacks on Bulgaria began on 19 November 1943. The raids, especially that of 30 March 1944 on the capital, Sofia, indicated clearly the shift in fortunes, and encouraged a decline in enthusiasm for continued support for Germany.[39]

## War with Japan

The great distances of the Pacific made it difficult for the Americans to bomb Japan, but securing bases from which Japan could be regularly bombed increasingly became a priority. Once the island of Saipan had been captured in July 1944, Japan was brought within range of the new, long-range B-29s, the Super Fortresses. Missions from Saipan against Japan began in November 1944.

Until then, the American navy had been more effective in damaging the Japanese economy, as well as the articulation of their empire. The USA became the most successful practitioner of submarine warfare in history. Unlike the Allies in the Atlantic, the Japanese failed to protect their maritime routes. They were less effective at convoy protection and anti-submarine warfare and devoted fewer resources to them, not least through not providing adequate air support for convoys. In 1944, American submarine attacks forced the Japanese to abandon many of their convoy routes. They failed to build sufficient ships to match their losses, their trade was dramatically cut, and the Japanese imperial economy was shattered. By the end of the war, American submarines had sunk 5.32 million tons of Japanese merchant shipping, and there was no area of Japanese overseas and coastal trade that was free from attack. This greatly increased the uncertainty that sapped the predictability that industrial integration depended on. Japanese losses made it difficult to move raw materials in the conquered areas, such as iron ore, oil and rubber back to Japan. It was also difficult to move troops rapidly within the empire. Thus the flexibility seen in the initial conquests had been lost. Expedients, such as postponing the maintenance of shipping and leaving garrisons to fend for themselves, proved deleterious for overall effectiveness.

The American submarine assault (which itself suffered considerable losses) was directed by signals intelligence, and was supplemented by the dropping of mines by naval aircraft, as well as by air attacks on Japanese shipping. In contrast, the Japanese achieved little with submarines, in part because they insisted on hoarding submarines for use against warships. This was an aspect of a questionable Japanese force structure in which battleships were overrated and submarines underrated.

The vast extent of the Pacific created unprecedented problems of warmaking and infrastructure. Substantial fleets had to operate over great distances and needed mobile support and maintenance. The scale of planning was large in space, time and resources. In August 1943, the Combined Staff Planners outlined a schedule culminating in an invasion or blockade of Japan in 1947. The Americans developed self-sufficient carrier task-groups (supported by effective at-sea logistics groups), which did not depend on a string of bases. Their problem-solving, can-do approach to logistics permitted the rapid advance across an unprecedented distance, with a lot of island-hopping that destroyed any chance that the Japanese might retain a defensive perimeter in the Pacific. Furthermore, the use, from 1944, of shipping as floating depots for artillery, ammunition and other *matériel*, increased the speed of army re-supply as it was no longer necessary to use Australia as a staging area. The seizure of islands provided additional forward-supply bases.

The Japanese continued building warships, but their numbers were insufficient and their navy lacked the capacity to resist the effective American assault. It also suffered from poor doctrine and an inadequate understanding of respective strategic options. Indeed, the deficiencies in Japanese planning are such that it is appropriate to focus on systemic failings. These included an inability to understand American policy and to respond to earlier deficiencies in Japanese strategy and operational planning.

There was a similar failure to develop more effective military methods on land. These failures focus attention on the cultural dimension of warmaking and on the extent to which they were reflected in institutional structures and practices. Thus, Japanese military culture becomes more than the practice of self-sacrifice that has attracted particular attention.

In operational terms, the Japanese also suffered from a serious shortage of trained pilots; it proved near impossible to train pilots fast enough to replace losses, a deficiency that became more apparent in contrast with the American situation. In addition, an organisational defect in the Japanese naval air arm made an air group integral to its ship with no reserve air groups to replace the strike element of carrier taskforces when they were destroyed.

In contrast, the ability to deploy carriers both in the south-west and the central Pacific reflected the extent to which superior American resources, and their effective use, permitted the simultaneous pursuit of more than one offensive strategy, and with a likelihood both of success and of an ability to overcome the defence and resist counter-offensives without having to call on reserves from other 'fronts'. Air power could be applied from the sea as never before. Multiple tasking included fighter combat to gain control of the skies, dive-bombing and torpedo attack to destroy ships, and ground attack to help amphibious operations, as well as the use of aircraft for transport and command-and-control functions. The development of carrier tactics reflected successful air–naval co-operation.

The Japanese planned a series of major clashes in 1944. An offensive from Burma was designed to forestall a British invasion, the prime objective, by overrunning the Imphal base area and destroying IV Corps, and, also, hopefully, to knock India out of the war by causing a rising. For this reason, Indian Nationalist forces played a major role in the advance. This operation was also designed to knock China out of the war by cutting its supply lines. This reflected Japanese awareness of Chinese dependence on such links, particularly for military supplies for their forces, and for the aircraft of their American allies.

## Conflict in China

To that end, the Japanese also launched Operation Ichi-Go with about 300,000 troops in South China in April. This was very successful in its more limited goal of overrunning airfields used by American planes in their bombing of Japan, and the Americans had to demolish the airbases and associated material that they had worked hard to establish. Changsa fell on 10 June to Japanese troops moving from Hankow, and claims by Claire Chennault, the American Commander of the China Air Task Force, that his planes would be able to stop Japanese advances were proved misleading. Kuomintang (Chinese Nationalist) ground resistance was initially good, but it was handicapped by a shortage of equipment, ammunition and food, and by the pace of Japanese success. Most of the large quantities of supplies the American Tenth Air Force had been flying into China were for the air assault on the Japanese, not munitions for the Chinese army, although, from the summer of 1943, the Americans, also, had been planning for a Chinese advance on Canton–Hong Kong, to link up with an American advance, via Formosa, to the Chinese coast, followed by joint operations to clear northern China and establish bases from which Japan could be attacked. The Americans had been confident that an air assault on Japan could make a major difference to the war. The first B-29 bombers that became operational were sent to China.[40]

In July 1944, however, the Japanese advanced south, but opposition strengthened as Hengyang was neared, in part because of the provision of supplies and the vigour of the air defence. Nevertheless, the city fell on 8 August, and this was followed by a marked decline in the fighting effectiveness of the now demoralised Chinese. Reluctant to fight, the Chinese retreated. Kweilin and Liuchow fell to the Japanese on 11 November, and Nanning soon after. The Japanese troops operating south from Hankow had met advancing forces from Indo-China, creating an overland route between central China and Indo-China, and thus a communications axis from Manchuria to Singapore that did not depend on sea links.

In November, the Japanese pressed on towards Kweiyang, Kunning and Chungking, although their success in advancing west into the interior of China was limited. Nevertheless, there was growing concern in the USA that Nationalist China, already weakened by corruption and inflation, would leave the war. That would not have led to the end of operations by the Chinese Communists, but they would have been less effective had the Japanese not also had Kuomintang forces to fight. The difficulty of holding down China was considerable, but the defeat of the Kuomintang would have permitted reliance on second-rank forces.

The Japanese operation severely damaged the Kuomintang army, not least because important areas that had produced both grain and recruitment had been overrun. The operation was one of the most far-reaching advances of that year, but was not really comparable to the advances in Europe because the resistance was far weaker. This reflected the character of the war in China, with Japanese advances generally not leading to battles, but rather to guerrilla resistance. Thus, in the summer of 1942, the Japanese had launched an advance into the provinces of Chekiang and Kiangsi, inflicting considerable damage and destroying airbases before retiring. As with the 1944 offensive, the 1942 attack was linked to American use of Chinese airbases: in 1942, the fact that the B-25s, launched from American carriers, that had bombed Japan on 19 April had flown on to China.

These campaigns continued to ensure that a disproportionate share of Japanese military resources were devoted to China. In addition, much of the army leadership remained more concerned about the apparent Soviet threat to Manchuria than about actual Allied advances in the Pacific, an area much of the army saw as a naval concern. The situation in China temporarily stabilised in December 1944 when a counterattack benefiting from American supplies east of Kweiyang stopped the Japanese, who were also affected by growing logistical problems.[41]

## War in the Pacific

In the Pacific, the Japanese aimed to destroy the spearhead of the advancing American fleet by concentrating their air power against it, the origins of what the Americans were to call (and victors' terms tend to stick) the Great Marianas Turkey Shoot of June 1944. The Japanese plan was for the American fleet to be lured into range of Japanese island airbases, while the naval air force was to be concentrated in order further to minimise the American lead in carriers. There was the hope that the decisive success of the Japanese fleet over the Russians at Tsushima in 1905 could be repeated. This reflected a more general conviction (see Hitler's attitudes to Kursk, 1943, and the Battle of the Bulge, 1944, and the Japanese's to Midway, 1942) that a decisive victory could be obtained on one front, which could overcome the role and impact of Allied resources. More specifically, this attitude arose from the sway of historical examples that supposedly represented national greatness and, even more, from the role of factors of will in Axis thinking. There was a conviction that victory would sap the inherently weaker will of opponents, and thus give the Axis the success to which they were entitled. Aside from the lack of political understanding underlying this policy, it was anachronistic militarily. Defeat in 1944 on one front would have delayed the Americans, but nothing more; and, by concentrating a target for the Americans, Japanese strategy made it more likely that the American attack would succeed in causing heavy casualties. The Americans had a better fleet, a far greater ability to replace losses, and far more capable leadership than the Japanese.

The campaigning in 1944 saw the collapse of the Japanese empire in the Pacific. Without air superiority, Japanese naval units were highly vulnerable. The Americans could decide where to make attacks, and could neutralise bases, such as Rabaul and its 100,000-strong garrison, and Truk in the Caroline Islands, that they chose to 'leapfrog'. This was part of the more general degradation of Japanese logistics and their lack of strategic capability. 'Leapfrogging' maintained the pace of the advance, lessened the extent of hard, slogging conflict and reflected the degree to which the Americans had the initiative.

From January 1944, the Americans successfully attacked the Marshall Islands. By the end of February, they had been brought under control, although some isolated positions were still held by the Japanese. The American success reflected the lessons learned at Tarawa. The Marshalls were a valuable asset to American naval and air power. The bases acquired made it easier to strike at the Mariana Islands.

That June, the American Task Force 58, with fifteen carriers and over 900 planes, covered an amphibious attack on the Marianas – Saipan, Tinian and Guam – leading, in the Battle of the Philippine Sea, to a struggle with the nine carriers and 400 planes of the Japanese First Mobile Fleet, the major battle the Japanese had sought. However, located by US radar, Japanese air attacks launched on 19 June were shot down by American fighters and by anti-aircraft fire from supporting warships, with no damage to the American carriers, while the Japanese also lost two carriers to American submarines; these submarines were now more effective than those of the Japanese in fleet support. The Americans were even more successful the following day, sinking or severely damaging three Japanese carriers with a long-range air attack in the failing light. The conduct of this mission reflected the American ability to accept, work with and minimise risk, in this case that planes would be lost on the return journey to, and landing on, their carriers. The Japanese carriers were protected by a screen of Zero fighters, but, as a clear sign of growing Japanese weakness in the air, this was too weak to resist the fighter aircraft that supported the American bombers. Although the Japanese still had a sizeable carrier fleet, once again the loss of pilots in the battle was a crippling blow. The Americans had benefited from prior knowledge of Japanese plans and from the failure of Japanese land-based aircraft in the Marianas to provide the navy with promised support.[42]

This victory enabled the Americans to overrun the Marianas, a decisive advance into the western Pacific. The resolution of the Japanese resistance was shown on Saipan, where nearly the entire garrison, 27,000 men, died resisting attack and which it took three weeks (15 June–9 July) to capture. The Japanese mounted a strong defence and also launched ferocious frontal counterattacks. Heavy casualties in the latter, however, greatly hit Japanese reserves on Saipan and made the American task less difficult than it would otherwise have been.

Both sides had seen Saipan, the best of the islands as a bomber base against Japan, as vital. Its fall led to the resignation of the Japanese cabinet on 18 July. Due to the role of the emperor, Hirohito, and the absence of a party equivalent to the Nazis, no Japanese politician enjoyed dominance equivalent to that of Hitler. Major defeat therefore had a serious political effect. Thus, the need to retain political control played a role in strategy.

On Tinian, where the Americans landed on 24 July, the Japanese also fought to the end, but the American attack was more effective and the island fell in a week, although, as elsewhere, for example on Guam, which was conquered on 21 July–10 August, those Japanese who were not killed fought on until the end of the war and, in some cases, beyond it. On all these islands, the terrain, particularly coastal cliffs, mountains and dense jungle, made the advance difficult. The Japanese lacked room to manoeuvre and thus to retreat. On Pacific islands, they could not fall back as they could, if obliged, in Burma or China, in 1945, and on the islands the density of troops and defensive fortifications was such as to make offensive progress very difficult. Further south, mobility, firepower and fighting quality brought the Americans and Australians further success in New Guinea. They relied heavily there on land-based air support.[43]

The conquest of the Marianas provided not only sites for airfields but also an important forward logistical base for the navy and for amphibious operations. The Americans used their naval and air superiority, already strong and rapidly growing, to mount a reconquest of the Philippines, their largest offensive in the Pacific during the war. It began in October, when Leyte was invaded, and continued in January 1945, when a large force was landed on the largest island, Luzon.[44]

In some respects, the Philippines were a cul-de-sac for a grand strategy focused on Japan. Saipan and Iwo Jima were a more important axis for air attack, although control of the central Philippines would increase the number of American bases in the western Pacific. The seizure of Taiwan would have been more important so far as affecting the war in China and, more crucially, helping to keep the pressurised and defeated Kuomintang in the war were concerned. However, the reasons for recapturing the Philippines were given added force by MacArthur's determination to reverse his flight from them in 1942. He insisted that the Americans had obligations to their Filipino supporters. Differences over strategy accentuated divisions between American policymakers. As critics of the Philippine campaign had feared, the invasion of the islands indeed led to a delay in the operations planned against Iwo Jima and Okinawa.

The invasion of the Philippines helped ensure a naval battle that secured American maritime superiority in the western Pacific, although, having obtained that, there was no real need to press on with additional landings in the already-isolated Philippines. In the battle of Leyte Gulf of 23–6 October 1944, the largest naval battle of the war, the Japanese fleet, in Operation Sho, sought to intervene by luring the American carrier fleet away and then using two striking forces to attack the landing fleet. This characteristically complex scheme, which posed serious problems for the ability of American admirals to read the battle (and for their Japanese counterparts in following the plan), nearly succeeded as one of the strike forces was able to approach the landing area and was superior to the American warships there. However, it retired and the net effect of the battle was heavy destruction of the Japanese fleet, with the loss of 4 carriers, 3 battleships, and 10 cruisers. In addition, Japanese air power in and near the Philippines was badly hit during the battle.[45]

From 25 October, the Japanese employed *kamikaze* (suicide) planes against American warships. Such attacks were a product not only of a fanatical self-sacrifice, but also of the limitations of the Japanese naval air arm. More generally, there had been a breakdown in strategic thought on the part of the Japanese; an inability, in the face of Allied power, to think through any option once the decisive naval battle had been lost. The destruction of naval assets made it difficult to think of any further large-scale action, and reduced the Japanese to a defensive–offensive predicated on a tenacious defence coupled with destructive suicide missions, both designed to sap their opponent's will. For the navy, 'the only effective weapon left was the *kamikaze*'.[46] The Japanese commanders in the Philippines and else-where were simply told to hold on to their positions. They received no logistical support. The weak government that had taken power after the fall of Tōjō in July had no plan other than for the Japanese military to die heroically. They felt unable to explain to the public that all had gone wrong and, like the Tōjō government, were very worried by domestic opposition, from both left and right.

## War in Burma

On their western front, both the Japanese and the British launched attacks. The creation of the South-East Asia Command in October 1943 had been designed to give effect to Churchill's wish to recapture Britain's lost colonies, and, specifically, to use amphibious operations to strike at the Japanese perimeter. The British Eastern Fleet was reinforced from the Mediterranean and from April 1944 attacked Japanese positions in what had been the Dutch East Indies. However, plans for invasions of Sumatra, the Andaman Islands and the Burmese coast all proved abortive.

The decisive clash occurred on the ground in Burma, where the Japanese were outfought in 1944. Having defeated a limited British offensive in the Arakan region, with a counterattack, Offensive Ha-

Go, launched on 4 February, that was designed to act as a diversion from the main offensive, the Japanese invaded north-east India in Operation U-Go, launched from 10–15 March. However, as in the Solomons and at Midway in 1942, the Japanese discovered that it was difficult to sustain or regain success once the dramatic advances of the early stages of the conflict had passed. They were over-confident and poorly prepared for a long struggle. The simplicity of their army's determined offensive tactics was wasteful of troops, while the army suffered from a poor logistical system, as well as from inadequate armour, artillery and air support.

In Burma/India, Japanese tactics were no longer adequate against better-trained British (as before, this refers to forces under British command) troops, able to control battles carefully and benefiting from high unit quality and superior logistics, air power and artillery. The vast expansion of numbers in the Indian Army, to over 2 million by the end of the war, provided the British with the necessary resources, but there had also been a fundamental change in training that reflected a rigorous evaluation of what had gone wrong both when the Japanese attacked in 1942 and, subsequently, in the First Arakan campaign. A full complement of basic training followed by jungle training, with a standardisation of training across the army in order to produce a consistent doctrine, had been insisted upon by the Infantry Committee report of June 1943. A more aggressive fighting style, mentally overcoming the jungle, patrolling no-man's land to deny it to the Japanese, seeking out Japanese concentrations, and responding to their infiltration tactics by using all-round defences, had been inculcated.

The British logistical situation had been improved, not least with road building, while the inroads of disease had been lessened. Malaria was largely overcome by the creation of Malaria Forward Treatment Units. These provided structured regimens for prevention and treatment, including the introduction of more effective drugs, especially penicillin and mepacine.[47] There had been a comparable build-up in air-force effectiveness.

The poorly commanded Japanese invasion was heavily defeated at their targets of Kohima and Imphal in March–July 1944. British defensive positions were held against frontal attacks from nearby trenches. Supplies were crucial for both sides: the Japanese needed rapid success and the capture of British supply dumps, as it was difficult to move forward large quantities of supplies along the jungle tracks they employed. Their practice of rapid advance did not allow sufficiently for a failure to overcome opposition, a situation which paralleled that of German *Blitzkrieg*. The Japanese failure to move forward sufficient supplies helped lead to starvation and furthered the inroads of disease. The Japanese lacked the necessary transport and air support. Combined with the British resistance, this led to casualties of over 53,000 (compared to 17,000 for the British).

The British depended heavily on air-supply, which, in turn, was affected by the weather. Even water had to be dropped for the Kohima garrison. Two divisions were airlifted from the Arakan to Imphal.[48] The quality of British command was higher than when Burma had been conquered by the Japanese in 1942. General William Slim, the Commander of 14th Army, was a winner: a successful strategist, also capable of selecting and supporting effective subordinates. A conviction that the Japanese could be defeated contributed powerfully to the victory. The low morale seen in 1942, in particular in Malaya and Singapore, had been replaced by a determination that was more impressive given the difficulties posed by terrain and climate. Morale could not suffice, as Japanese failure showed, but the fact that its absence no longer undermined the British was crucial to their fighting quality. Slim ably exploited the miscalculations of the Japanese advance in order to employ attrition to gain a decisive result.[49]

The defensive success at Kohima and Imphal was exploited as the retreating Japanese were attacked: the British maintained the pressure despite the coming of the monsoon in May. The Japanese defeat, one of the most serious suffered by their army, provided a basis for the British invasion of Burma from December 1944. Further east in Burma, the American-Chinese units of the Northern Combat Area Command advanced in order to open supply routes to China, but, after initial successes, they were badly exhausted in May–August 1944 by the lengthy defence by the outnumbered Japanese garrison of Myitkyina.

Fighting in the close terrain and heat of Burma was hard. Lieutenant-General Sir Henry Pownall noted, 'It is bound to be a slow business, I fear. That jungle is so infernally thick you literally cannot see ten yards into it, and to winkle out concealed Japs, one by one (and they have to be killed to the last man) is the devil of a business'. A British Military Mission report on how best to fight the Japanese had suggested in April 1944 that 'each individual infantry soldier must be trained to be a self-reliant big game hunter imbued with a deep desire to seek out and kill his quarry'.[50] Fortunately for the Allies, the atom bomb was to save them from such a final battle in Japan.

The campaign in Burma does not play a major role in discussion of the war, and in Britain the 14th is known as the 'Forgotten Army'.[51] In part, this is understandable. There were no accompanying naval battles, and the campaign did not contribute directly to the air attack on Japan, although it had an indirect impact from the role played in securing supply routes for American airbases in China. Furthermore, just as the Japanese advances in China in 1944–5 did not lead to Japanese victory in the war, so Japanese success in Operation U-Go would not necessarily have had such an effect, let alone have made a major impact on the crucial Pacific campaigns. Given their logistical problems, it is dubious that the Japanese could have exploited victory in U-Go. Indeed, it would probably have remained a frontier campaign, comparable in some respects to the Japanese advance to the Aleutians, which had also been at the extreme of Japanese logistical range and had not been exploited. Allowing for this, the achievement in defeating the Japanese in Burma was considerable, and the British were to prove more successful in doing so there than the Americans proved on Luzon, although circumstances were different, not least the Japanese willingness to engage in Burma. Penney noted in June 1945 that American losses at Okinawa had made them appreciate the British victory in Burma more;[52] and yet, as the Americans prepared to invade Japan, it remained a strategic irrelevance.

## 1944 reviewed

A combination of the Allied goal of unconditional surrender by Germany and Japan with the resolve of their opponents' leaderships and their grip over their populations ensured that the war would go on; although it was no longer viable for Hitler to hope that a defeat of the Second Front would enable the Germans to concentrate on and defeat the Soviet forces. The Axis was in a parlous condition. There was no effective co-operation or coordination between Germany and Japan, and the German alliance system in Europe had collapsed.

The Axis leadership was also very poor. Hitler was increasingly succumbing to his range of psychological problems, and his diminished grasp on reality exacerbated the difficulties of German command. His lack of interest in a negotiated end to the war, by a separate settlement with the Soviet Union or the Western Allies, was based on distrust of Stalin and was, in part, vindicated by his opponents' stress on unconditional surrender, but it arose from 'a world-view which had completely abandoned Clausewitz's ideas of the relationship between war and policy, and by denying the possibility of defeat, and therefore of negotiated terms, invited the total destruction of his own land and people'.[53]

In addition, there were serious flaws with Hitler as an operational commander. Whatever his skills as an overseer of attack, Hitler was a 'disaster'[54] as a commander of the defence due to his unwillingness to yield territory and his consequent preference for the static defence. By concentrating decision-making and being unable to match Stalin's ability to delegate (or indeed his more measured response to failures in 1941–2), Hitler ensured that there was no alternative way to provide sound command decisions. Divisions within the German military leadership testified to grave concern about the course of the war and the consequences of earlier support for Hitler.[55]

The July Bomb Plot, an attempt, on 20 July 1944, by military conspirators to assassinate Hitler, seize power and negotiate peace, narrowly failed when the bomb went off but did not kill him. This failure greatly weakened the critics of Hitler among the army. Had Hitler indeed been killed, the cohesion of the Nazi regime would have collapsed. Unlike civilian conspirators, the army had the organisation and strength to seize power. The potential for success was illustrated in Paris, where SS and Gestapo leaders were arrested by supporters of the plot. The political aftermath of an army seizure of power would have been far less clear, but failure ensured it would be a fight to the finish. A suitable sentence to end a chapter, but, as a reminder that the war years involved more suffering than that caused by conflict, in 1944 Bengal was threatened by a major famine, and the British needed to divert shipping to move grain there.

In every field, the strength of Allied resources was readily apparent. That year, the USA alone produced 89 million tons of steel, about half the world's total production. 1944 ended with the Axis in a far weaker situation than at its start, although the fundamentals were no different. The Axis were the weaker alliance, they were on the defensive, and they were unable to match the forces deployed by the Allies, particularly the USA and the Soviet Union. The war had now been carried up or close to Germany's frontiers, although the Germans and Japanese remained in occupation of large amounts of conquered territory, including Norway, Denmark, most of the Netherlands, much of Poland and part of Yugoslavia, as well as Malaya, the Dutch East Indies and most of Burma and the Philippines.

Both Germany and Japan had lost the war at sea and in the air. The latter ensured that ground and sea units could not be protected by the Axis, a situation that had tactical, operational and, at sea, strategic consequences. It also meant that the German and Japanese homelands could not be protected. The consequences, in terms of damage to industry and infrastructure and harm to civilian morale, were not under the control of the Axis regimes. Instead, they were dependent on the effectiveness of Allied doctrine and operations and on a civilian response to bombing that Axis regimes struggled to influence.

Having survived the July Bomb Plot, Hitler was able to take greater control over the army than he had wielded hitherto. He was even more convinced than hitherto that he was intended by destiny to save Germany. Furthermore, the greater role of Nazi fervour in appointments to, and promotions in, the army after the Bomb Plot helps explain why the army went on fighting when success appeared very unlikely. Soldiers were convinced that they had to protect Germany from the Soviets, who were presented as murderous Asiatic hordes, but they also fought in a determined fashion against Anglo-American forces. In addition, the SS became more powerful in the Nazi regime and German society, further increasing the oppression of those deemed traitors and helping further the implementation of total war. Appointed 'Reich Plenipotentiary for Total War', Goebbels introduced the sixty-hour week.

In 1944, the Axis had lost more territory and more troops than in 1943, and the Second Front had proved far more successful than Hitler had anticipated, although German resilience had been under-estimated by the Western Allies. It had also proved impossible for the Axis powers to reverse earlier Allied successes, most importantly that in the Battle of the Atlantic. Nor was it possible to launch a second version of the Kursk offensive. The Germans no longer had the resources to launch such an attack on the Eastern Front. The Bulge offensive on the Western Front was not on the same scale, and its context was a far more desperate one. The Germans were unable to challenge Allied control of the sea effectively, while the Allied air offensive had at last started to make inroads on German munitions production. Axis failure was registered in the loss of allies such as Finland. In July 1944, the Fascist pro-Japanese government of Field Marshal Pibul Songgram in Thailand fell, to be replaced by a ministry more sympathetic to the Allies.

Yet there was still much that was unclear at the beginning of 1945. The problem of conquering Japan appeared particularly trou-bling given the willingness of Japanese units to fight to the death, the large proportion of their army that had not yet been engaged, and the extent to which it was unlikely that the Chinese or, unless they intervened, the Soviets would be able to prevent the reinforcement of Japan from China and Manchuria.

Aside from that, it was unclear how long it would take to vanquish Hitler. He was determined to fight to the finish, and was unwilling to heed contrary advice. The prospect of a Nazi redoubt in Alpine Germany troubled some observers, while there was growing concern about what Soviet triumph in Eastern Europe would mean for the future shape of the continent. Conflict between Communists and Royalists had broken out in Greece. The course and consequences of the campaigns of 1945 seemed far from inevitable.

## NOTES

1  W.S. Dunn, *Soviet Blitzkrieg: The Battle for White Russia, 1944* (Boulder, Colorado, 2000).

2 J.K. Zawodny, *Nothing but Honour: The Story of the Warsaw Uprising, 1944* (Stanford, 1978).

3 H.P. Willmott, *When Men Lost Faith in Reason. Reflections on War and Society in the Twentieth Century* (Westport, Connecticut, 2002), pp. 124–8.

4 S. Newton, *Retreat from Leningrad: Army Group North, 1944–1945* (Atglen, Pennsylvania, 1995).

5 J.T. Gross, *Revolution from Abroad: The Soviet Conquest of Poland's Western Ukraine and Western Belorussia* (Princeton, 1988).

6 E.D. Smith, *The Battles for Cassino* (1975); J. Ellis, *Cassino: The Hollow Victory* (1984).

7 Alexander to Brooke, 26 January 1944, LH. Alanbrooke papers, 6/2/19.

8 G.W.L. Nicholson, *The Canadians in Italy, 1943–1945* (Ottawa, 1956), is of value for the whole campaign. See also B. McAndrew, *Canadians and the Italian Campaign, 1943–1945* (Montreal, 1996).

9 P. Verney, *Anzio, 1944: An Unexpected Fury* (1978); C. D'Este, *Fatal Decisions: Anzio and the Battle for Rome* (1991).

10 Brooke to Sir Henry Maitland Wilson, Supreme Commander, Mediterranean, 2 August 1944, LH. Alanbrooke papers 6/3/6.

11 D. Orgill, *The Gothic Line* (1967); D. Graham and S. Bidwell, *Tug of War: The Battle for Italy, 1943–1945* (1986).

12 R. Miller, *Nothing Less than Victory: The Oral History of D-Day* (2000).

13 G. Hartcup, *Code Name Mulberry: The Planning, Building and Operation of the Normandy Harbours* (Newton Abbot, 1977).

14 O'Connor to Lieutenant-General Sir Allan Harding, Chief of Staff of Allied Armies in Italy, 19 August 1944, LH. O'Connor 5/3/37.

15 D.I. Hall, 'From Khaki and Light Blue to Purple. The Long and Troubled Development of Army/Air Co-operation in Britain, 1914–1945', *RUSI Journal*, 147, no. 5 (October 2002), p. 82.

16 I. Gooderson, *Air Power at the Battlefront: Allied Close Air Support in Europe 1943–4* (1998).

17 LH. Alanbrooke papers, 6/2/35, pp. 1, 5, 9, 29.

18 C. D'Este, *Decision in Normandy* (1983); M. Hastings, *Overlord: D-Day and the Battle for Normandy* (1984); M. Reynolds, *Steel Inferno: I SS Panzer Corps in Normandy* (New York, 1997); S. Weingartner (ed.), *The Greatest Thing We Have Ever Attempted: Historical Perspectives on the Normandy Campaign* (Wheaton, Illinois, 1998); R. Hart, *Clash of Arms: How the Allies Won in Normandy* (Boulder, Colorado, 2001).

19 M. Blumenson, *The Battle of the Generals: The Untold Story of the Falaise Pocket: The Campaign that Should Have Won World War II* (New York, 1993).

20 C.B. MacDonald, *The Battle of the Huertgen Forest* (Philadelphia, 1963); A. Kemp, *The Unknown Battle: Metz* (1981).

21 M. Van Creveld, *Fighting Power: German and US Army Performance, 1939–1945* (Westport, Connecticut, 1982), is less persuasive than M.D. Doubler, *Closing with the Enemy: How GIs Fought the War in Europe, 1944–1945* (Lawrence, Kansas, 1994). On the Germans, see S.G. Fritz,

*Frontsoldaten: The German Soldier in World War II* (Lexington, Kentucky, 1995).

22  D. Raser, *And We Shall Shock Them: The British Army in the Second World War* (1983); S. Bidwell and G. Dominick, 'The Second Round: 1939–1945', in *Fire Power: British Army Weapons and Theories of War, 1904–1945* (1982).

23  C. Stacey, *The Victory Campaign: The Operations in North-West Europe, 1944–1945* (Ottawa, 1960).

24  S.D. Badsey, 'The American Experience of Armour 1919–53', in J.P. Harris and F.H. Toase (eds), *Armoured Warfare* (1992), p. 142.

25  C.B. MacDonald, *The Battle of the Bulge* (1984); T.N. Dupuy, D.L. Bongard and R.C. Anderson, *Hitler's Last Gamble: The Battle of the Bulge* (New York, 1994); D.S. Parker, *Battle of the Bulge. Hitler's Ardennes Offensive: The German View of the Battle of the Bulge* (1997).

26  C. Whiting, *The Battle of the Bulge: Britain's Untold Story* (Stroud, 1999).

27  F.C. Pogue, *The Supreme Command* (Washington, 1954).

28  R. Lamb, *Montgomery in Europe 1943–45: Success or Failure?* (1983).

29  S. Hart, *Montgomery and Colossal Cracks: The 21$^{st}$ Army Group in Northwest Europe, 1944–5* (Westport, Connecticut, 2000).

30  Penney to Major-General John Sinclair, Director of Military Intelligence, War Office, 2 May 1945, LH. Penney 5/1.

31  For his defence of his strategy, see D.D. Eisenhower, *Crusade in Europe* (1948).

32  LH. Alanbrooke papers, 6/2/35.

33  M.J. Neufeld, *The Rocket and the Reich: Peenemünde and the Coming of the Ballistic Missile Era* (Washington, 1995).

34  W. Murray, *Strategy for Defeat: The Luftwaffe, 1933–1945* (1985); S.L. McFarland and W.P. Newton, *To Command the Sky: The Battle for Air Superiority, 1942–4* (Washington, 1991).

35  G.P. Gentile, 'General Arnold and the Historians', *Journal of Military History*, 64 (2000), p. 179.

36  R. Schaffer, *Wings of Judgment: American Bombing in World War II* (Oxford, 1985); S. Garrett, *Ethics and Airpower in World War Two* (New York, 1993).

37  N. Gregor, 'A *Schicksalsgemeinschaft*? Allied Bombing, Civilian Morale, and Social Dissolution in Nuremberg, 1942–1945', *Historical Journal*, 43 (2000), pp. 1,051–70.

38  A.C. Mierzejewski, *The Collapse of the German War Economy, 1944–1945* (Chapel Hill, 1998).

39  The best general account of the subject is R.J. Overy, *The Air War, 1939–1945* (1980).

40  H. Feis, *The China Tangle: The American Effort in China from Pearl Harbor to the Marshall Mission* (Princeton, 1953).

41  D. Wilson, *When Tigers Fight: The Story of the Sino-Japanese War, 1937–1945* (1982); J.C. Hsiung and S.I. Levine (eds), *China's Bitter Victory: The War with Japan, 1937–1945* (Armonk, 1992).

42  W.Y'Blood, *Red Sun Setting* (Annapolis, 1980).

43  S.R. Taaffe, *MacArthur's Jungle War: The 1944 New Guinea Campaign* (Lawrence, Kansas, 1998).

44  S.L. Falk, *Liberation of the Philippines* (1971); W. Breuer, *Retaking the Philippines* (New York, 1986).

45  E.P. Hoyt, *The Battle of Leyte Gulf: The Death Knell of the Japanese Fleet* (1972).

46  G.W. Baer, *One Hundred Years of Sea Power. The U.S. Navy, 1890–1990* (Stanford, California, 1993), pp. 261–2.

47  D.P. Marston, *Phoenix from the Ashes: The Indian Army in the Burma Campaign* (DPhil., Oxford, 2001).

48  H. Probert, *The Forgotten Air Force: The Royal Air Force in the War against Japan 1941–45* (1995).

49  C. Malkasian, *A History of Modern Wars of Attrition* (Westport, Connecticut, 2002), pp. 104–8.

50  Pownall to Ismay, 26 April 1944, LH. Ismay 4/26/2; PRO. WO. 33/1819, p. 50.

51  R. Callahan, *Burma, 1942–1945* (1978); L. Allen, *Burma: The Longest War, 1941–45* (1984); D. Smurthwaite (ed.), *The Forgotten War: The British Army in the Far East 1941–1945* (1992).

52  Penney, conversation with Dr. Ripley, U.S. Office of Strategic Services, 6 June 1945, LH. Penney 5/2.

53  B. Bond, *The Pursuit of Victory. From Napoleon to Saddam Hussein* (Oxford, 1996), p. 154.

54  A.W. Purdue, *The Second World War* (1999), p. 150.

55  M. Cooper, *The German Army, 1933–1945: Its Political and Military Failure* (1978).

# CHAPTER SEVEN

# The fall of the Axis

In 1945, the Thousand Year Reich came to an end, followed by the Japanese empire. There is a certain inexorable inevitability about the demise of both, but it is necessary to remember that the final course of both struggles was far from inevitable, that the year saw bitter fighting, and that many troops and civilians died.

## The conquest of Germany

In Europe, the Red Army finished its advance from the Volga to Berlin, driving on indeed to the Elbe, a distance greater than that achieved by any force in Europe for over a century. Against bitter resistance, the Soviets were victorious in the Vistula–Oder Offensive of January–February 1945. Breaking out from their bridgeheads across the Vistula, the Soviets again indicated the ability of their army to make rapid progress in winter conditions, although they were helped by greatly outnumbering the Germans in troops and equipment: Army Group A was outnumbered by about 2.2 million troops to about 400,000. Heavy German casualties in 1944 had lessened the available manpower and diluted fighting quality, not least because the replacement regiment system had broken down.

Attacking from 12 January, the Soviets fought their way through the German defence lines, greatly helped by plentiful artillery, in which their margin in numbers was about 7.5 to 1. Rapidly advancing Soviet tank forces (margin in numbers about 5.5 to 1) then exploited the victory, in what had become a pattern of success in 'deep operations'. Warsaw fell on 17 January and Krakow on 19

January, and the Oder was reached on 31 January. The Red Army was able to establish bridgeheads across the river at the start of February.

However, as with other advances, there were growing problems with supplies, while strong German resistance in Silesia also helped narrow the front of advance. When the offensive finished in early February, the Soviets were close to Berlin (35 miles), but the presence of German forces to the north (East Prussia and East Pomerania) and south (Upper Silesia) ensured that a strengthening of the position on the flanks in March, as well as re-supply of the forces in the main axis of advance, would be required before there could be an advance on the Nazi capital. Breslau, the fortified capital of Silesia, held out until 7 May, but the state of its garrison – without air cover or tanks – testified to the condition of the German army.

The last stages of the war demonstrated the continued strength of Soviet operational art. This stressed firepower, but also employed mobile tank warfare. Attrition and manoeuvre were combined in a coordinated sequence of attacks that reflected Soviet operational skill. This can be seen in the conquest of Poland, much of which was completed in January 1945: the Red Army used large numbers of tanks, which were able to exploit opportunities prepared by short and savage artillery attacks. The individual Soviet tank armies gained space to manoeuvre and this prevented the Germans from consolidating new defensive positions. For forces that had broken through their opponents, mobility enhanced the ability to prevent their opponents from falling back in order. Mobility replaced the sequence of new front lines that World War One advances had had to face with the open battlefield, in which retreating opponents had to rely on defensive hedgehog positions that could be encircled, if the momentum of the offensive could be maintained. The limit of the new advance was often that of maintaining petrol supplies, as in the Red Army's advance through Poland in early 1945.

Responding to Soviet requests and seeking to show that they were providing help, British and American heavy bombers attacked cities that were rail nodes to the rear of the front, particularly Magdeburg and, most damagingly, on 13–14 February, Dresden. The heavy civilian casualties accorded with the intention of causing chaos.

The Soviet delay in resuming the drive on Berlin was accentuated by poor weather in March, and enabled the Germans to build-up their defences west of the Oder in February and March. However, the Soviets themselves built up their forces as well as widening their bridgeheads across the Oder.

The Soviets followed up in April with the crowning Berlin Operation. Keen to benefit from competition, Stalin launched two Fronts to take Hitler's capital: 1st Belorussian under Zhukov and, to its south, 1st Ukrainian under Koniev. By deleting boundary lines between the Fronts' advances, Stalin gave them an added inducement to compete. The attacks were mounted in the morning of the 16 April, but Zhukov's troops encountered well-prepared defences benefiting from the Seelöw Heights west of the Oder as well as from the delay in the Soviet advance since early February. On 16 April, Zhukov accompanied his attack with the use of 143 searchlights designed to dazzle the Germans. In fact the air was so thick with rubble from the Soviet barrage that the searchlights could not penetrate. The Soviets were also hampered by the night-time German abandonment of the first line of defences before the attack was launched. This ensured that the Soviet artillery had less impact initially than had been anticipated. Zhukov's failure to make progress on the first day led him to commit his armour, which he had held back for exploitation, too early, ensuring heavy losses from German anti-tank guns. Although eventually successful, Zhukov's Front had taken both heavy casualties and more time than had been anticipated.

The continued Soviet use of frontal attacks, particularly on the Seelöw Heights on 16–18 April, was, by Western standards, wasteful of manpower. This practice contributed to the Soviets having military casualties far greater than that of any combatant. The April frontal attacks were also accompanied by an extensive use of armour and artillery. Zhukov, in particular, had massed a formidable amount of the latter: about 9,000 guns and 1,400 rocket launchers.

Having breached the German defence belts, the Soviets advanced to encircle Berlin from north and south, completing the encirclement on 25 April. The city centre was attacked the following day. The Red Army fought its way into the centre, with large numbers of German troops, many recently conscripted boys and old men, fighting on amidst the heavily bombarded rubble, although they knew that their cause was hopeless. The Soviets used particularly intensive artillery fire throughout the operation.

Hoped-for relief could not be obtained: the forces Hitler called on, the Ninth and Twelfth Armies, were both weak and were themselves under great pressure. The Soviet offensive on Berlin was supported by advances to north and south, and German troops in the region were fully engaged. With the Soviets storming the bitterly defended Reichstag, Hitler, convinced that he had been let down by the German people and military, committed suicide on 30 April. Other Nazi leaders followed. On 2 May, the remaining German forces in Berlin surrendered. Other Soviet forces had advanced to the Baltic coast and the Elbe.[1]

Further south, the German counter-offensive from Lake Balaton towards Budapest, Operation Spring Awakening, launched on 5 March, had been fought to a halt by 15 March.[2] The Soviets benefited from their resources, their ability to hastily create defensive positions, and the impact of mud on the German tanks. Advancing Soviet forces overran Slovakia, while, on 13 April, others finally captured Vienna after bitter fighting in the city. The Soviet forces in Austria did not subsequently advance far; there was certainly nothing to compare with the advance of American troops across southern Germany and into Austria.

Meanwhile, Anglo-American forces had advanced across the Rhine in March. The Germans had made a major effort to defend their country west of the Rhine, but that had led to major losses in fighting west of the Ruhr and in the Saarland in February and March. The former proved difficult for the Allies, not least due to the number of rivers, the poor weather and the tenacity of the resistance; but, once the Allies attacked along the entire line, the Germans found it difficult to reinforce hard-pressed sectors. The withdrawal of German troops to face the Soviets helped the Western Allies. Cologne fell on 5 March and the Ludendorff rail bridge across the Rhine at Remagen two days later. This gave the Americans a bridgehead across the river: German counterattacks and the use of V-2 rockets failed to destroy the bridge.[3]

Once the Rhine had been crossed in strength, German resistance became much weaker. As in 1944, the Allies benefited from the breakout into a more mobile stage of conflict, and in addition, in 1945 the Germans were badly affected by the accumulated losses of campaigning in the West since the previous June. Their capacity for mounting a counter-offensive had been gravely weakened, while their forces were short of manpower, equipment and petrol, lacked air support, and were heavily outnumbered in tanks. Heavy Allied strategic air attacks were having a devastating effect, and were also making German failure readily apparent.

The Americans advanced from the Remagen bridgehead, while Anglo-American forces crossed the lower Rhine near Wesel on 24 March in an operation coordinated with an Anglo-American parachute landing.[4] German military cohesion broke down as units were isolated by advancing Allied forces. The German army did not fight very well once the Rhine had been crossed: morale was low, and the total Allied control of the air greatly weakened German resistance. The German Army Group B defending the Ruhr was encircled on 1 April and what was left there (317,000 troops) surrendered on 18 April. There was no force available to mount a counterattack.

Anglo-Canadian forces on the northern flank of the advance cleared the eastern Netherlands and advanced into northern Germany, crossing the Weser on 5 April. Thereafter, there were further advances in Holland and Germany, with a crossing of the Elbe on 29 April, Hamburg falling on 3 May, and an advance to the Baltic at Lübeck (which fell on 2 May), designed in part to block Soviet troops from advancing into Denmark. British conviction of Nazi iniquity was fortified by the liberation of the concentration camp of Bergen-Belsen.

Meanwhile, the Americans had reached the Elbe (near Magdeburg) on 11 April. The encirclement of Army Group B ensured that there was a massive gap in the German defences, and that resistance was limited. American forces in central Germany advanced east, capturing cities that would subsequently be handed over for Soviet occupation, including Leipzig on 19 April; although there was no advance on Berlin, a decision that was subsequently criticised as helping the Soviets to establish a more powerful position for the Cold War.[5] American and Soviet troops made contact near Torgau on the Elbe on 25 April.

In southern Germany, although forces in Nuremberg put up a strong resistance, there was a rapid American advance to the Danube, which was crossed on 22 April, and an even more rapid advance thereafter. Munich was captured on 30 April, and American units advanced into Austria, taking Linz, Salzburg and Innsbruck, and moving through the Brenner Pass to join up, on 4 May, with American forces advancing from Italy. The fall of Hitler's eyrie at Berchtesgaden on 4 May made it clear that there would be no last-ditch resistance, based on a National Redoubt, in the Alps.[6]

The Allied forces that had advanced through Trent to the Brenner were part of the breakout in northern Italy. Operations there had been delayed by the strength of German resistance and by the winter, with little change in the front line after the stopping of the American advance on Bologna in late October 1944, although the 8th Army had slowly moved up the east coast to, and past, Ravenna in December 1944 and January 1945, albeit in the face of firm resistance benefiting from the series of rivers the British had to cross. The failure of the Allies on the Italian front to hamstring German policy was shown in December 1944 when Hitler was able to launch his Ardennes attack without having to withdraw forces from Italy.

The Allied offensive in Italy resumed on 9 April 1945. The 8th Army slowly fought its way through the German defensive positions and the Argenta Gap, while the Americans broke through the mountains south-west and west of Bologna, reaching the Lombardy plain.

The Germans had lines to fall back on in Italy – the Po, Adige and Alpine Lines – but their cohesion was now broken, and the Allied advance created a wider front for operations. The Allies were rapidly able to exploit their advantage, the Americans advancing on a number of axes, including via Modena to Parma and Piacenza, as well as north to Lake Garda, Mantua and Vicenza, and north-east to Padua. As the German position disintegrated, the Allies were able to advance in all directions: the Americans to Milan (29 April), Turin (2 May) and along the Ligurian (Mediterranean) coast, where German resistance had been hitherto most successful, to Genoa (27 April), and the British to Venice (29 April).

German defeats across Europe had already revived the Italian resistance, which had been bloodily suppressed by the Germans the previous winter. The partisans liberated Genoa, Milan and Turin ahead of the Allied army. With Mussolini shot by partisans on 28 April while trying to flee to Switzerland, the demoralised remains of his Fascist forces ceased fighting. On 29 April, the German commander in Italy agreed an unconditional surrender. It took effect on 2 May, the day in which British troops reached Trieste, blocking the advance of Tito's Communist forces.

The Germans were still in control of large areas, including Norway, Denmark, most of Austria and much of southern Germany, but they had been totally defeated. The *Luftwaffe* had been outfought, and the lack of flying training and fuel had gravely compromised its capability. Although there were still large numbers of U-boats, they were unable to inflict serious losses on Allied shipping, although, had new types become operational, they would have posed a more serious challenge.

Based at Flensburg, Hitler's successor, Admiral Dönitz, wanted to maintain resistance to the Soviets while negotiating terms with Britain and the Americans, a measure that he hoped would enable more Germans to escape Soviet occupation, but, on 5 and 6 May, the Western Allies insisted on unconditional surrenders. On 7 May, the Germans, indeed, surrendered unconditionally, the surrender becoming effective the next day.

The surrender process, however, was not without serious problems. The capitulation agreed on Lüneburg Heath on 4 May, for German units in the Netherlands, Denmark and north-west Germany, was rejected by the commander of the garrison on the Danish island of Bornholm, and he did not surrender until 9 May, when Soviet bombing attacks on the previous two days was followed by the arrival of warships. Other, larger, German forces fought on near Prague until 11 May against a massive Soviet army, much of it recently used against Berlin. The Americans had occupied Pilsen on 6 May, but held back from advancing on Prague, as they had earlier done on Berlin. German forces across Europe, from Brittany to Courland and Norway to the Channel Islands, had all surrendered by 12 May.[7] Fears that U-boats would continue operating proved unfounded.

## The collapse of Japan

Japan took longer to defeat. In the Pacific, the Americans could choose where to land, but the fighting and logistical problems of operations on shore were formidable, and Japanese determination to fight on led to heavy casualties. This was seen both in the Philippines and on the islands of Iwo Jima and Okinawa. The Japanese on the Philippines did not surrender after the Americans landed on Luzon on 9 January. Although the Japanese XIV Area Army had more than 0.25 million troops, its condition reflected the degradation of the Japanese war machine. There were only about 150 operational combat aircraft to support it, and their planes and pilots could not match the Americans in quality; most were destroyed by American carrier planes before the invasion. Naval support had been destroyed the previous autumn. The troops lacked food and ammunition and the relatively few vehicles available had insufficient fuel.

Rather than engaging the Americans where they were likely to be strongest – in the invasion zone and the plains between there and Manila – Yamashita deployed his troops to take advantage of areas of difficult terrain. The naval garrison of Manila, however, refused to evacuate the city and vigorously defended it, leading the Americans to turn to an extensive use of artillery. Combined with Japanese atrocities, this may have led to the death of 100,000 Filipino civilians. Manila was not completely regained until 3 March, although American troops had entered the city on 4 February.

Japanese forces, which held out in northern Luzon until the end of the war, were able to make little effective contribution to the war effort other than tying down Allied forces and causing heavy casualties: the American army alone suffered 145,000 casualties. This attritional end was an important Japanese goal, although they, in turn, suffered heavily, not least from starvation and disease. The Luzon operation was accompanied by other attacks in the extensive Philippine archipelago. With space at a premium and with knowledge of the end, it is easy to neglect such attacks in order to focus on the preparations for the assault on Japan, but they are of importance not least for the light they shed on relative capability and on strategic goals. The Americans were keen to use the Philippines as a base for the invasion of Japan. The islands they had already captured were crucial as bases for air attack, but they were not large enough to provide the staging areas required. While gaining such positions in central Luzon, particularly Clark Field and Manila Bay (where Corregidor fell on 28 February), the Americans also needed to ensure the security of shipping passages. This led to a series of amphibious attacks on the islands of the region. Samar was invaded on 19 February, Palawan on 28 February, and other islands in March and April. American skill in amphibious operations, in the coordination of air and sea support, and in the rapid securing and development of bridgehead positions was demonstrated and enhanced. Although the scale was very different, this continual process was a useful preparation for landings in the Japanese archipelago.

Iwo Jima and Okinawa were seized in order to provide airbases for an attack on Japan. This bland remark gives no guidance to the difficulty of the conquests and the heavy casualties involved in defeating the well-positioned Japanese forces, who fought to the death with fanatical intensity for islands seen as part of Japan, although under heavy pressure from the attacking American marines with their massive air and sea support. The Japanese were also skilful defenders, well able to exploit the terrain, not least by tunnelling into Iwo Jima. This ensured that the bombing and shelling that preceded the landing of the marines there on 19 February inflicted only minimal damage. As a consequence, the conquest of the island was slow and bloody, and much of the fighting was at close quarters. The Japanese had created a dense network of underground fortifications and this not only vitiated the effects of American firepower, but also made a fighting advance on foot difficult, not least because the network provided the Japanese with a myriad of interconnected firing positions. The Japanese had sufficient artillery, mortars and machine guns to make their defences deadly. Their use of reverse-slope positions also lessened the impact of American firepower.

On Okinawa, where the Americans landed on 26 March, they dropped napalm into the entrances of Japanese positions. The Americans also made extensive use of tank-mounted flame-throwers in order to clear positions. Although the circumstances were very different to operations elsewhere, the successful use of flame-thrower and other tanks depended on effective co-operation with infantry, which provided crucial protection for the tanks. Demolition teams of combat engineers also proved an important part of this well-integrated force. The heavy casualty rate inflicted by the defenders of both islands, the vast majority of whom died in the defence, led to fears about the casualties that an invasion of Japan would entail. Although much of Iwo Jima had fallen within two weeks, the time anticipated for its capture, it took thirty-six days to conquer the island and more than one-third of the marines employed were killed (5,391) or wounded (17,372); 22,000 Japanese troops were killed. On Okinawa, the Americans lost 7,613 dead and 21,807 wounded, while the Japanese lost 110,000 dead and 7,400 prisoners. Resistance there did not cease until 30 June. The Japanese decision to rest on the defensive on land and not to use suicide attacks there made the American task more difficult.[8]

The Japanese sought to inflict as many casualties as possible and also hoped that the operations would provide them with an opportunity to inflict serious damage by air and sea attacks on American warships, thus limiting their ability to invade Japan. *Kamikaze* attacks were responsible for the sinking and damage of numerous warships, but not enough to have a strategic impact. In defending against *kamikaze* attacks, the Americans benefited from the large number of fighters carried by their numerous carriers and from the radar-based system of fighter control. Bomber attacks on Japanese airbases also helped.

The Japanese sent their last major naval force, led by the battleship *Yamato*, on a *kamikaze* mission, with only enough oil to steam to Okinawa, but it was intercepted by American bombers and the *Yamato* and five accompanying ships were sunk on 7 April. The vulnerability of surface warships without air cover was amply demonstrated. The battleships on which the Japanese had spent so much had become an operational and strategic irrelevance.

As a result of its loss of sea and air power, Japan was now vulnerable to invasion. Its position was an indication of the great value of naval power. Although the Japanese still occupied large areas in East and South-East Asia, these forces were isolated. American submarines operated with few difficulties in the Yellow and East China Seas and the Sea of Japan. Carrier-borne planes attacked Japan, dominated its air space and mined its waters, while warships bombarded coastal positions. On 24 July, for example, American and British carriers launched 1,747 planes to attack targets around the Inland Sea. In addition, from both carriers and Clark Field on Luzon, Formosa could be bombed.

American naval and amphibious operations benefited from their mastery of logistics, not least in ensuring the availability of sufficient oil. The Americans could plan where they wanted to mount an inva-sion. Just as the Battle of the Atlantic had ended in Allied triumph, the naval war in the Pacific had been decisively won. Although, despite logistical limitations, the British Pacific Fleet played a successful role alongside the Americans in 1945,[9] this was very much an American triumph. They had borne most of the struggle and were to dominate the post-war Pacific.

## Air attack on Japan

Meanwhile, the air assault on Japan had been stepped up. Initially, the American raids had been long distance and unsupported by fighter cover. This led to attacks from a high altitude, which reduced their effectiveness. The raids that were launched were hindered by poor weather, especially strong tailwinds, and difficulties with the B-29's reliability, as well as the general problems of precision bombing within the technology of the period.

From February 1945 there was a switch to low-altitude night-time area bombing of Japanese cities, a policy which reflected the views of General Curtis LeMay, the commander of the 21st Bomber Group. The impact was devastating, not least because many Japanese dwellings were made of timber and paper and burned readily when bombarded with incendiaries, and also because population density in the cities was high. Fighters based in Iwo Jima (three air hours from Tokyo) from 7 April 1945 could provide cover for the B-29s, which had been bombing from more distant Saipan since November 1944. Weaknesses in Japanese anti-aircraft defences, both planes and guns, eased the American task. LeMay was able to increase the payload of the B-29s by removing their guns. Although the Japanese had devel-oped some impressive interceptor fighters, especially the Mitsubishi AbM5 and the Shiden, they were unable to produce many, due to the impact of Allied air raids and of submarine attacks on supply routes, and were also very short of pilots.

In 1944–5, American bombers destroyed over 30 per cent of the buildings in Japan. Over half of Tokyo and Kobe were destroyed, and nearly half of Yokohama. On 10 March 1945, in the first major low-level raid on Tokyo, more people were killed than in the atomic bomb attack on Nagasaki that was to follow. The death, in that raid, of over 83,000 people in terrible circumstances was accompanied by another 1 million becoming homeless. The raid showed the fire-power that the Americans had available: 334 B-29s were used; 14 were lost. The rate of destruction was far higher than in the bombing of Germany. There were further heavy raids on Tokyo on 13 and 19 April and 23 and 25 May. Similarly, there were heavy raids on Nagoya on 12 and 20 March and 14 and 16 May. There, and else-where, the loss, pain and disruption caused by casualties and homelessness were accentuated by the cumulative nature of the pres-sure and the lack of any apparent response or recourse. Large numbers were evacuated from the cities, which exacerbated the general disruption. Furthermore, cities throughout Japan were bombed. The combined effect was to spread devastation and economic ruin, to wreck communications, and to weaken seriously the Japanese people, state and war economy.[10]

The cumulative nature of the attack was seen in the destruction of Japanese transport. Mining badly hit Japanese coastal shipping, with the dropping of about 4,000 mines in the Shimonosekei Strait in March–July 1945, hitting the movement of merchant shipping through this major route to the ports of the Inland Sea. In response, the Japanese switched to rail, but it, in turn, was hit by attacks on marshalling yards, bridges and other targets. Had the war lasted to 1946, the destruction of the rail system would have led to famine as it would have been impossible to move food supplies.

Bombing culminated in the dropping of atomic bombs on Hiroshima and Nagasaki on 6 and 9 August, respectively, as a result of which over 280,000 people died, either at once or, eventually, through radiation poisoning. This transformed the situation, leading the Japanese, on 14 August, to agree to surrender unconditionally; although that also owed something to Soviet entry into the war, which removed any chance that the Soviets would act as mediators for a peace on more generous terms.[11] At the Potsdam Conference (17 July–2 August), the Allies had issued the Potsdam Declaration, on the evening of 26 July, demanding unconditional surrender as well as the occupation of Japan, Japan's loss of its overseas possessions and the establishment of democracy in the country. The alternative threatened was 'prompt and utter destruction', but, on 27 July, the Japanese government decided to ignore the Declaration.

The use of atomic bombs was to be very controversial, but seemed justified given the likely heavy Allied casualties that would arise from an invasion. MacArthur told Penney in April 1945 that his troops had not yet met the Japanese army properly, and that when they did they were going to take heavy casualties.[12] The Japanese homeland army was weak – poorly trained and equipped, and lacking mobility and air support – but the heavy Japanese and Allied losses on Iwo Jima and Okinawa suggest that the use of atom bombs was necessary in order both to overcome a suicidal determination to fight on, and to obtain unconditional surrender.[13] General Marshall considered using atom bombs in tactical support of a landing on Kyushu. This was seen as the site for the first landings in Japan, and it was there that the Japanese had concentrated most of their forces.

A rapid and complete victory seemed necessary in order to force Japan to accept terms that would neutralise its threat to its neighbours. In addition, it was necessary to secure the surrender of the large Japanese forces in China and South-East Asia. The dropping of the atom bombs showed that the Japanese armed forces could not protect the nation, and was therefore a major blow to militarism.

Critics of American policy argue that the dropping of the bombs represented an early stage in the Cold War, with their use designed to ensure peace on American terms and both to show the Soviet Union the extent of American strength – in particular a vital counter on Soviet numbers on land – and to ensure that Japan could be defeated without the Soviets playing a major role. This may have been a factor, but there seems little doubt that the prime use of the bombs was to ensure a rapid surrender that obviated the need for a costly invasion and a lengthy continuation of the conflict. Truman wrote on 9 August, 'My object is to save as many American lives as possible but I also have a human feeling for the women and children of Japan'.[14]

The Germans and Japanese had both been interested in developing an atomic bomb, but neither had made progress comparable to that of the Allies. The *Uranverein*, the German plan to acquire nuclear capability, was not adequately pursued, in part because the Germans thought it would take too long to develop. The German conviction that the war would, or could, be finished long before the bomb would be ready was encouraged by their successes in

1939–41, but was an instance of over-confidence affecting the development of new technologies. The Germans were also affected by hostility to what the Nazis termed 'Jewish physics', as well as the consequences of over-estimating the amount of U235 required.[15]

## Conflict in Burma

The bombing offensive on Japan had not prevented further Allied campaigning on the ground. From December 1944, the British had invaded Burma. Their drive on the Irrawaddy valley was successful. Slim, the British commander, proved one of the best generals of the war, with his ability to out-think the Japanese and then to implement plans in an area where terrain and climate combined to make operating very difficult. Heavy rain badly hit transport routes. Diseases such as scrub typhus were also a major problem. These conditions also affected the Japanese, who suffered, in addition, from the weakness of their supply system.

Bridgeheads to the north of Mandalay were established on 11 January 1945, and to the west and south from 13 February. The British exploited this in late February and March, advancing to seize Meiktila (3 March), the major Japanese supply base in central Burma, and then Mandalay (19 March). The Japanese mounted a major counter-offensive to regain Meiktila in March, but, supported by aerial supplies and ground-support aircraft, the British beat them off. As in the Pacific, the Japanese were willing to fight to the death, although their unit cohesion was affected by the Allied advance, not least by the impact of air power. In contrast, the nationalist Indian National Army fought poorly and many surrendered without firing a shot. The Burma National Army defected to the British in April.

Slim followed up his success in central Burma, which reopened the Burma Road to China, with an advance from Meiktila down the Sittany valley and then, via Pegu, on Rangoon that was supported by an amphibious landing, and by another advance to the east of the Irrawaddy. Another force had advanced down the Arakan coast to Gwa. Rangoon was captured on 3 May. Throughout, British operations on land were supported by naval action, while the British fleet also launched attacks (especially with aircraft and submarines) on Japanese positions and shipping.

After the fall of Rangoon, it was necessary for the troops to recu-perate and re-supply. Thereafter, it was unclear whether the British would continue to campaign overland, into southern Burma and/or Siam, against the large Japanese forces in the region, or would mount an amphibious advance on Malaya and Singapore, the recapture of which was seen as important to British prestige, or would, instead, focus on the planned invasion of Japan. In September 1944, Admiral Sir Geoffrey Layton, Commander-in-Chief Ceylon, had written of

> the vital importance of our recapturing those parts of the Empire as far as possible ourselves. I would specially mention the recapture of Burma and its culmination in the recovery of Singapore by force of arms and not by waiting for it to be surrendered as part of any peace treaty...the immense effect this will have on our prestige in the Far East in post-war years. This and only this in my opinion will restore us to our former level in the eyes of the native population in these parts.

Admiral Louis Mountbatten, Supreme Commander of South-East Asia Command, strongly agreed.[16]

In the event, Operation Zipper, an amphibious invasion of western Malaya, was planned for 9 September 1945. It would prob-ably have led to heavy casualties, both British and Japanese, but was made unnecessary by the Japanese surrender.

## China and Indo-China

In China, in one of the largely forgotten campaigns of the war, the Japanese had resumed the offensive. In February, they captured the railway line from Canton to Hanyang, increasing the depth and logistical strength of their position in southern China, while, the following month, they advanced further north towards the American airbases at Laohokow (which fell on 8 April) and Ankang, only being halted by a counterattack on 19 April. Another counterattack, on 8 May, blocked an advance on the airbase of Chihkiang, and this battle near Changteh helped persuade the Japanese to pull back in south China. The Japanese also succeeded in increasing their power in

French Indo-China. Aware that the French colonial administration was increasingly moving towards resistance, and concerned about American intervention, the Japanese overcame the French garrisons in March 1945, and persuaded the Emperor of Annam (for the whole of Vietnam) and the kings of Cambodia and Laos to declare independence.

## Australian attacks

Japan still held much of its empire at the close of the war, although Australian forces had mounted a series of amphibious attacks on the island of Borneo in May–July against very varied opposition. Their target was the oilfields near Tarakan and Balipapan and in Brunei, seized on 1 May, 10 June and 1 July, respectively. As the Japanese were no longer able to transport oil from Borneo to Japan, its value to them was limited, and there was subsequently to be criticism in Australia of the wastefulness of the attacks, but had the war continued it would have proved useful to the Allies.

In addition, the campaign enabled the Australians to indicate their continued importance to the Allied war effort. Indeed the war ended with a much closer strategic relationship between the USA and Australia. British influence had receded. In 1951, Australia and New Zealand were independently to enter into a defence pact with the USA (ANZUS). Similarly, the reliance, in the last stage of the war in Luzon, on Filipino units to bear much of the brunt of the conflict, while American troops were withdrawn to prepare for the invasion of Japan, helped look towards the granting of independence of the Philippines in 1946.

## The Soviet–Japanese war of 1945

On 8 August 1945, two days after the first atom bomb was dropped on Hiroshima, the Soviet Union declared war on Japan and invaded Manchuria, as Stalin had promised, at the Yalta Conference that February, to do three months after the war in Europe had ended. The Japanese were outnumbered in Manchuria, particularly in artillery, tanks and aircraft, and they were also outfought. The Soviet forces were better trained and many had had combat experience in

Europe. Aided by skilful deception techniques, they seized the initiative and advanced rapidly to envelop their opponents. Soviet armoured columns concentrated on advancing through the Greater Khingan Range of mountains, where the Japanese were weakly deployed. Their campaign bridged aspects of German *Blitzkrieg* with Soviet Cold War plans for invasions of Western Europe. While the forces of the Trans-Baikal Front crossed the Greater Khingan Range, invading Manchuria from the west, the First Far Eastern Front advanced from near Vladivostok, driving on Harbin. In contrast, the units and commanders from the Far East, who had not seen recent combat and were deployed in the Second Far Eastern Front to the north of Manchuria, operated in a more cautious fashion.

Thanks to the wartime build-up in military preparedness, the Soviets had far more weapons than the Germans had had in 1940 when they attacked France: they deployed 1.5 million troops, 4,370 aeroplanes, 5,500 tanks and 28,000 pieces of artillery. In contrast, the Japanese had 267,000 troops, with another 243,000 in reserve, but very few weapons, including only 50 frontline aircraft. The Japanese forces lacked combat experience and were deficient in mobility, firepower and communications.

The Japanese fought tenaciously in Manchuria, although their planning was disorientated by the speed of the Soviet advance. The Japanese had failed to appreciate the advances the Soviets had made in 1943–5 in developing and sustaining 'deep operations'. In particular, the Japanese underrated Soviet mobility and inaccurately assumed that the Soviets would need to stop for re-supply after about 250 miles, providing the Japanese with an opportunity to respond to the Soviet advance. The Soviets, in fact, were able to maintain the pace of advance. The Japanese used the suicide tactics already seen by the Western Allies. Soldiers carrying explosives detonated them against tanks. Fighting fiercely in defence, the Japanese also launched bitter counterattacks. Their resistance was, however, greatly affected by the announcement, on 14 August, of the Japanese surrender. The commanders in Manchuria decided to go on fighting, but, on 17 August, a direct order from the emperor ensured compliance.

The confusion in the Japanese response from 14 August had helped the Soviets to make further advances. They increased the pace of their operations, using airborne detachments to seize important cities and airfields, and pushing forward their tanks, many of which were refuelled by air. A tank force that had crossed the Gobi Desert joined up with Chinese Communist forces near Beijing. Harbin and Shenyang (Mukden) fell on 20 August and Liaodong (Port Arthur) two days later. Over 0.5 million Japanese troops and civilians captured in 1945 were sent to camps in Eastern Siberia, where more than 60,000 died in the harsh Arctic conditions. More than 80,000 Japanese troops had been killed fighting in Manchuria. In comparison the Soviets lost 8,219 dead and 22,264 wounded.

The Soviet offensive included an advance overland, from 12 August, into north Korea as far as the 38$^{th}$ Parallel, supported by amphibious operations, as well as the conquest of southern Sakhalin and the Kurile Islands, both of which indicated Soviet amphibious capability. Southern Sakhalin was invaded both overland and by amphibious forces. Most of the Kuriles were invaded from the north but the southernmost ones were occupied by troops that had been involved in the Sakhalin operation. On the island of Shimushu in the Kuriles, the Japanese used the tactics they had displayed in the Pacific against the Americans. The rest of the group fell after the Japanese surrender, although, there and elsewhere, some groups continued to resist – in Manchuria and the Kuriles until 1 September. The following day, the Japanese signed the surrender document on board the American battleship *Missouri*, which was appropriately moored in Tokyo Bay. American occupation troops had started to land from 28 August.

The Manchuria campaign was as much part of the early stages of the Cold War as of the close of World War Two, although General Patton was regarded as premature when he made clear his support for the maintenance of German military capacity as a future aid against the Soviets. The Soviet advance weakened the American position in East Asia and, in particular, helped ensure that the USA would be unable to determine the future of China. To match the Soviet invasion of north Korea, the Americans landed troops from Okinawa on 8 September and occupied the south. Stalin was trying to ensure that the Soviet Union was best placed for what he saw as a future confrontation with Western capitalism. Already, in mid-1944, planners for the British Chiefs of Staff had suggested a post-war reform of Germany and Japan, so that they could play a role against a Soviet Union whose ambitions in Eastern Europe were arousing growing concern. The following May, Penney noted the claim that the USA and Britain wished to build up Japan as a bulwark against the Soviet Union, with whom they would be at war relatively soon.[17] Differences over the future of Poland had proved a particular source of tension in Allied diplomacy. These and other differences had had a major impact on debates about strategy. Churchill's support for operations in the Balkans owed much to a wish to pre-empt a Soviet advance there. He had failed to prevail with the Americans. They were clearly taking the leading role in the Western Alliance, and this affected the choice of military and political strategies. Brooke had commented in August 1944:

> the Americans now feel that they possess the major forces at sea, on land and in the air, in addition to all the vast financial and industrial advantages which they have had from the start. In addition they now look upon themselves no longer as the apprentices at war, but on the contrary as full blown professionals. As a result of all this they are determined to have an ever increasing share in the running of the war in all its aspects.[18]

America was even more to take the lead in resisting Communism in the Cold War.

## NOTES

1 C. Duffy, *Red Storm on the Reich* (1991); T. Le Tissier, *Zhukov at the Oder: The Decisive Battle for Berlin* (Westport, Connecticut, 1996) and *Race for the Reichstag* (1999).

2 M. Reynolds, *Men of Steel: The Ardennes and Eastern Europe 1944–45* (Staplehurst, 1999).

3 K. Hechler, *The Bridge at Remagen* (New York, 1957).

4 P. Allen, *One More River: The Rhine Crossings of 1945* (1980).

5 The decision is defended in S.E. Ambrose, *Eisenhower and Berlin, 1945: The Decision to Halt at the Elbe* (New York, 1967).

6 H. Essame, *The Battle for Germany* (1969); C.B. MacDonald, *The Last Offensive* (1973).

7 C.F. Brower (ed.), *World War II in Europe: The Final Year* (1998).

8 I. Gow, *Okinara, 1945: Gateway to Japan* (New York, 1985); C.H. Yahara, *The Battle for Okinawa* (New York, 1995).

9  J. Winton, *The Forgotten Fleet* (1970); D. Brown (ed.), *The British Pacific and East Indies Fleets* (Liverpool, 1995).

10  K.P. Werrell, *Blankets of Fire: U.S. Bombers over Japan during World War II* (Washington, 1996).

11  H. Feis, *The Atomic Bomb and the End of World War II* (Princeton, 1966); R.B. Frank, *Downfall: The End of the Imperial Japanese Empire* (New York, 1999).

12  Penney to Sinclair, 2 May 1945, LH. Penney 5/1.

13  G. Feifer, *Tennozan: The Battle of Okinawa and the Atomic Bomb* (New York, 1992); J.R. Skates, *The Invasion of Japan: Alternative to the Bomb* (Columbia, South Carolina, 1994), esp. pp. 254–7.

14  D. McCullough, *Truman* (New York, 1992), p. 458.

15  M. Walker, *German National Socialism and the Quest for Nuclear Power, 1939–1945* (New York, 1989).

16  Layton to First Sea Lord, 13 September, Mountbatten to Layton, 15 September 1944, BL. Add. 74796.

17  Penney to Sinclair, 2 May 1945, LH. Penney 5/1.

18  Brooke to Sir Henry Wilson, Allied Commander in Chief in the Mediterranean, 2 August 1944, LH. Alanbrooke 6/3/6.

# CHAPTER EIGHT

# *Contexts*

The coming of a second world war, more global in its scope than the first, gave a renewed boost to the role of states and the mobilisation of governments. The mobilisation of national resources led among the combatants to state direction of much of the economy, although the effectiveness of this varied. It was necessary to produce formidable amounts of equipment, to raise, train, clothe and equip large numbers of men, as well as considerable, though smaller, numbers of women, to fill their places in the workforce, and to increase the scale and flexibility of the economy. In the non-totalitarian societies, free trade and largely unregulated industrial production were both brought under state direction. Economic regulation and conscription were introduced more rapidly and comprehensively than in World War One. The experience of state intervention in that conflict ensured that it was more effective in World War Two. Yet greater 'effectiveness' was frequently oppressive, and is, anyway, difficult to assess.

## A global war

One aspect of effectiveness reflected the more widespread nature of World War Two, although many of the states that declared war on Germany only played a modest role in the conflict. Most of these states were in Latin America, where entry into the war reflected American influence in the region. This was readily apparent in December 1941. The USA declared war on Germany on 11 December, as did Cuba, the Dominican Republic, Guatemala,

Nicaragua and Haiti; Honduras and Salvador following next day, and Panama, Mexico and Brazil in 1942. The entry of the last owed much to German attacks on Brazilian shipping. Other states delayed, Bolivia and Colombia until 1943, and Ecuador, Paraguay, Peru, Uruguay, Venezuela, Chile and Argentina until 1945. Other late entrants were Liberia in 1944, and Saudi Arabia and Turkey in 1945.

Of these states, Brazil played the biggest combat role, sending 25,000 troops to Italy. Brazil, the most strategic of the South American states, also played an important role in operations against U-boats in the South Atlantic, and was the recipient of three-quarters of the American Lend–Lease aid to Latin America. Mexico sent units to the Philippines in 1944, and, in addition, about 0.25 million Mexicans served in the American military.[1] However, other states still played an important role by providing raw materials, such as oil from Venezuela, as well as air and naval bases, and by allowing use of their air space. New airbases were developed by, and for, the Americans in Cuba, the Dominican Republic, Haiti and Panama. These bases were used to oppose the destructive U-boat campaign in the Caribbean, which began in February 1942, as well as against U-boat operations in the Atlantic. The war was important to Latin America for economic development, especially in industry, for the lessening of European (largely British) economic influence, and for the revival in raw material exports, as wartime demands brought a revival after the 1930s Depression.

Latin America was not the only region distant from the centres of conflict to feel the impact of the war. In the Arctic, the quest for meteorological information that would be of value in particular for air operations over Europe led to the establishment of German weather stations in Greenland, Labrador and Spitzbergen. When found, these were the subject of successful Allied attacks, for example in Spitzbergen in 1941 and 1942 and Greenland in 1944

Round the Pacific and the Indian Ocean, the entry of Japan into the war in 1941 ensured that areas that had not had to fear invasion in World War One, especially Australia, Canada, India, New Zealand and the USA, had to take defensive precautions. Coastal defences were erected, for example on the coasts of Australia and New Zealand, while large numbers of inhabitants of Japanese descent were interned because of suspicions about their loyalty. All 23,000

Japanese-Canadians in British Columbia were forced to move from the coast, while over 110,000 Japanese-Americans from the three Pacific coast states were interned. These suspicions were mistaken, but reflected a widespread concern about a recently coined term, 'fifth columns'. It was believed that the Axis powers made use of sympathisers to engage in sabotage, as well as to demoralise the population, and this concern was heightened after the collapse of France in 1940. The consequent reaction to those termed enemy aliens was an aspect of the total warfare of the period and of the extension of governmental controls that was readily adopted.

Fears of invasion brought home the war even more directly than the losses of men on distant battlefields also seen in World War One. In 1942, the pace of the Japanese advance, and its extent, which included the bombing of Darwin and the seizure of some of the Aleutian Islands off Alaska in June, led to anxiety and alarmism on both the West Coast of the USA and in Australasia that had a potent psychological impact. Fear and paranoia helped lead to hatred.

## German ideology and brutality

For Hitler, peace and war were part of the same process, and the peacetime years had seen an active moulding of society to further the goals of conflict. Nevertheless, much of the German economy was not geared for war until conflict began. An extensive conversion of industrial capacity began with the outbreak of hostilities, as the Germans tried to mobilise their massive industrial base for a long period of fighting. However, they faced many difficulties, not least too many competing agencies being involved, particularly in 1939–41. Their highest level of armament production did not come until September 1944, towards the close of the war. This was despite devastating Allied bombing, but reflected the time it took for the rationalisation plans of Albert Speer, who had been appointed Minister for Armaments and Munitions in February 1942, to come to fruition.

Once the Soviet Union had been invaded in 1941, the conflict was more stridently presented within Germany as a people's struggle, and one that was seen in millenarian terms as a fight for racial mastery and a contest of wills. This helped ensure that Nazi ideology was at the centre of the military struggle and also influenced the way in which the war was waged, particularly the brutality shown to Russians and in occupied areas in Eastern Europe.

The major role of the SS in creating élite military units – the Waffen-SS – indicated the close relationship between ideology and the German war effort. Over 800,000 men served in the Waffen-SS, and it became an important part of Germany's fighting forces, serving under the operational command of the army, although it was a separate structure, and the role of the army in recruitment within Germany ensured that much of the Waffen-SS, especially from 1943, was recruited from non-Germans.[2] Attempts have been made to argue that Nazi influence was largely restricted to SS units, and that the professionalism of the rest of the military kept ideological factors at bay. It has also been suggested that the combat units of the Waffen-SS did not share in the brutality displayed by other SS units in the occupied countries.

These arguments continue to be pushed hard, and have been seen by some commentators as an attempt to rehabilitate the German war effort. Sensitivity about this became especially acute at the close of the 1990s and the beginning of the 2000s, with claims that the Germans were moving away from the earlier recognition of the malign nature of their wartime conduct. This was linked to political factors, with Edmond Stoibl, the unsuccessful Christian Democratic candidate for the German Chancellorship in 2002, being seen as a defender of the reputation of the *Wehrmacht* and an exponent of reparations for the Sudeten Germans who were driven from Czechoslovakia after Germany's defeat in 1945.

The attempt to rehabilitate the wartime conduct of the Waffen-SS[3] and of the German military is unconvincing; and the same is true for the brutal Japanese military, which treated prisoners and civilians alike in a callous and cruel fashion. Operation Barbarossa in 1941 was accompanied by the instruction to execute all political commissars with the Red Army and by a decree that promised soldiers exemption from prosecution if they were responsible for crimes against civilians. Many German commanders issued orders calling on their troops to annihilate Hitler's targets. Hitler was committed to a total reordering of the Soviet Union, including a demographic revolution of slaughter and widespread resettlement, and a widespread change to Soviet geography. Leningrad and Moscow were to be destroyed and new German-populated settlements created. The genocidal treatment of the Jews from 1941 was not an exception, but rather the culmination of a totalising ideological militarism. This had implications not only for the conduct of the war by the Germans, but also for the home front; although conscription lessened the distinction between the two. The brutality shown to those judged unacceptable within Germany and the harsh treatment of dissidents were regarded not only as necessary but also as part of the Nazi mission.[4] Much of the German navy, especially the submarine service, also provided eager support for Nazi attitudes and policies.[5]

Brutalisation extended to the military. Whereas, in World War One, the Germans had officially executed 48 of their soldiers, in World War Two nearly 20,000 were executed for desertion alone. The Soviet Union treated its soldiers with even greater brutality. The extent to which this helped maintain cohesion and fighting quality among troops with low morale is open to debate. In practice, brutality reflected the character of the regime. The Soviet Union also executed unsuccessful generals. 'Punishment units' were employed in particularly dangerous attacks, and they suffered very high rates of casualties. The Western Allies followed a very different regime, and this was also seen in contrasting attitudes towards prisoners of war.

Troops, as well as civilians, also responded to the new circumstances of war, particularly the role of air power. Some Allied aircrew that parachuted from damaged planes over Germany were lynched by civilians. In April 1943, Penney recorded lunch with Lieutenant-General Carl Spaatz, the American commander of the Allied North Africa Air Forces:

> Discussion arose on rights or wrongs of shooting men who had baled out of aircraft and are on their way to earth or sea. Spaatz had heard that his boys had started it the day before in the Straits chiefly owing to a report that they had received that the Boche thought them soft and squeamish. Mary C.'s [Air Vice-Marshal 'Maori' Coningham, Commander of the Desert Air Force] views were that the Boche did it regularly, ethics did not arise and we should do

it if the pilots etc. were going to fall into their own lines or into the sea ie. anywhere where they were not going to be eliminated as far as further flying was concerned. Spaatz and Kueter not so sure, again not on ethical grounds but on danger of diverting aircraft from their proper mission in order to protect their own pals who had taken to their parachutes. I always thought that there was some understanding that once in a parachute drop you were immune. Entirely illogical and inconsistent with total war. Same applied to American slaughter of Jap. [*sic*] soldiers in the sea after sinking the big convoy in the Solomons area.[6]

## Resistance

The German and Japanese treatment of occupied areas testified to the character of the total war and, in turn, affected the course of the conflict; although there were important variations in occupation practice. These reflected the geopolitical and ethnic considerations that affected the details of Axis policy, as well as the contrast between civil and military occupation, and variations within both. Allowing for this, much of the civilian population was treated harshly, and large numbers with great cruelty.

Brutalised, many of the defeated were not prepared to accept the verdict of battle, so that German and Japanese occupation practices encouraged resistance, particularly, in the case of the Germans, in the Soviet Union, where, initially, there had been only limited popular resistance and, instead, a willingness to see if the unpopular Communist regime collapsed and if the replacement was any better. However, the genocidal thrust of German policy affected regular army as well as SS units, leading to a war of annihilation in which killing became an end in itself. Largely as a result, civilian casualties were higher in the Soviet Union than in any other country.[7] The Italians were less brutal in the Balkans than the Germans.

The Soviets had not prepared for partisan warfare, partly because of confidence in their military and its ability to defend the Soviet Union, and partly because of suspicion of the idea of the nation in arms: people's warfare was associated with Stalin's former rival, Leon Trotsky, who was assassinated by a Soviet agent in Mexico in 1940.

Once the Germans had invaded, there was confusion about how best to organise and control partisan activity, and the rapidity of the German advance made it difficult to organise a response. In contrast, thanks to their experience of resisting the Kuomintang government, the Chinese Communists were better prepared for guerrilla opposition, although a rigorous study of their effectiveness has not been encouraged by subsequent myth-making.

Eventually, there was a high level of resistance activity directed against the Germans and their local allies across much of Europe; as well as against the Japanese, particularly across much of China. Much resistance was passive, particularly the evasion of regulations, and this had serious consequences for the effectiveness of the Axis war economy. There was also active resistance. Some was non-violent, for example strikes and demonstrations. Thus, in 1944, a Dutch railway strike was timed to help Operation Market-Garden.

There was also violent resistance. In Poland and occupied areas of the Soviet Union, there was extensive partisan activity, helped by the vastness of the area in question, the difficult nature of the terrain – for example the Pripet Marshes – and the harshness of German rule. The history of this resistance was for long complicated by its role in the mythic presentation of the war. Communist scholars emphasised the extent of popular participation in resistance and the central role of the Communist Party, and neglected differences within the resistance and the degree to which large sections of the population did not offer support.[8]

More recently, different perspectives have been offered.[9] Most of the early partisans were, indeed, Communist Party or Communist Youth League members, but many were ineffective. Indeed the search for supplies played a central role in their activity. Furthermore, many partisans deserted. Some early partisan opposition came from units of the Red Army that had been cut off by the German advance, and from units from the People's Commissariat of Internal Affairs (NKVD, secret police), but, with time, partisan support became far more widespread. On 3 July 1941, Stalin ordered guerrilla activity when he proclaimed a 'patriotic war' against the Germans. The winter counter-offensive proved more effective in rallying support as it showed that German victory was not inevitable. There was also a marked increase in partisan activity from

August 1942, particularly in attacks on trains in White Russia and the Bryansk Forest. Increasingly, partisan groups acted in large units, moving from base areas in order to mount raids. This helped to spread the impact of opposition from the forested and swamp areas, where it was strong, to others, such as southern Ukraine, where the natural cover and political circumstances were less supportive.[10]

Terrain and natural cover were not only a factor in Eastern Europe and in the Japanese empire. In France, they also helped account for variations in resistance activity, with, for example, less in the flat and well-cultivated Loire Valley than in the Massif Central.[11] However, other factors also played a role. The discouraging nature of reprisals, particularly the shooting of large numbers of civilians when German troops were killed, was important, but so also were the detailed configuration of local politics and society and its relationship with the complex dynamic of collaboration and resistance. In France, Vichy enjoyed more support than it would subsequently be prudent to note, while there was also a concern with the immediate needs of family and community that discouraged resistance. There was a willingness as well as a need to negotiate relations with the German occupiers, and, as long as armed resistance was avoided, this was possible for French communities; although Jews were often the victims of this process.[12]

Where it occurred, partisan activity contributed to the sense of the alien character of the occupied territories. This particularly affected the Germans in Eastern Europe and the Japanese in China, because of their vastness, the strength of prior racial indoctrination and attitudes and the intractable nature of opposition. These all contributed to the brutality of German rule and the savage response to resistance, although it would be misleading to suggest that partisan activity was responsible for harsh rule: from the outset, the Germans had a set of beliefs, attitudes and policies that contributed to this. However, a sense of disorientation, perhaps alienation, among ordinary soldiers contributed to their implementation of such attitudes. At the same time, not all German troops and officials responded in this fashion, and most who did not comply were not punished. This variety in response highlights the issue of individual responsibility and removes from the guilty the argument that they were in some way passive victims of an all-powerful system and ideology.

Partisan activity in some countries was lessened by serious rivalries. In western White Russia, there was rivalry between Polish and Soviet partisans, and this was an aspect of a more widespread tension within areas that had been part of the Soviet Union but which contained large numbers of non-Russians. Ethnicity was very important to the detailed configuration of local politics and society. The Germans won some support among Russians and even more among non-Russians, particularly in Ukraine.[13] Indeed, resistance to the reintroduction of Soviet rule continued there long after the German collapse. In Vilnius, which had been part of Poland in 1922–39, the unit of the Polish Home Army that had played a major part in freeing the city in July 1944 was sent to a Soviet Gulag (slave labour camp). Some, who were able to resist, fought back. In Yugoslavia, the Communists, led by Josip Tito, competed with the Chetniks under Dragoljub Mihailović, with a full-scale civil war breaking out in November 1942.[14] Resistance groups also fought each other in China, Albania and Greece. Again, political rivalries between Communists and conservative nationalists were crucial.

The situation in the Balkans (as indeed in China) was made more complex by frequently ambivalent relations between sections of the resistance and the occupying power. This was accentuated by the reliance of the Germans on local allies and of the Japanese on de facto truces. In France, there were major divisions among the resistance, including, although not only, between the Communists and Charles de Gaulle's Free French; and these overlapped with variations in attitudes towards Vichy and the Germans.[15]

These differences complicated the task of foreign assistance, although less in France than in the Balkans. The British established the Special Operations Executive (SOE) in July 1940 in order to help resistance, and it made a major contribution in France and the Balkans, although in the Netherlands the success of German counter-intelligence thwarted SOE efforts. Aside from intelligence and sabotage operations, the SOE and its supporting special-duty air squadrons delivered close to 0.5 million small arms to the French resistance.[16]

As the Germans withdrew from the Balkans in 1944, conflicts within the resistance became more apparent, particularly in Greece. The difficulty of operating against resistance groups was recalled by a signaller who was among the British troops flown from Italy to Athens in December 1944 in order to contain ELAS, the left-wing Greek People's Army of Liberation:

> The enemy were just the same as any other Greeks as far as we knew, they didn't have any uniform as such.... It was a situation that was quite completely different to the way we had been used to fighting.... As an average infantryman, one of the first questions that you ask is 'Which way is the front?' So that you know if the worst comes to the worst which way you can go to get out of the bloody place. In this sort of situation, which is a typical urban 'battlefront', it's all around you.[17]

British intervention prevented ELAS from seizing Athens, but the conflict between ELAS and Royalist forces spilled over into the post-war Greek Civil War. In Greece, as in many other areas, there was no clear division between the war and the post-war world. The role of the Communists in the resistance owed much to their earlier organisational strength and, in some countries, to their experience of acting as a banned movement.

The resistance to German occupation across Europe was hit by the scale, energy and brutality of the German response. The Germans were deliberately brutal. Thus the mortal wounding, by Czech agents trained by the SOE, in Prague, on 27 May 1942, of Reinhard Heydrich, the Deputy Head of the SS, who had become Reichsprotektor of Bohemia and Moravia in September 1941, led rapidly to the execution of 2,000 Czechs, and, after Heydrich's funeral, Hitler ordered the wiping out of a community in order to teach the Czechs subservience. The village of Lidice was selected, all the men were shot, the women were sent to concentration camps and the children either gassed or selected for Germanisation. Even the dogs were shot. The village was burned down and bulldozed. The Germans made no effort to conceal the act. They saw it as an exemplary act designed to teach obedience, and carefully filmed their activities.

The better-armed Germans were generally able to defeat partisans in open conflict, as in the spring of 1942 when Stalin insisted that the partisans hold positions in the rear of Army Group Centre, or when the Germans suppressed major uprisings in Warsaw, Slovakia and the Vercors plateau in France, all in 1944. Partisan formations were vulnerable to German air power. In addition, the Germans were usually successful in maintaining control of their supply lines.

Large numbers of troops, however, had to be deployed in order to limit resistance operations or to prevent their possible outbreak, for example in the Bryansk Forest in early 1943; although, on the Eastern Front, frontline troops were rarely diverted to act against partisans. On 1 January 1944, German, Bulgarian and quisling (local allied) forces in Yugoslavia amounted to 360,000 men. Most of those troops could not have been readily deployed on the Eastern Front, and the military value of allied forces was not, on the whole, very high. However, such forces were useful for occupation duties. Some German troops could have been freed for frontline tasks elsewhere had they not had to engage the resistance. In France, although the *Milice Française* was available, from January 1943, to help suppress opposition to Vichy, the Germans played the major role in opposing the resistance. 10,000 German troops suppressed the Free Republic of the Vercors on 19–22 July 1944.

Aside from the suppression of resistance, many areas under partisan control were so in part because the Germans and the Japanese chose not to deploy troops to occupy them. Nevertheless, the resistance still achieved much. Most important, as with the Allied air offensive, was the diversion of large amounts of German resources to dealing with the threat, as well as the need to adopt anti-partisan policies that affected the efficiency of German rule and of economic and transport activities. The Allies also benefited from large quantities of crucial intelligence, for example on defences, troop movements, bomb damage and the development of German rocketry. In addition, considerable damage and disruption were inflicted by sabotage and by guerrilla attacks. This was most useful when coordinated with Allied operations, such as in support of the Soviet offensive in early 1942 and in fighting near Kursk in 1943. In 1944, the cutting by partisans of transport links by which the Germans might move troops complemented the Allied air offensive in preparing for the Normandy landings by isolating forces in the area and making it difficult to move up reinforcements.[18]

Resistance also achieved the vital political goal of weakening collaboration and undermining co-existence. This isolated the German and Japanese (and allied) militaries, and also made the new order appear transient. Resistance activity reflected and contributed to the way in which the war affected the people of Europe. Denmark might have fallen to the Germans in a day, but that was not its wartime history. Instead, especially from 1943, thousands of attacks were launched by the resistance, hitting the rail system and tying up many German troops in defensive tasks. This changed Denmark 'from a German vassal state' into an active source of opposition to the Axis.[19] However, helped by the opportunities offered by the terrain, the Norwegian resistance was more effective both in causing damage and in tying up German forces: in response to the resistance, although far more to the apparent threat of British invasion, the occupation force was over 200,000 strong.

Resistance to Japanese occupation varied in response to the configuration of local politics. The Western colonial powers had enjoyed only limited popular support, and resistance to Japanese rule appears to have been far higher in China. Nevertheless, despite Japanese attempts to win support by creating puppet regimes and appealing to anti-Western nationalism, for example in the Dutch East Indies, the harshness of their rule compromised support, and this harshness was exacerbated as the Japanese military situation deteriorated, a deterioration that, in turn, also compromised support. Thus, in the Philippines, resistance by American and Filipino troops who had not been captured in 1942 was supported by civilians alienated by Japanese occupation practices. Outside China, this was the most prominent guerrilla movement against the Japanese,[20] although the British-backed guerrillas in the Karen Hills of Burma proved an important aid in the closing stage of the war.

The Allies made efforts to stir up resistance and to organise sabotage in Japanese-occupied areas; but the task was more difficult than in Europe, in part because of the distances involved and resulting logistical problems, but, in large part, because there was no equivalent to the governments-in-exile and popular resistance movements from which they benefited in Europe. Nevertheless, SOE, the American Office of Strategic Services, and Special Operations Australia supported guerrilla operations, for example by the Malayan People's

Anti-Japanese Army.[21] In China, much of the resistance was organised by the Communists. For the Allies, against both Germany and Japan, there was a tension between intelligence gathering and sabotage.

The Germans and Japanese were far less successful in developing resistance movements as the Allies advanced. The speed of the Nazi collapse and the movement's dependence on Hitler were crucial, but so also was the absence of unoccupied bases from which resistance could be encouraged and supplied. Nevertheless, the Werewolf movement did inflict some damage in 1945–6, killing a few officials who co-operated with the Allies, particularly the Mayor of Aachen, as well as some Allied officials and troops.[22] A far more sustained resistance was mounted to the imposition and subsequent brutalities of Soviet rule in Ukraine, especially western Ukraine, and the former Baltic republics. Its suppression took years, involved large numbers of troops and also much harshness, including the deportation of large numbers of people from the western Ukraine. The emperor's surrender in Japan ensured that there was no resistance to occupation there.

## The German war economy

The degree of resistance to German control in occupied Europe was, in part, an aspect of the way in which German policy helped threaten its resource base. The cruel nature of German control dissipated support and encouraged labour non-cooperation. Rather than mobilising female labour in Germany thoroughly, and in response to the use of much of their young adult male population in the military and to high casualty levels on the Eastern Front, the Germans preferred to use slave labour – an inefficient, as well as a cruel, policy. Millions of foreign workers, especially Soviet, Polish and French, were brought to Germany, while, elsewhere in occupied Europe, workers were forced to work in often brutal conditions in order to produce resources for Germany. The need for the labour of prisoners led the Germans to cease being so murderous to Soviet prisoners in October 1941, although their working conditions, which, from 1944, included less than 1,000 calories of food daily, were such as to lead to high death rates. Aside from prisoners of war, 5.7 million foreign workers were registered in the Greater German

Reich in August 1944; combined with the prisoners of war, they provided half the workforce in agriculture and in the manufacture of munitions.[23] The deportation of workers to work in Germany met with evasion and opposition, as in Belgium, encouraged recruitment for the resistance, as in France, and further compromised the acceptability of German control and of collaborators, let alone the idea of a Nazi-led New Europe.

Regimes allied to Germany could not protect their citizens from conscription for such purposes, nor ensure that their resources were not expropriated for German ends. Although the degree and type of exploitation across occupied and allied Europe varied in accordance with German policy, Nazi ideology and Hitler's personal interventions, there was a common experience not just of exploitation but also of a degree of helplessness in influencing or restraining the frequently arbitrary nature of demands. This situation deteriorated further, as German demands rose after it became clear that Barbarossa had led not to a swift victory but, instead, to an intractable commitment to a conflict on a far larger scale. As a result, the appeal of co-operation with Germany declined, although an understandable reluctance to trust Stalin restricted the options available to collaborators in Eastern Europe.

The use of slave workers was not a way to ensure labour commitment or efficiency. Furthermore, the horrendous programmes of genocide pursued by the Germans absorbed revenues that might otherwise have been devoted to the war. Thus, trains were used to transport victims to the concentration camps, rather than to move military supplies. This was an aspect of the preference for ideology over practicality.

Although the Germans were quite happy to use the forced labour of non-German women, Hitler was reluctant to conscript women for the industrial workforce. His conservative social politics led him to see German women as wives and mothers. The conservatism of the Nazi regime was taken further in the allied and puppet regimes. These, for example Slovakia under Monseigneur Tiso, Hungary under Admiral Horthy, Romania under General Antonescu and Vichy France under Marshal Pétain, drew on conservative elements that sought as little change as possible, and their social politics did not lend themselves to an effective gearing of the state for war.

Hitler's attitude towards work by women was but part of the more wide-ranging failure of the Axis powers to mobilise their resources, a failure that owed much to the social assumptions of their leaderships and to their mistaken expectation of a speedy victory. Göring proved incompetent in his direction of economic planning in 1936–8, and serious inefficiencies in munitions production continued, although there was considerable improvement from 1941 and, even more, 1942, as Speer sought to introduce greater coordination between companies in order to ensure that weapons production was facilitated. In April 1942, Speer established a Board for Central Planning, designed to provide central control over the use of raw materials. Despite Allied air attacks, armament production rose markedly until the summer of 1944 (and tank production continued to rise until January 1945), but the weakness of government direction was still a factor, and, more generally, 'the economy failed to rise to the challenge of a large-scale war as it did in Britain, the United States and Russia'.[24] For example, Daimler-Benz, a major company, was unwilling to commit itself too heavily to armament production before or during the war, as the conflict would lead to victory, or, later, defeat, and, in either case, it was necessary for the company to plan for peace.[25] Soviet manufacturing units were under greater government control.

The Germans also failed to exploit mass-production techniques as successfully as their opponents, because they put a premium on responding to military requests for custom-made weapons, rather than on mass production of a more limited range of weapons. Thus, there was a large number of models of tanks, and their parts were not all mutually compatible, a situation that made maintenance difficult. This was further exacerbated by the development of self-propelled guns and their use alongside tanks. The German attitude towards the standardisation of weapon types reflected a military culture that emphasised duty and tactics, not logistics (nor indeed intelligence), a political culture in which there was a reluctance to understand the exigencies and potential of the economy, and a simple expectation that it would produce resources as required, without consultation, and to order.

The Germans were also fascinated with potent weapons – moving towards bigger and bigger tanks and guns – rather than with weapons that were less effective individually but easier to produce in massive quantities. The complexity of German weaponry often precluded simple field repairs and elementary servicing by untrained staff, whereas both were possible with Soviet tanks. The limitations in the mechanisation of the German army arose in part from the same problem, although there was the more general issue of an industrial base that was small compared to that of the USA. The Germans had mechanised key units, which were designed to act as the apex of *Blitzkrieg*, but this led to an army that was unbalanced, with most units obliged to rely on horses.[26] Such a force structure was a particular weakness when the army was on the defensive and its opponents could choose where to attack.

In addition, Hitler's interventions in the allocation of resources for weapons production and, subsequently, in the use of weapons, were frequently deleterious, and in keeping with his naivety and failure as a strategist. He squandered the German lead in jet-powered aircraft, ordering that the Me-262 should not be used as an interceptor of Allied bombers, despite its effectiveness in the role; although there were also serious difficulties with the plane's engines. Hitler was convinced that, late in the war, Germany would suddenly produce a wonder weapon that would win the war; such a weapon existed in the atom bomb, but Germany missed the chance of developing it.

Aside from weaponry issues, there were also serious organisational deficiencies stemming from Hitler's intervention. In particular, the building up of SS military units, from 1942, hit the provision of equipment, particularly tanks, for the army; as, to a lesser extent, did the creation of *Luftwaffe* field divisions. Hitler's distrust of the army led him to place too little reliance on experienced commanders and expert advice. Most SS generals were unable to provide this.

The Todt Organisation was another aspect of the personalised institutional politics, ambitious policymaking and cruelty of the Nazi regime. Developed by Fritz Todt (1892–1942), an architect and engineer who was close to Hitler and, in 1940, became Minister of Weapons and Munitions, this Nazi body was responsible for a massive construction policy that included the *Westwall*, built from 1938 to deter Allied attack while Hitler conquered Poland. Other works included the Atlantic Wall, begun in 1942 and intended to resist Allied invasion, submarine pens, airfields, and repairing and improving transport links. At the same time, most of the workers were malnourished prisoners of war or forced labour, while the organisation was used against partisans and, in late 1944, was armed for the defence of Germany. Vast quantities of concrete were poured in the cause of *Festung Europa* (Fortress Europe), a German phrase, used from 1942, that testified to an ability to create a major system of fortifications, although, in the event, it was rapidly breached by Allied air and land forces.

However inefficient, the German regime was able to direct and enforce a major expansion in the war economy, and a devotion of activity and production to the war, with personal consumption levels pushed down below those in Britain and the USA, although, thanks to the exploitation of occupied areas, German living standards were supported by a multitude of transfer benefits, including food, draft horses and agricultural workers. Nazi Party members were the best fed. Similarly, rice consumption in Korea and the Philippines was pushed down in order to feed the Japanese. However, moving food and other supplies to Germany and Japan lessened support for them in occupied and allied areas, and increased resistance. The conscription of labour accentuated crises in food supply in occupied areas. In Vichy France, rationing became more severe, and the regime became associated with shortages, queuing and the black market: the daily bread ration was reduced from 350 grams per person from September 1940 to 275 grams from January 1942.

Starting from far weaker industrial bases, Italy and Japan were less able than Germany to create effective military-industrial supply systems that met their needs. This contributed to Italian failure and a general sense that the war had gone adrift.[27] Thus, the Italians were unable to sustain the relative air strength built up in the first decade and a half of the inter-war period because their industrial base lacked the ability to raise production as well as to keep pace with developments in aircraft technology. Much of the air force in 1940 was obsolete, and newer planes were less effective than their British counterparts. As a result, the arrival of the *Luftwaffe* units made a major difference to the air war in the Mediterranean. By using German engines, the Italians did begin to make effective fighters from 1941, but in insufficient numbers;[28] 1941 was the peak year for Italian aircraft manufacture, and in 1942 and early 1943 this fell markedly. There were problems with capital availability, expertise and production facilities.

The more serious Italian problems were strategic and operational, not least poor command on land and a failure to integrate land and sea forces. These, rather than the availability of weapons, led to their failures in East Africa and Libya, and the same was true in the Mediterranean, where the Italians were outfought, desptie their navy including a number of modern warships and submarines.

The deficiencies of the Japanese military-industrial system were cruelly exposed by conflict with the USA, particularly in terms of naval strength. Even without that, the Japanese army was characterised by inadequate equipment, not least a lack of mechanisation. Japan had inadequate resources and industrial capacity. This limited its ability to respond to the challenges of the war, not just in terms of production, but also in terms of developing effective new weaponry.[29]

Japan's economic base was far weaker than that of the USA, but considerably stronger than that of China. Far more of China's industrial infrastructure had been overrun than was the case for the Soviet Union, but, in addition, the pre-war Chinese economy was weak in many areas of industrial production. This ensured that China was dependent for advanced weaponry, such as modern aircraft, on American aid.

## The Soviet Union

The Allied response to the needs of war was more effective than that of the Axis, certainly as measured by aggregate production of weapons; although China was unable to manufacture much higher-level weaponry. Amongst the Allies, the Soviet system most closely approximated to that of Germany in its use of compulsion and coercion. Those deemed unacceptable within the Soviet Union, including peoples such as the Crimean Tatars, who were seen as insufficiently anti-German, if not collaborators, were harshly treated. The Gulags continued to be full of the victims of Stalin's terror, and they were used to help meet demands for forced labour. Slave labour in the Gulags involved possibly 10 per cent of the Soviet population in March 1939, and there were possibly about 1 million deaths per year in the Gulags during the war, although, both then and subsequently, the situation was kept secret. Conditions were very harsh, with beatings, starvation rations and the severe cold of the majority of the camps, many of which were in the harsh terrain of Siberia, particularly near Vorkuta and in the Kolyma valley. Fresh influxes of prisoners came from the territories occupied by the Soviet Union in 1939–40, especially Eastern Poland and the Baltic republics. Once the war was over, Soviet prisoners of war released from German camps were sent to forced-labour camps, as they were judged suspect. There was similar harsh treatment of those who had fought for the resistance: after the war, such independence was crime.

Labour discipline was part of a close control of the Soviet economy, particularly of industry and transport. This enabled the government to enforce considerable adaptability on both. From the late 1920s, the Soviets had developed industrial production and mining in, or east of, the Urals, which were beyond the range of German air attack. This looked back to a long tradition of production in the Urals that had been greatly encouraged in the early eighteenth century under Peter the Great, but was stepped up under Stalin, such that about one-third of Soviet coal, iron and steel production was there. The Ural metallurgical industry proved of particular importance during the war. Major new industrial capacity was also developed near Novosibirsk in south-western Siberia, and new plants were built in Soviet Central Asia. The movement east took industry closer to raw materials and energy infrastructure, but exacerbated the serious transport problems of the Soviet system. The evacuation of industrial plant from threatened areas was a formidable undertaking. It is claimed that it involved nearly 1.5 million railway wagons in the second half of 1941. This evacuation of plant, combined with destruction through war and scorched-earth policies, ensured that the Germans did not benefit in economic terms from their conquests to the degree they anticipated.

It was particularly in the Soviet Union that the mobilisation of resources involved a marked degree of direction of the economy, including all aspects of resource allocation and labour. Already an autocracy, the Soviet system sustained the war effort, despite the loss of many of its leading agricultural and industrial areas to German advances in 1941 and 1942. Indeed, although Soviet production statistics should only be used with care, in the first six months of the war, the Soviet economy lost areas producing 68 per cent of its iron, 63 per cent of its coal and 58 per cent of its steel; as well as 40 per cent of its farmland, including, in Ukraine, much of its most fertile area. These losses were accentuated by scorched-earth policies in areas that seemed vulnerable to German occupation. Combined, they were but part of the profound wartime disruption caused by unexpected invasion. In agriculture, the Soviets found it necessary to encourage individual enterprise, although the constraints of an auto-cratic system remained in place.

By the spring of 1942, the Soviets had regained pre-war produc-tion levels of weaponry, and thereafter it greatly increased. This ensured that German forces were outnumbered in every weapon type, and, increasingly, by enormous margins. The productivity of the Soviet system helped overcome the inherent limitations of a planned economy, especially under an authoritarian regime ruling in response to a mixture of ideology and paranoia. The Soviets proved particularly effective in the manufacture of artillery, tanks and ground-support planes, but was less effective in transport equipment, such as rolling stock and, even more, lorries (trucks), while strategic bombers and shipping were not Soviet priorities. As a result, *matériel* from the West, especially lorries, was of particular importance for Soviet logistics. The inefficiencies of the Soviet system, which included inadequate quality control and training in industry and poor maintenance in the military, however, exacerbated the difficul-ties created by conscripting skilled workers and by using unskilled workers in industry, to ensure high breakdown and replacement rates for weapons. More generally, the variability of such rates lessens the value of tables of weapons manufacture. As an example of the resources available to Soviet forces, the troops transferred from Europe to invade Manchuria in 1945 left their tanks behind and were equipped with new ones in Siberia, thus reducing transport burdens on the Trans-Siberian Railway and greatly speeding up the transfer, although there were bottlenecks at the depots because so many troops demanded tanks at once.

The build-up of the Soviet war economy had deleterious conse-quences after 1945, as this vested interest directly contributed to the large share of resources and investment directed to the military, and, thus, to the inability of the Soviet Union to satisfy consumer demands, particularly once post-war growth greatly slackened in the 1970s; although all government figures for Soviet economic performance are open to question.[30]

## The USA

Shifts in the distribution of manufacturing plant also played a role in the USA, but the character of industrial mobilisation was very different to the situation in the Soviet Union. In part, this was because the USA had not been invaded and subjected to the conquest of much of its industrial capacity, but there was also a very different political background. The dynamic of the American response relied on lightly regulated capitalism, not coercion. Having had cool relations with much of American business during the 1930s, President Roosevelt turned to them to create a war machine, a task that was doubly difficult because there had not been a military build-up in the 1930s comparable to that of the Axis powers. The American army was in a particularly poor state, and smaller in 1939 than that of Portugal, although Portugal had a larger overseas empire.

In 1939, Congress agreed a major increase in military expenditure. Part of this was directed at creating a larger manufacturing base for war material. The War Resources Board was established in 1939, in order to ready industry for a war footing, and the Office of Production Management under William Knudsen, head of the car manufacturer General Motors, followed in 1941. Turning to business for co-operation in rearmament led to a lack of coordination, and numerous failings in the quality of munitions were exposed by the Truman Commission in 1941; but this was rectified by the establishment of the Office of War Mobilisation in May 1943. Furthermore, the Americans benefited from their already-sophisticated economic infrastructure, which helped in the adaptation of the economy for war production.[31] Although care is needed before pushing any comparison, there is a parallel between the operational flexibility that the Americans frequently displayed in combat and that of their economy.

The USA surmounted the domestic divisions of the 1930s in order to create a productivity-orientated political consensus which brought great international strength. This consensus enabled America to go on holding elections, as the constitution decreed, including a presidential election in 1944 (in which Roosevelt won with 53.4 per cent of the popular vote). In contrast, there was no general election in Britain until after the war with Germany had ended; although by-elections did occur to fill vacancies in the House of Commons and these led to defeats for the government. As authoritarian regimes, the Soviet Union and the Axis regimes did not expose their governments to the scrutiny of the electorate. In America, the war did not see hard-fought adversarial politics, and there was no equivalent to the bitter divisions over policy seen on the Union side during the Civil War, not least in the 1864 election, or, later, during the Vietnam War. This reflected a far greater sense of outrage and unity of purpose; although it is important to note the continuation of party divisions and their linkage to questions of military policy. Thus, Roosevelt was bitterly criticised for the failure of preparation seen at Pearl Harbor.[32]

The resources, commitments and pretensions of the American federal government grew greatly during the war, and taxes and government expenditure both rose substantially. Government spending totalled $317 billion, and nearly 90 per cent of this was on the war. One consequence was a major growth of the federal capital, Washington, which developed as the government bureaucracy grew. The population there rose in response to the influx of federal workers. Many were women, who were employed as clerks, and the presence in the city of large numbers of young single women was typical of the extent to which the war had a widespread impact on detailed social patterns.

The development of Washington and the federal bureaucracy were aspects of a wartime expansion that continued into the post-war world, and serve as a reminder of the danger of treating the war years as separate to those of peace. The continuation of this expansion owed much to the Cold War with Communism, but there was also a clear contrast between the response to the Depression, which had led to much more modest expansion in government, and the marked expansion that resulted from World War Two. There was also a pronounced shift in authority and power from state to federal government.

In the USA, the attitude and techniques of the production line were focused on war and fuelled by massive capital investment and capacity expansion, as well as by a policy of keeping skilled workers at their jobs. The Americans produced formidable quantities of munitions – $186 billion worth – and an infrastructure to move them. Such production was necessary. Equipment was destroyed or broke down, while the rate of consumption of munitions was high: over 1 million tons of 105 mm ammunition was used in the battle for Okinawa; and, throughout the war, especially in the Philippines in 1944, American army operations in the Pacific were affected by problems in ammunition supply.[33]

Aircraft and ship productive capacity and production greatly increased. In 1941–5, the USA produced 297,000 aeroplanes and 86,000 tanks. The capability of the war economy was amply shown in shipbuilding, which was crucial to the global scope of Allied power and to operational capability. Most of the 42 million tons of shipping built by the Allies during the war was constructed by the Americans. The British shipbuilding industry was affected by German bombing, as well as by serious problems of resource supply and allocation, and the capacity for expansion was limited. The Soviet industry was badly affected by German occupation. Canadian production increased, but it was the Americans who were responsible not only for much of the new shipping but also for the rapid response to needs and for the expansion in types. Many of the new American vessels were Liberty ships, built often in as little as ten days, using prefabricated components on production lines. This was an aspect of the rapid design and production methods that characterised American weaponry development, as with the introduction of the bazooka. By March 1944, the USA was producing one aircraft every 294 seconds. All-welded ships replaced riveting, speeding up production.

In contrast, the Japanese made scant use of welding. Their shipbuilding industry also suffered from resource problems, including a lack of steel, poor plant and weak organisation, including an absence of standardisation. Despite losing oil tankers with a total tonnage of 1,421,000, mostly to German submarines, which inflicted particular damage to American inshore shipping on the Atlantic coast in the early months of the year, the tonnage of the American oil-tanker fleet rose from 4,268,000 tons in 1942 to 12,875,000 tons in 1945. The flexibility of American society helped directly: by 1944, 11.5 per cent of the workers in the shipbuilding industry were women. Shipbuilding capability also had a dramatic impact on the number of warships, and this was seen as very important. In 1944, Ismay wrote to Churchill:

> the war we have to wage against Japan is of an entirely new type. It is no mere clash of opposing fleets. Allied naval forces must be so strong in themselves, and so fully equipped to carry with them land and air forces, that they can overcome not only Japanese naval forces but also Japanese garrisons supported by shore-based air forces...the bigger the Allied fleet free to seek out the enemy, the better the chances of destroying the Japanese fleet.[34]

Between Pearl Harbor and the end of the war, no fewer than 18 fleet carriers, 86 light fleet or escort carriers, 8 battleships, 46 cruisers, 349 destroyers and 203 submarines were among the warships commissioned into the American navy.

As another example of the extent to which the war led to new demands, the American Army Map Service produced over 500 million maps, while, despite having its offices in Southampton badly bombed in 1940, the British Ordnance Survey produced about 300 million maps for the Allied war effort. Air power led to an enhanced demand for accurate maps, in order to plan and execute bombing and ground-support operations. There was a premium on cartographic expertise. Walter Ristow, Chief of the Map Division of the New York Public Library, became head of the Geography and Map Section of the New York Office of Military Intelligence, while Armin Lobeck, Professor of Geology at Columbia, produced maps and diagrams in preparation for Operation Torch.[35]

Industrial expansion affected American demographics and society. The populations of Washington, Oregon and, in particular, California, where many of the new American shipyards and aircraft factories were located, rose considerably, and the economy of California greatly changed. By the end of the war, 8 million Americans had moved permanently to different states, while large numbers had worked away from home for shorter periods. Some were African-Americans: about 700,000 African-American civilians left the South permanently, especially for California. The opportunities that war industrialisation provided for African-American workers helped loosen racial, as well as gender and social, relations. However, much segregation remained, and racial tension was exacerbated by housing shortages and volatility in the labour market that reflected migration. This led to serious outbreaks of violence, particularly in Detroit in June 1943 (but far from only there). Roosevelt responded by sending in federal troops.[36]

In the armed forces, the War Department was unwilling to establish racially-integrated military units, and there was opposition to using African Americans in combat roles or as officers. Most African Americans served in service roles, for example in aircraft maintenance or as mess men. These policies reflected racist attitudes that were weakened as the need for more combat troops was appreciated, but segregation remained central to military policy until Truman changed it in 1948.[37]

War with racist Axis regimes made some Americans uncomfortable about segregation, and the government was anxious to maintain the support of African-American politicians and workers, although other Americans did not make any connection. The mobility in attitude and experience that stemmed from the war encouraged conservative responses on the part of some. In March 1944, Roosevelt's absentee voting bill, designed to help the soldiers vote, was defeated in favour of a state-dominated voting plan designed to restrict the vote by African-Americans. In the longer term, and with important contributions from post-war causal factors, the mobility in attitude and experience powerfully helped develop both the desire for change on the part of African-Americans and a growing willingness on the part of government, the military and many Americans to respond positively.

The same was true for Native Americans. Large numbers served in the military or left reservations to work in industry, while women took over male jobs. Native American average annual income rose about 250 per cent in 1940–44. The Nationalities Act passed in October 1940 granted Native Americans citizenship, and they thus became subject to conscription.

The new economic geography of the USA included new communication routes that were outside the range of submarine attack. Pipelines were laid from Texas to the industrial centres of the North-East, including the 'Big Inch' from Houston to New York, in order to lessen the need for coastal shipping. The coastal inland waterway system was improved. Both steps were designed to lessen vulnerability to German submarines. In 1942, the Alaska Highway was built in order to provide an overland route through Canada to the American bases there. Although there was much use of rail, and improvements in rail capacity, during the conflict, wartime mobilisation contributed to the longer-term shift towards roads in the USA. They were a more flexible communication system.

For American companies, gross corporate profits rose markedly, helping fund investment. For American workers, average wages rose far more than the cost of living, helping ensure that at the individual, as well as the corporate and national, level the war saw America become far stronger and more prosperous. This was an absolute as well as a relative increase. It provided a stable tax base for greater government expenditure, and also helped enable the USA to remain a net creditor during the war and thereafter; while all the other warring states were debtors. Britain lost a quarter of its national wealth during the war, and was the world's greatest debtor nation by 1945.

Aside from the availability of massive resources, especially oil, the extent of manufacturing capacity, and the fact that their industry was not being bombed as those of the other combatants were, the Americans benefited from a relative lack of need for imports. This contrasted greatly with the situation in Japan and Britain. Both of the latter required imports of raw materials, oil and food.

In turn, American industry produced massive quantities of goods for allies, including 55,000 aeroplanes, 18,000 of which went to the Soviet Union. The Allies benefited more than their opponents from the provision of munitions and other supplies to members of the alliance under strain, although German military support helped prevent an earlier Italian collapse. The movement of military supplies between the Allies made a significant impact in particular operations: in North Africa in 1942, the British benefited from American tanks. Large quantities of Anglo-American supplies were provided to the Soviets. They helped compensate for particular deficiencies. Thus, American jeeps and trucks provided a valuable degree of mobility for Soviet forces. However, there were heavy losses to German attacks on shipping moving supplies from Britain to the Soviet Arctic port of Murmansk. It was far less hazardous to move supplies to the Soviet Union via Alaska or, even, Persia (Iran), but there were serious logistical problems involved in both routes, as well as the problems of access to the war zone once the supplies had arrived.

There were also important exchanges of knowledge among the Allies, particularly between Britain and the USA. The Tizard mission sent to the USA in 1940 provided valuable British technology, including a prototype cavity-magnetron. This was central to the development of microwave radar.[38] The exchange of intelligence under the BRUSA (Britain and the USA) agreement of May 1943 was important.[39]

Like America, Australia, Canada and New Zealand benefited in their wartime industrial mobilisation from the absence of attack on their manufacturing centres. Thanks to production for the war, Canadian gross national product more than doubled in 1939–45, while federal government expenditure rose from $680 million in 1939 to $5,136 million in 1945. The War Measures Act was used to regulate industrial activity, and the Wartime Prices and Trade Board set wages and prices and allocated scarce commodities, although the regulation of the workforce through the National Selective Service had only limited success.[40] The Canadians supported a major war effort that tends to be overlooked when the Allies are treated in terms of Britain, the USA and the Soviet Union. There was a vast expansion in the Canadian armed forces. At the outbreak of war, there were fewer than 9,000 regulars, alongside 2,700 reservists and 51,000 militia. In contrast, 1,086,343 men and women were enlisted during the war, and a military that had not been equipped for war was provided with the necessary equipment.[41]

The development of industries in Canada and Australasia was linked to a longer-term decline in dependence on imports of British manufactures. The war also accentuated the tendency for increased economic (and strategic) co-operation between Canada and the USA.

## Britain

Britain showed the impact of the war on an hitherto non-authoritarian society. The outbreak of war led to the passage of the

Emergency Powers (Defence) Act of 1939, which extended the power of government. That year, conscription was introduced and new ministries were created for Economic Warfare, Food, Home Security, Information, Shipping and Supply, Power and Production. National wage-negotiating machinery did not, however, prevent a serious miners' strike in early 1944. Industrial production, however, increased markedly, while unemployment fell substantially.

Farming provided a good example of the new interventionist character of British government. The industry was subject to a hierarchy of control. Each county was administered by a separate War Agricultural Executive Committee, the members of which were appointed by the Ministry of Agriculture, and was, in turn, divided into districts controlled by district sub-committees. Unlike in World War One, the policy of encouraging tillage (cultivated land) was imposed as soon as the war began. By 1945, tillage was 55 per cent more than the 1935–9 average, leading to a greater production of grains, which reduced the need for food imports. Information and labour direction were both part of the process. In June 1940, a farm survey was begun in order to assess productive capacity, and a more comprehensive survey followed from the spring of 1941. Farmers were provided with labour, especially young women from the Land Army and, later, prisoners of war, and with machinery. The latter helped to ensure that World War Two established modern agriculture in Britain, although it was the great expansion in American agricultural production that was of particular value to the Allies, not least in providing food for Britain and the Soviet Union.

In Britain, the Soviet Union and elsewhere, the war also saw a major increase in urban allotments. These were very important as a source of potatoes, vegetables and meat (chicken and pigs), although animals were also kept in backyards. Aside from providing food, allotments indicated the way in which the war effort demanded full attention. Leisure was restricted, as workers farmed their allotments in the evening and at weekends. In Japan, strenuous efforts were made to cope with the impact on food imports of Allied attacks on shipping, but the same attacks also cut fertiliser imports, hitting agricultural productivity, while many farm workers were conscripted. By 1943, average consumption of food in Japan was falling, a fact that exacerbated the already brutal treatment of Allied prisoners.

In Britain, the war also transformed the state's relationship with society. Everything was brought under the scrutiny of government. Food rationing, for example, remoulded the nation's diet in accordance with nutritional science as well as the availability of particular types of food, and of substitutes for others: people were pushed to eat hitherto unappetising, but available, products. There was also advice on how best to cook what was available. The war brought the end of consumption of foods from occupied areas, for example greatly affecting the types of cheese eaten (French cheese could not be obtained), and also those from distant colonies and other foreign sources, as shipping was in short supply. Thus, a generation grew up without tasting bananas.[42]

Rationing in Japan also allowed the state to rank citizens on need; a process also clearly seen in the Soviet Union, where dependants got the least. Rationing helped lead to the spread of black markets, as in Finland. There, as in other states, state expenditure, taxation and inflation rose rapidly. Finland also demonstrated the more general process of extended state control. Aside from rationing and higher taxation, prices, rents and wages were all brought under control, compulsory labour service was introduced and strikes were banned.

Rationing rested on a theory of equality. The war encouraged an inclusive notion of nationhood on the part of all combatants. A language of inclusiveness and sharing,[43] and a stress on the 'home front',[44] made social distinctions seem unacceptable, and this helped condition post-war politics. In Britain, this led to a welfare state, in which support for healthcare and unemployment assistance would be the responsibility of the state and be provided free to all, in other words paid for by the taxpayer.

These changes were introduced by the Labour government elected on 5 July 1945. The electorate's rejection of Winston Churchill, who had been the Prime Minister since 10 May 1940, throws light on the wartime home front. Churchill's rousing oratory, bulldog spirit and sheer capacity for work had made him the motive force of the government, as well as its respected public face. However, partly as a consequence of his focus on the war and his own self-confidence, Churchill was insufficiently sensitive to shifts in the public mood towards attitudes and policies associated with the Labour Party. His unwillingness to give any immediate commitment to legislation based on Sir William Beveridge's report of December 1942 on Social Insurance and Allied Services, which had called for state-supported security 'from the cradle to the grave', had significant political results. On 16 February 1943, 119 MPs went into the division lobby against Churchill over the issue, while in the 'little General Election', as the press termed the six by-elections in January and February 1943, the Conservative vote dropped in four of the seats.

In May 1945, the Labour Party conference turned down Churchill's suggestion that the wartime coalition continue until Japan was defeated. Churchill formed a caretaker government that lasted until the general election, but this gave Labour an increase of 10 per cent on its pre-war share of the vote, and its first clear parliamentary majority. This reflected political, social and cultural shifts during the war. State control, planning and Socialism increasingly seemed normative. Trade union membership had risen by 50 per cent during the war, while the role of Labour in the wartime coalition was important to its revived standing and provided an apprenticeship in power.

The extent to which the war brought change, including a measure of democratisation, was also seen in Western colonies. It affected not only civilians, but also the military. In India, there was a major shift in military culture, with a determined attempt by the British to promote Indians as well as recruitment from races hitherto seen as lacking in martial quality. Japanese propaganda helped win over small numbers of the colonial military, as on Horsburgh Island in the Cocos group, where, on 8–9 May 1942, a few Ceylonese troops mutinied in an unsuccessful attempt to hand it over to the Japanese.[45]

## Total war

World War Two was not only a 'total war'; the populations involved were also *told* it was a total war. State control or influence over the means of propaganda ensured that the greater access of the public to information, through mass literacy and ownership of radios, helped to create national views, or impressions of them, in accordance with the view of the state. In Britain, the British Broadcasting Corporation (BBC) played a major role in supporting the war effort, not least by successfully reaching outside the middle class and encouraging a sense of common experience and purpose. Radio comedy presented working-class life as in no way inferior,[46] and wartime films were notable for their gritty realism and 'bulldog spirit'. Cinema realism was also important in creating an image of a 'people's war', as were films such as *Dawn Guard* and *Millions Like Us*.[47] In addition, nearly 1,900 official films were produced in Britain during the war, mostly by the Ministry of Information and many by the Crown Film Unit. Their propagandist documentaries were a major success.

Interest in the course of the war greatly increased public knowledge of distant areas. When war broke out in Europe in 1939, maps of Europe sold out in the USA, and the public use of maps increased at the New York Public Library. The war also led to an enormous increase in press cartography. The *New York Herald Tribune*, *New York Times*, *New York Daily News*, *Christian Science Monitor*, *Chicago Tribune* and *Milwaukee Journal* all had their own cartographers, and their maps were reproduced in other newspapers. German firms such as Justus Perthes and Ravenstein produced detailed war maps for the German public.

American mapmakers sought to make clear what were to Americans often very distant and unknown regions. It was also important to counter isolationism by linking these regions to American interests. The war globalised American public attention, and maps played a major role in the process. The orthographic projections and aerial perspectives used by Richard Edes Harrison brought together the USA and distant regions and helped create a new look to the world, one particularly appropriate to an age of air power. The preface to his *Look at the World, The Fortune Atlas for World Strategy* (New York, 1944) explained it was intended 'to show *why* Americans are fighting in strange places and *why* trade follows its various routes. They emphasise the geographical basis of world strategy'. Pearl Harbor led Americans to a new sense of space, which reflected both vulnerability and the awareness of new geopolitical relationships. Roosevelt's radio speech to the nation on 23 February 1942 made reference to a map of the world in order to explain American strategy. He had earlier suggested that potential listeners obtain such a map, leading to massive demand and also to increased newspaper publication of maps. The dynamic appearance of many war maps, for example those in *Life* and *Time*, with their arrows and general sense of movement, helped to convey an impression that the war was not a static entity at a distance, but, rather, was in flux, and therefore could encompass the spectator, both visually, through images of movement, and, in practice, by spreading in his or her direction.[48] Frank Capra's film *Prelude to War*, produced by the Film Production Division of the American Army, used maps to underline the theme of challenge: the maps of Germany, Italy and Japan were transformed into menacing symbols, while the world map depicted the New World being surrounded and then conquered.

Greatly influenced by the success of British propaganda in World War One, Hitler used propaganda effectively, although it helped mobilise people for only so long. Under Josef Goebbels, the Minister of Propaganda, there was an intensive programme of controlling and organising culture in order to disseminate Nazi themes and foster public support. Film production was carefully controlled, and cinema newsreels were also important. German radio was also carefully controlled, and the government encouraged the production of inexpensive sets. Radio broadcast the German classics (apart from those composed by Jews, such as Mahler and Mendelssohn) and presented the Third Reich as the bulwark of civilisation. For this reason, a major effort was made to keep orchestras playing. Radio and cinema were also carefully controlled in Japan.

In Britain, culture was also conscripted, in part in an attempt to maintain civilian morale and to associate the war effort with the defence of civilisation. The Ministry of Information established a War Artists' Scheme. Several thousand paintings and drawings were commissioned. Some showed bomb damage, including work by John Piper and Graham Sutherland's *Devastation in the City* (1941), while Henry Moore and Feliks Topolski depicted people sheltering from German air raids in tube stations. Artists found less demand for landscapes and portraits. For many authors, also, the war provided the occasion for a shift to a new seriousness. Dorothy L. Sayers, best known for her earlier detective novels about Lord Peter Wimsey, produced a series of radio plays about the life of Christ, *The Man Born to be King* (1941–2).

This seriousness did not drown out other themes or styles. The war years saw the introduction into Britain of vigorous jive and jitterbug dances by American soldiers. Michael Tippett's oratorio *A Child of our Time* (1944) incorporated African-American spirituals. The Nazis, in contrast, banned jazz. They disliked both its musical freedom and the African-American background, and saw jazz as symptomatic of American decadence. The German and Japanese failure to understand the vitality and energy of American society and culture was an important aspect of the inaccurate mindset of their leaderships. This greatly affected strategic planning by leading to an underrating of American resolve. Jazz helped provide the sound of the war, reflecting America's role as her forces brought their music with them to areas where they were based, most obviously Britain in the build-up to D-Day and Germany with the occupation.

The war indeed affected all sections of society. In Britain, in response to the threat of German bombing, there were mass evacuations of children from the major cities at the outset of the war; 690,000 alone from London. This was the biggest state-directed move of civilians in British history and the cause of much disruption. Many children were separated from their parents, and their allocation to new surrogates was not always a happy one. Later in the war, in response to Allied bombing, there was also to be a large-scale evacuation from German cities to southern Germany.

The mobilisation and inclusiveness so frequently stressed in discussion of the impact of the war on Britain were not always successful. Although there has been insufficient work on the subject, not least because the sources are elusive, there is evidence, for all combatants, of large numbers who sought to evade or profit from regulations, creating, for example, an extensive black market in rationed goods in Britain and elsewhere.

There were also war economies that, as a whole, failed to meet the growth rates of other major combatants, most prominently Italy. There, the government was unable to introduce an effective mobilisation of resources. Taxes did not become realistic, there was only limited direction of the large industrial combines, and both weapons and weapons systems were delivered in insufficient quality and quantity. Partly for these reasons, it proved difficult to rebuild the military after early losses against Greece and Britain; although Italian forces still played an important role at El Alamein, and, indeed, in Tunisia in 1943.

## Home fronts

Bombing, evacuation, rationing and single parenting brought much hardship on the home fronts of the combatants. The elderly faced a number of serious challenges, including the absence of children, while, conversely, young children grew up without fathers.[49] Women bore the brunt of queuing, balancing the family budget, coping with the black market, and feeding and cooking with few resources. In addition, the war contributed to a greater flexibility in social conventions. There was more freedom for women, because far more were employed, frequently away from home; because of an absence of partners, and, in many cases, fathers; and, in part, because of different attitudes. In Britain, the last was indicated by wartime surveys, while films such as *Waterloo Road* (1944) and *Brief Encounter* (1945) suggested that the war was offering new possibilities for relationships between the sexes, even at the cost of marriages. Divorce rates rose, as did illegitimacy.[50] This was true also of areas distant from the zone of conflict. In Prince Edward Island in Canada, where many airmen trained, a sense of the transience of life as well as the breakdown of self-restraint for many men and women led to a marked rise in the rate of illegitimacy.

In America, women played a major role in the economy, while others served in the military, including ferrying planes.[51] The war also led to a questioning of gender and racial roles and positions, and to pressure on established social mores; although there was also a reluctance to embrace change. Thus, day-care centres operated at only a quarter capacity, as, despite encouragement, the vast majority of women with young children continued to be reluctant to work. Women at work faced a male-dominated environment, and suffered accordingly in working practices and relative pay.[52]

In Canada, the National Selective Service, established in 1943, focused at first on single women. Married women were subsequently sought, not least through the Day Nurseries Agreement, but its day-care facilities were only introduced in Ontario and Québec.[53] In New Zealand, by 1943, nearly one-third of factory workers were women. A Women's Land Service was created. Much of the female entry into the workforce was voluntary, but state direction was also used. As elsewhere, it was not only a case of more women working in New Zealand, but also of a change in the nature of the female workforce. Domestic service fell greatly, while factory and white-collar work rose, and some women were promoted to positions of authority in the workplace, rarely reached before. Domestic service also became far less common in Britain, where it had been particularly important among unmarried women and also significant for unmarried men. Taxes hit the ability to employ servants, but conscription, the allocation of workers and the ethos of collective service were also important.

The impact of the war was harsher in some other states. The Soviet Union was very ready to see women as a direct resource for the war effort, and one that should be controlled by the state. All able-bodied city women aged from 16 to 50 who were not students or looking after children under 8 were put under government direction in 1942, and thousands, uniquely, fought on the front line. Soviet propaganda made much of this, as it also did of women partisans. This contributed to the idea of an all-inclusive war effort. The number of women working in Soviet industry greatly increased, and many worked in heavy industry. Working conditions in Soviet industry were frequently harsh. Unmarried young women were also used to replace skilled male workers who entered the Japanese military, while non-working women were encouraged to do volunteer and civil-defence work, contributing to the regimentation of Japanese society.

Women in occupied countries also found themselves subject to enforced work, as well as to serious changes in their living arrangements and to the myriad circumstances that determined lifestyle and social status. German occupation ensured that the war greatly increased pressure on French women. This raised their consciousness; many had to confront the experience of being single, as large numbers of men were prisoners or sent to work in Germany.[54] Women played a major role in France, and elsewhere, in resistance activities.[55] Conversely, women who had relationships with German soldiers were frequently treated brutally after liberation. This arose through popular action, as in France, where many were paraded naked, their heads shaved and with swastikas marked on their bodies, and/or as a result of official policy, as in the Soviet Union, where such women were arrested.

Aside from numerous losses through bombing, bombardment and other acts of war, large numbers of women were casualties in other ways. Malnutrition affected many, reducing resistance to disease and leading to skeletal deformities, difficulties in childbirth and other problems. There was much sexual oppression. Large numbers of women were used as prostitutes, or, as the Japanese termed them, comfort women. There are no reliable statistics for the numbers used to staff the brothels for soldiers opened from 1938, but they are estimated at over 100,000, mostly Koreans and many quite young.[56]

Large numbers of German women of all ages were raped, particularly gang-raped, by Soviet forces in 1944–5, causing a major rise in female suicide as well as very high rates of venereal disease. Although they were well aware of what was going on, Soviet leaders made little effort to encourage a more sympathetic treatment of German civilians. There were also numerous rapes of German women who fled or were expelled from Eastern Europe after the war, for example from the Sudetenland in Czechoslovakia. The range of those attacked at the close of the war was very wide. In Nice, Italian-owned shops and naturalised Italians thought to be anti-French were the victims of explosions,[57] while, in Poland, Jews who had escaped the Nazis fell victim to anti-Semitic pogroms staged by Poles.

During the war, the Germans themselves had slaughtered women and children as part of their genocidal attacks on Jews, gypsies and others their regime sought to extirpate. Indeed both women and children were apt to be selected for immediate killing in the concentration camps because they were regarded as having less to offer in terms of work than men, many of whom were sent to the labour camps. The Japanese had followed a policy of slaughter in China. Thus, their 1942 offensive into Chekiang and Kiangsi led to the killing of about 250,000 Chinese and the use of biological warfare. Large numbers of Chinese civilians were killed by the Japanese when Singapore fell that year.

## Conclusion

In a variety of ways, the problems of fighting World War Two put major pressures on contemporary societies. For political and military leaders, it was clear, as it had been in World War One, that a rapid

12 R. Gildea, *Marianne in Chains: In Search of the German Occupation* (2002).

13 M. Dean, *Collaboration in the Holocaust: Crimes of the Local Police in Belorussia and Ukraine, 1941–1944* (Basingstoke, 2000).

14 W. Roberts, *Tito, Mihailovic and the Allies, 1941–1945* (New Brunswick, New Jersey, 1973); J. Tomasevich, *The Chetniks: War and Revolution in Yugoslavia 1941–1945* (Stanford, 1975).

15 J.F. Sweets, *The Politics of Vichy France: The French Under Nazi Occupation* (Dekalb, Illinois, 1976).

16 M.R.D. Foot, *SOE in France* (1966) and *SOE: An Outline History* (1994); D. Stafford, *Churchill and Secret Service* (1997); W.J.M. Mackenzie, *Secret History of SOE* (2000).

17 P. Hart, *The Heat of Battle: The 16th Battalion Durham Light Infantry – The Italian Campaign, 1943–1945* (1999), pp. 201–2.

18 M. Hastings, *Das Reich: Resistance and the March of the 2nd SS Panzer Division through France, June 1944* (1981).

19 K.J.V. Jespersen, *No Small Achievement. Special Operations Executive and the Danish Resistance 1940–1945* (Odense, 2002), p. 515.

20 U.S. Baclagon, *The Philippine Resistance Movement against Japan* (Manila, 1966).

21 C.G. Cruickshank, *SOE in the Far East: The Official History* (Oxford, 1983); D.W. Hogan, *U.S. Army Special Operations in World War II* (Washington, 1992); R.J. Aldrich, *Intelligence and the War Against Japan: Britain, America and the Politics of Secret Service* (Cambridge, 2000).

22 P. Biddiscombe, *Werewolf! The History of the National Socialist Guerrilla Movement, 1944–1946* (Cardiff, 1998).

23 U. Herbert, *Hitler's Foreign Workers: Enforced Labor in Germany under the Third Reich* (Cambridge, 1997).

24 R.J. Overy, 'Hitler's War and the German Economy: A Reinterpretation', in A. Marwick, C. Emsley and W. Simpson (eds), *Total War and Historical Change: Europe 1914–1955* (Buckingham, 2001), p. 157.

25 N. Gregor, *Daimler-Benz in the Third Reich* (New Haven, 1998).

26 R.L. DiNardo, *Mechanized Juggernaut or Military Anachronism? Horses and the German Army of World War II* (Westport, Connecticut, 1991).

27 M. Knox, *Hitler's Italian Allies: Royal Armed Forces, Fascist Regime, and the War of 1940–1943* (Cambridge, 2000). For a searching analysis of differences between the regimes, see M. Knox, *Common Destiny: Dictatorship, Foreign Policy, and War in Fascist Italy and Nazi Germany* (Cambridge, 2000).

28 J. Thompson, *Italian Civil and Military Aircraft, 1930–1945* (Los Angeles, 1963).

29 D.C. Evans and M.R. Peattie, *Kaigun: Strategy, Tactics, and Technology in the Imperial Japanese Navy, 1887–1949* (Annapolis, 1997).

30 R.W. Thurston and B. Bonwetsch (eds), *The People's War: Responses to World War II in the Soviet Union* (Urbana, Illinois, 2000).

31  K.E. Eiler, *Mobilizing America: Robert P. Patterson and the War Effort, 1940–1945* (Ithaca, 1997).

32  M.V. Melosi, *The Shadow of Pearl Harbor: Political Controversy Over the Surprise Attack, 1941–1946* (College Station, 1977).

33  H.P. Lepore, 'Contribution to Victory. The Distribution and Supply of Ammunition and Ordnance in the Pacific Theater of Operations', *Army History*, no. 34 (1995), pp. 31–5.

34  Ismay to Churchill, 16 March 1944, LH. Alanbrooke 6/3/8.

35  A.C. Hudson, 'The New York Public Library's Map Division Goes to War, 1941–1945', *Geography and Map Division: Special Libraries Association Bulletin*, 182 (Spring 1996), pp. 2–25.

36  D.M. Kennedy, *Freedom from Fear: The American People in Depression and War, 1929–1945* (Oxford, 1999), pp. 747–93; H. Sitkoff, 'The Detroit Race Riot of 1943', *Michigan History*, 53 (1969), pp. 183–206.

37  J.M. MacGregor, *Integration of the Armed Forces, 1940–1965* (Washington, 1981); B.C. Nalty, *Strength for the Fight* (New York, 1986).

38  D. Zimmerman, *Top Secret Exchange: The Tizard Exchange and the Scientific War* (Montreal, 1996).

39  B.F. Smith, *The Ultra-Magic Deals and the Most Secret Special Relationship* (Novato, California, 1993).

40  C.P. Stacey, *Arms, Men and Government: The War Policies of Canada 1939–1945* (Ottawa, 1970); M.D. Stevenson, *Canada's Greatest Wartime Muddle: National Selective Service and the Mobilization of Human Resources During World War II* (Montreal, 2001).

41  C.P. Stacey, *Six Years of War: The Army in Canada, Britain and the Pacific* (Ottowa, 1955).

42  I. Zweiniger-Bargielowska, *Austerity in Britain: Rationing, Controls and Consumption, 1939–1955* (Oxford, 2000).

43  M. Honey, *Creating Rosie the Riveter: Class, Gender, and Propaganda During World War II* (2nd edn, Amherst, Massachusetts, 1985).

44  The best introduction is provided by J. Noakes (ed.), *The Civilian in War: The Home Front in Europe, Japan and the USA in World War II* (Exeter, 1992). See also E.R. Beck, *The European Home Fronts, 1939–1945* (Arlington Heights, Illinois, 1993).

45  N. Crusz, *The Cocos Islands Mutiny* (Fremantle, 2001).

46  S. Nicholas, *The Echo of War: Home Front Propaganda and the Wartime BBC, 1939–45* (Manchester, 1996).

47  P.M. Taylor (ed.), *Britain and the Cinema in the Second World War* (London, 1988).

48  W. Ristow, 'Journalistic Cartography', *Surveying and Mapping*, 17 (1957), pp. 369–90; M. Mandell, 'World War II Maps for Armchair Generals', *Mercator's World*, 9/4 (1996), pp. 42–5; J. Ager, 'Maps and Propaganda', *Bulletin of the Society of University Cartographers*, 11/1 (1977), p. 8; A.K. Henrickson, 'The Map as "Idea": the Role of Cartographic Imagery during the Second World War', *American Cartographer*, 2 (1975), pp. 19–53.

49  W.M. Tuttle, *Daddy's Gone to War: The Second World War in the Lives of American Children* (Oxford, 1993); L. Holliday, *Children's Wartime Diaries. Select Writings from the Holocaust and World War II* (1995).

50  G. Braybon and P. Summerfield, *Out of the Cage: Women's Experiences in Two World Wars* (1987); J. Harris, 'War and Social History: Britain and the Home Front during the Second World War', *Contemporary European History*, 1 (1992), pp. 17–35; H.L. Smith (ed.), *Britain in the Second World War: A Social History* (Manchester, 1996).

51  M. Merryman, *Clipped Wings: The Rise and Fall of the Women Airforce Service Pilots: WASPS of World War II* (New York, 1998).

52  S.M. Hartman, *American Women in the 1940s: The Home Front and Beyond* (Boston, 1982); R. Milkman, *Gender at Work: The Dynamics of Job Segregation by Sex during World War II* (Champaign, Illinois, 1987).

53  R. Pierson, *'They're Still Women After All': The Second World War and Canadian Womanhood* (Toronto, 1986).

54  H. Diamond, *Women and the Second World War in France, 1939–1945: Choices and Constraints* (London, 1999).

55  M.C. Weitz, *Sisters in the Resistance: How Women Fought to Free France, 1940–1945* (New York, 1995).

56  G. Hicks, *The Comfort Women: Japan's Brutal Regime of Enforced Prostitution in the Second World War* (1994).

57  E. Criseyda, *'L'Occupation à la manière latine': Italians in Nice, 1942–43* (MPhil. Thesis, Oxford, 2002), p. 70.

# CHAPTER NINE

# *Struggle reviewed*

## Resources and contingencies

Allied victory in World War Two is frequently discussed in light of their ability to out-produce the Axis, an approach that can make the result of the struggle seem inevitable, and that also accords with a powerful current of general work on war by historians seeking to find a wider analytical pattern, if not a systemic explanation of results. The role of resources in war can be seen in a number of lights. The focus can be on quantity or quality of weaponry, on enhanced strategic, operational and tactical capability, on the consequences for particular campaigns, and on aggregate consequences for the war as a whole, or for particular aspects of it. For example, American production, not least of ships, helped counteract the serious problems created by the boldness of Allied strategic planning, which had paid insufficient attention to logistical realities. This was a particular problem in Churchill's case: his emphasis on operations in the Mediterranean had serious logistical implications, as it was more distant from British bases than France. The American preference for concentrating on a cross-Channel invasion of France was more appropriate in terms of resource availability and resulting logistical capability.[1]

Allied planning also owed much to the quantity of fuel available. In contrast to the situation today, the USA in 1941 produced about two-thirds of the world's oil, and had refining capacity to match, while the Soviets were responsible for about another 10 per cent. America's role in the oil industry was matched by its ability to develop and utilise oil-related technology, such as mobile, flexible pipelines. Other states that were prime producers, such as Mexico and Venezuela, were part of the Allied economic system, while Axis access to neutral supplies was anyway prevented by blockade. The Axis was in a better position as far as coal was concerned, although the Allies were still responsible for the majority of world supplies.

The role of resource availability and utilisation in determining the result of the war is capable of different interpretations. Alongside the undoubted impact of resources, their actual availability did not overcome the role of the contingent in the short term, and, in war, the long term is really only a series of short terms. In addition, the contingent fact of war helped mould the long-term resource base, socio-economic structures and political cultures of the combatants.

Alongside resources, the conflicts also included multiple contingencies and counterfactuals, such as what if Hitler had not declared war on the USA in 1941; or what if Stalin had acted on his fears about being left in the lurch by the Western Allies and had settled with Hitler, as he considered doing? This is a reminder of the danger of basing an account of the conflict preponderantly on resource availability. Assessing the resources available to both sides is a misleading approach, if only because it underrates the contingent nature of the sides, although other factors also played a role. The combatants had different understandings of what victory entailed, with a consequent impact on political and military strategy. Their operational methods reflected this and were, in part, shaped by war aims. These political factors were not extraneous to the course of the conflict.

Discussion of contingency can be taken further by focusing on areas and groups that offer a different perspective to that of the macro scale, and that are all too often forgotten, for example Albania, for which the official account of the war, actively propagated during the post-war Communist Hoxha regime, was so politicised as to lessen greatly its value. Instead, a more complex picture emerges if attention is paid to the role of the early non-Communist resistance movements in Albania. Initially, the Germans in 1943–4 were more effective in Albania than the Italians, who occupied it in 1939–43, in winning support. Opposition to the Serbs in nearby Kosovo proved popular with some Albanians, but, ultimately, the Germans failed to maintain order in Albania and Kosovo through the use of allied Albanian forces.[2]

Yet it is important not to neglect the role of resources, particularly in the second half of the war, by when the role for political contingency had diminished. The war became less fluid than it had been in its first two years, because Hitler's mindset and the Allies' response helped ensure that the conflict ended through unconditional surrender, rather than the unilateral negotiations that might otherwise have been a response to his failure to defeat the Soviet Union in 1941. The Germans were unable to translate their central position into lasting political or military success, because, due to Hitler's attitudes, peace was not an option. This helped to give an attritional character to the later years of the war, but, even then, differences in war aims, operational culture, force structure and resource availability combined to ensure great diversity in conflict. The attritional character of the war in Europe was particularly pronounced on the Eastern Front, not least because it was the land sector in which conflict lasted longest:

> fighting on the eastern front bore a greater resemblance to the hard pounding of the Great War than it did to combat in the west. The technology had changed, but the human mass and cost remained constant. In the Second World War the western front [of 1914–18] was in the east.[3]

The Germans had not planned for such an outcome, for neither their military nor its doctrine nor the military-industrial complex was prepared for the lengthy conflict that resulted. Instead, the Germans sought the *Kesselschlacht* (battle of encirclement and annihilation) that they had pursued in earlier conflicts and, as in 1914, there was no plan B, and a failure to give adequate weight to other possibilities.[4]

The absence of adequate mechanisation affected the effectiveness and range of German advances; although, even had there been more vehicles, there were the issues both of their maintenance and, more seriously, of the availability of petrol. Furthermore, German doctrine was based on the notion of a rapidly obtained decisive land battle. This goal was realisable if the opposing power was readily accessible, focused its strength on the army, lacked adequate space in which to retreat or manoeuvre, and accepted the same doctrinal suppositions. These factors were absent in the case of Britain, the Soviet Union and the USA; and German warmaking was the story of failure of will: the inability to make opposing states accept German assumptions. Will could not be a substitute for a failure to set sensible military and political goals.5

Although the situation was not identical, similar points can be made about Japanese warmaking. The Japanese were involved in an attritional struggle in China even before they attacked the USA; although, by 1941, it was not of an intensity comparable to that of the struggle to come with the Americans. With the 'Germany First' policy, the USA planned for a limited war with Japan initially. However, the pressures of domestic assumptions for a full commitment were important. Furthermore, the consequences of allocating sizeable forces to resist Japanese advances, for example at Guadalcanal, led to the commitment of military assets that produced their own impetus for advances.[6] This interacted with inter- and intra-service military politics, helping ensure that more of the American combat effort against the Axis in 1942–3 was a matter of 'Japan First' than might be anticipated by reference to 'Germany First'; although that was far less apparent in the air.

The role of factors other than simple economic capacity in military success can be seen in weapons procurement. Unlike the Germans, the Americans and Soviets concentrated on weapons that made best use of their capacity because they were simple to build, operate and repair, for example the American M-1 Garand infantry rifle and Sherman M-4 tank, and the Soviet 120 mm Type 38 mortar. In contrast, German tanks were complex pieces of equipment and often broke down, compromising their operational value. Much German armour was no better than Soviet armour, although, for long, the British and Americans had inadequate tanks. The British Infantry Mark I, Matilda, Valentine and Churchill tanks suffered from inadequate armament, and all bar the last were undergunned. The best German tanks were technically better in firepower and armour in 1944, the Tiger and Panther, for example, being superior in both to the Sherman, but the unreliability and high maintenance requirements of the Tiger tank weakened it. The quality gap that favoured the Germans against the Anglo-Americans was closed by late 1944 and 1945, as new Allied tanks, particularly the heavily gunned American M-26 Pershing,[7] appeared, while the

Americans also benefited in late 1944 from the introduction of high-velocity armour-piercing shells for their tank armament. This helped compensate for the earlier American emphasis on tanks that were fast and manoeuvrable.

Alongside tanks, it is also necessary to consider the consequences of motorising anti-tank weaponry. The resulting self-propelled tank destroyers had a major impact: effective German versions were matched by American destroyers armed with 76 mm and 90 mm guns.

The Allies had important advantages in artillery and in motorised infantry. The former was particularly important, because, as in World War One, more battlefield casualties were killed by artillery fire than by any other weapons system. Artillery was more effective than in the earlier war because of better shells and fuses, for example proximity fuses, which were used by the Allies in land warfare from the Battle of the Bulge. Benefiting from impressive guns, such as the American 105 mm howitzer, Allied artillery was more intensive and overwhelming in firepower, although the British lacked an adequate modern heavy artillery. The British, Americans and Soviets were very keen on using big artillery bombardments to accompany their offensives (the Soviets had particularly plentiful artillery), and the Germans, who used artillery when they could, had no real answer. The Japanese relied on the terrain, frequently digging in underground. Artillery fire, particularly that of the Americans, benefited from improved aiming and range that reflected not only better guns but also radio communication with observers and meteorological and survey information. The Americans, with their high-frequency radios, were particularly adept at this. The use of self-propelled and mechanised guns increased the mobility of artillery. In the Pacific, Allied firepower was largely provided by warships and air attacks, although the plunging fire of mortars was important to conflict on the islands.

The Germans were not without good weapons, although their value depended on fighting conditions. For example, in Eastern Europe, the impact of the effective German long-range anti-tank guns was lessened by the close distances of actual engagements. However, in the MG-42, introduced in 1942, the Germans had a flexible, easy-to-use machine gun. This gave considerable strength to their defensive positions, and made it important to suppress their fire before they were stormed. The Americans first used the Bazooka anti-tank rocket in 1942 but failed to upgrade it as tanks got heavier. The Germans, however, developed the design into the more powerful Panzerschreck rocket grenade. They also developed the hand-held Panzerfaust rocket launcher. The British lacked a satisfactory anti-tank weapon.

American weapons production was closely linked to the objective of movement. American forces were motorised to an extent greater than those of any other state, and this was not only a question of the armour. Although German success in 1940 had led American tank commanders to foster a doctrine in which their forces alone brought success, American force structure and training was organised by General Lesley McNair, the head of the Army Ground Forces, to emphasise combined-arms attacks.[8] American infantry and artillery were also motorised, which helped maintain the pace and cohesion of the advance. The British, Germans, Japanese and Soviets could not match this integration.

American mobility was intended to allow for 'triangular' tactics and operations, in which the opposing force was frontally engaged by one unit while another turned its flank, and a third, in reserve, was poised to intervene where most helpful. British commentators were impressed by the value of motorised infantry, and, in late 1944, some individual commanders, such as Lieutenant-General Sir Richard O'Connor,[9] sought to find ways to follow suit. In its planning in 1940–2, the Vichy army had responded to German victory in 1940 by planning for a more motorised force, so that the infantry and artillery could move at the same speed as the armour.[10]

American force structure and tactics were a direct product of the economy's ability to produce weaponry and vehicles in large numbers, and were closely related to American logistical capacity. The force structure and logistics also helped ensure the strength of the economy, as the relatively small number of combat divisions, eighty-nine, made it easier to meet demands for skilled labour. The flexibility of both economy and military were mediated by that of American society. This included institutional and cultural factors, such as the widespread existence of management abilities stemming from the needs of the economy, as well as a high degree of appointment and promotion on merit (albeit not as far as African-Americans were concerned). In addition, there were widely disseminated social characteristics, including a can-do spirit, an acceptance of change, a willingness to respond to the opportunities provided by new equipment, a relative ease with mobility and a self-reliance that stemmed from an undeferential society.

The contrast with Germany was readily apparent, not least in the use of foreign labour. About 220,000 Mexican labourers gained work in American agriculture, their conditions, like those of African-Americans, incomparably better than the groups that were not equal participants in the Nazi and Japanese worlds. Similarly, workers could, and did, strike in the USA and UK, whereas in Germany and the Soviet Union labour discipline was ruthlessly enforced. The British used Italian prisoners as agricultural labourers, but their working conditions were not harsh, and, indeed, allegedly, did not preclude intimate relations with some local women.

At both tactical and operational levels, mobility and firepower were seen by the Americans as multipliers that compensated for relatively few troops. These facets had resource and logistical implications, not least in the need for oil, ammunition and shipping. Thus, the *relatively* small size of the American combat arm increased its mobility, although there was need for a substantial backup.

Allied resource superiority affected the conduct of the war, at the strategic, operational and tactical levels. For example, as the Americans advanced across France in 1944, they generally did not storm villages and towns where they encountered resistance. Instead, they stopped, brought in aerial, armour and artillery support, and heavily bombarded the site before moving in, with limited loss of American life; although this does not lessen the contribution made by their effective infantry. To some British commentators, the Americans were overly keen on waiting to bring up artillery, a course that could lead the Germans to disengage successfully and retreat. However, American artillery moved forward close to the line of advance, while the British had learned in North Africa the wisdom of methodical preparation and superior firepower when closing with the Germans, Montgomery used artillery and air support to preface his attacks in 1944–5, and American fighting quality had increased greatly since the Kasserine pass.

Resource superiority made it easier for the Americans to support combined-arms operations, although it was also necessary to have the relevant doctrine and training. In part, this entailed knowing how best to respond to the combined-arms tactics of opponents. The Germans proved unable to do so, their moving armour proving particularly vulnerable to Allied close-air support, which helped to close the capability gap the Germans had initially benefited from. This was an instance of the manner in which resource factors were very important in providing the basis for successful combined-arms operations, although, again, they could not provide the necessary doctrine.

The difficulty of making general statements about military style is underlined, however, by the different conclusions of detailed studies. Thus, American fighting quality in the winter of 1944–5 has been underlined in a study of the Vosges campaign, but questioned for the Huertgen Forest operation. Command skills in the latter have been questioned.[11] Such differences reflect not only scholarly emphasis but also the frequently underrated issue of variations between units, as well as the extent to which particular command decisions could accentuate the nature of such differences. The relatively small size of the American army also ensured a lack of reserve divisions, and the resulting duration of combat without a break for individual units in 1944–5 created serious difficulties.

The course of the conflict amply demonstrated the value of doctrine and training. Major-General Eric Dorman-Smith, Deputy Chief of General Staff for the British Eighth Army in North Africa in 1942, saw this as a crucial factor in conflict there in 1941:

> In the Middle East Command, during the autumn of 1941, there arose the tactical heresy which propounded that armour alone counted in the Desert battle, therefore the British...should discover and destroy the enemy's equivalent armour, after which decision the unarmoured infantry divisions would enter the arena to clear up what remained and hold the ground gained.

Dorman-Smith contrasted this with Rommel's *Afrika Korps*, and its tactical preference for a 'mixed formation of all arms', and attributed

British deficiencies to the sway of generals with a cavalry background: 'the romantic cavalry mystique of horsed warfare' led to 'basic tactical fallacies...the dichotomy between the unarmoured infantry divisions and the relatively "uninfanterised" armoured divisions.'[12]

Armoured divisions that were balanced between the arms were effective, rather as the Napoleonic division and corps had been. The British eventually adapted their doctrine and closed this capability gap, although the initial doctrine for infantry–armour operations imposed by Montgomery was flawed and required change after the problems encountered in Normandy in 1944.[13] In February 1945, Montgomery argued that close co-operation with infantry was needed in order to overcome anti-tank guns: 'I cannot emphasise too strongly that victory in battle depends not on armoured action alone, but on the intimate co-operation of all arms; the tank by itself can achieve little'.[14] Commanders of armoured units urged their officers to wait for support rather than charging in. This was a sensible response to the German skill in defensive warfare, particularly the careful siting of guns in order to destroy advancing tanks. In July 1944, O'Connor, the commander of 8th Corps in Normandy, instructed the commander of an armoured division to

> go cautiously with your armour, making sure that any areas from which you could be shot up by Panthers and 88s are engaged. Remember what you are doing is not a rush to Paris – it is the capture of a wood by combined armour and infantry.[15]

The development of close-air support capability, doctrine and tactics was also very important for the Allies, particularly for the British and Americans.

The importance of industrial resources for weaponry on the battlefield lent point to strategic bombing of factories and economic infrastructure, and ensured that victorious powers sought to seize manufacturing plant. The Soviets took large quantities from eastern Germany and Manchuria once they had conquered them in 1945. The location of resources also played a role in military planning. Romania's importance to the powers owed a lot to the Ploesti oilfield, Hitler's major source of oil; while, planning for the German offensive in 1942, Hitler included an advance on the Soviet oilfields at Baku. This advance ensured there was less armour available for operations near Stalingrad and also increased the vulnerability of the German offensive to flank attack. Concern about oil also helped explain the British seizure of control in Iraq and Persia in 1941, as well as the Japanese drive to gain Borneo, Sumatra and, to a lesser extent, Burma in 1942. Fuller pressed the importance of seizing the Ruhr, the leading German industrial region, and, in his General Situation memorandum of 21 January 1945, Montgomery wrote, 'The main objective of the Allies on the western front is the Ruhr; if we can cut it off from the rest of Germany the enemy capacity to continue the struggle must gradually peter out'.[16]

## The application of science

Both industrial production and the capability of weapons and weapons systems benefited from applied science. Scientific advances were used by all the major powers, but with differing results. The most dramatic was the atom bomb, which not only closed World War Two, but also played a major role in helping determine post-war military planning and geopolitics. However, the atom bomb was just the culmination of an intense period of rivalry in invention and application which affected capability and combat on land, at sea and in the air.

Science was indispensable for the rapid development of radar, which, in Britain, evolved from the rather crude Chain Home (CH) stations, which played a major role in helping the defenders in the Battle of Britain, to the sophisticated cavity-magnetron discovered in 1940. Radar was used successfully in escort vessels and aircraft in the fight against submarines. Microwave radar was the most effective counter to the U-boat because the Germans were not able to develop suitable countermeasures in time. The Germans experienced a major shock when they discovered that the British were using microwaves. Until then, German scientific orthodoxy was sceptical of their value, and no priority had been given to the production of the transmitting valves necessary for microwaves.

There was a major difference in scientific cultures between the two sides. In contrast to the teams of scientists of the Western Allies,

275

who were free to handle their own affairs, German technical staff were frightened of being proved wrong and being exposed to ridicule. The Germans were, however, more successful in interfering with Allied offensive radar, thus introducing the new technique of electronic warfare in which attackers and defenders strove to outwit each other. Nevertheless, accurate attacks on pinpoint targets could only be made after post-war scientific advances. In the Pacific, despite extensive research, the Japanese lacked their opponents' advantage in radar, an advantage that proved very important in naval conflict.[17]

The range of scientific application included developments in fertilisers and food preservation designed to improve the production and use of food. Import substitution was another field for food science, as synthetic foodstuffs were manufactured and substitutes developed, as they also were for clothes and shoes. Scientific advances were not always utilised, as anticipated threats were not always realised. Thus, the Allies put much effort into anti-gas precautions, but, unlike in World War One, the Germans did not use such weaponry.

Overall, the Allies were more successful in developing and applying effective weapons technology, particularly in air and sea warfare. Their ability to use the scientific skills of Jews and other refugees who had fled Germany and occupied Europe, not least in the atom bomb programme, testified to another aspect of the consequences of Hitler's racist policies. Research by the Germans and Japanese included brutal experiments on prisoners to discover the impact and nature of gas, bacteria, freezing, malaria, tuberculosis and other cruel experiments, for example in bone grafting. There was no consent, much cruelty, and, not that this would have been any justification, the scientific value was minimal.

## Destruction and cities

A very different aspect of the brutality of the struggle was that which arose from the destruction to the urban environment, an important part of the devastation of housing stock and marked reduction of national wealth that the war gave rise to. Cities had been razed before and destruction employed as a method of war, but, thanks to the role of air power and the range of the struggle, the scale of the damage in

World War Two was unprecedented. In Europe, the assault on cities began with the German terror-bombing of Warsaw, while the Japanese had inflicted great damage on Chinese cities, such as Shanghai, before the Americans bombed their cities. Destruction affected not only cities, but also much that entailed and reflected human values and social cohesion. Thus, religious buildings were fought over and destroyed in large numbers, most famously the ancient Benedictine monastery at Monte Cassino, which became a key feature in the well-defended German Gustav Line in Italy, and was heavily damaged by Allied bombing and artillery in early 1944.[18]

The destruction of prominent buildings was also, in many cases, a deliberate aspect of an assault on national memory, cohesion and morale. This was seen with both the German and the Soviet treatment of Ukraine.[19] The German assault on Jewry included a deliberate destruction of Jewish knowledge, culture and locations, for example synagogues. Having demonised Jews, Slavs and other supposed opponents, the Germans were in the dangerous position of feeling both strength and weakness towards them. They were able to plan and execute a barbarous rolling massacre that reflected the one-sided nature of a power relationship in which the perpetrators of slaughter were in no physical danger. At the same time, they were driven on not only by their vicious ideology but also by a sense of the challenge posed by the large numbers they now controlled. Thus, paradoxically, the weakness of Nazism played a major role in the Holocaust.[20] Due to their racist paranoia, unlike other imperial powers, the Germans lacked the willingness and ability to elicit consent: in Eastern Europe, only some groups were designated for collaboration.

At a less malign level, the Germans systematically looted occupied Europe for artistic treasures that were then designed to glorify their own regime. Over 13,000 paintings were seized from Warsaw alone. This was an aspect of a more widespread pillage, as well as of the seizure of assets that characterised many German leaders. Göring was a particularly vigorous kleptomaniac. Hitler also rewarded generals with money and other assets.

Urban devastation was largely due to air attack, which ensured that cities far from the range of opposing armies, such as those in Britain and Japan, were devastated. In addition, both artillery and ground fighting were more destructive than is generally appreciated. The scenes of rubble photographed in Berlin and Stalingrad were repeated to devastating effect elsewhere, for example in Warsaw in 1944 and Manila in 1945,[21] albeit not always on the same scale. Cities that survived much damage, for example Kyoto, Paris and Prague, were those that had not been bombed or shelled.

This is a reminder of the limitation of discussing conflict largely in terms of campaigns and battles of movement in open country, important as those were. In fact, part of the fighting took place in cities. These proved a terrain that was intractable for armoured warfare, as the German tanks discovered in Warsaw at the outset of the war in Europe. Linked to this was the frequency of sieges of towns and cities, which, by their importance and the relative ease of defending them, lent themselves to use as fortified positions. They were not to be of importance in the German *Blitzkriege*, but, in the conflict in the East, the siege of Leningrad was the key event in the campaign in northern Russia, while sieges of Sevastopol were crucial to those in the Crimea, and so on. Rommel felt it important to capture Tobruk before he advanced towards the Nile.

## Conflict re-evaluated

Such sieges can be viewed in two lights. It can be argued that, like the Napoleonic and Franco-Prussian Wars and World War One, the fate of fortified positions and unfortified cities was settled by the war of movement, the fall of Singapore for example following that of Malaya, the two captures of Manila following successful landings in Luzon, and the battle of Berlin following the Soviet destruction of the German positions to the west of the Oder. In Italy, the German defence was based on defensive lines in mountainous terrain and not on cities. Alternatively, it can be argued that fortified positions, such as Leningrad and Stalingrad, helped anchor defences that curtailed, and could help determine, campaigns of movement. This debate related to the more general one of the respective merits of attack and defence.

A re-evaluation of World War Two should have at its core an emphasis not on new weaponry, but on fighting quality involving the effective use of established weaponry. This is an account not about a paradigm shift in twentieth-century warfare resulting from the role of aircraft and tanks, important as they were, but rather about the need, in addition, to consider the continued value of artillery and infantry and, also, of effective tactical, operational and strategic coordination of arms. In place of a fascination with the machine and the modern, there is need for an awareness of the importance of effectiveness and change within established military traditions and practice.

Planning and command skills and, more generally, the ability to articulate and integrate different arms, a long-established aspect of effectiveness, became more important with the greater range of available technology. Thus it became necessary to integrate infantry, artillery and armour successfully, as well as air and land, air and sea, and land and sea forces. This was necessary not only to achieve success in the attack, but also in defence. In February 1943, Admiral Sir Dudley Pound, First Sea Lord in the British Admiralty, noted:

> At the moment we are doing all we can to produce super long-range aircraft so that we can cover the whole of the Atlantic from one side to the other, as there is no question but that if you can put aircraft over the U-boats during the day, it prevents them getting into position for their night attacks. I am hoping very much that we shall be able to blast them out of their operational bases in the Bay of Biscay [by air attack].[22]

More generally, a stress on the campaigns in the war, especially on fighting qualities and command skills, ensures that there is due attention to the defeat of the Axis on land and sea and in the air. There is also a more general point about the value attached to fighting. If the Axis defeat is regarded as inevitably flowing from the extent of Allied resources, then the difficulty of the task is underrated, while there is the risk that the resource issue is in some fashion employed to extenuate Axis warmaking.

In practice, it is possible to point out, for example, not only the extent of American shipbuilding capability and the consequent ability to replace losses and secure naval superiority in the Pacific, but, also, the extent to which the Japanese navy remained a dangerous arm after Midway and had to be both beaten in battle and weakened by the attack on the Japanese war economy.[23]

## The lessons of the war

The evaluation of the war was not only of scholarly interest. In the aftermath of World War Two, the campaigns were carefully scrutinised for indications about how best to wage war in what appeared to be the imminent conflict between the Soviet Union and the group of non-Communist powers that allied in 1949 in the North Atlantic Treaty Organisation (NATO). As the Americans demobilised after World War Two, the already powerful Soviet military became relatively stronger. The prospect of a Soviet advance into Western Europe was accentuated as growing East–West divisions were accompanied by Soviet-backed seizures of power in Eastern Europe by local Communists. To offset this, it appeared that the West would have to rely on air-delivered nuclear bombs. The Americans had the only ones in the world, but the British also set in train a programme to acquire nuclear capability. The question whether the American use of nuclear weapons in 1945 meant that there had been a paradigm shift in military capability and warmaking attracted attention.

This situation was transformed in 1949 when the Soviet Union, unexpectedly, exploded a nuclear bomb. As a result, the military situation appeared radically different to that in World War Two. Doctrines and arithmetics of nuclear threat and deterrence came to play a major role in military planning, and the use of nuclear weapons appeared to outweigh conventional capability, particularly the overwhelming Soviet strength in Europe. However, the possibility that the threat of nuclear devastation would prevent either side from using it led to revived interest in conventional operations. The Americans took a close interest in the experience the Germans had acquired in fighting the Soviet Union. In the 1950s they persuaded *Luftwaffe* commanders to write a series of reports. In addition, Franz Halder, head of the German army's General Staff in 1938–42, was employed by the American army's Historical Division for fourteen years. Both Soviet and NATO forces came to focus on manoeuvre warfare, and there was great interest on both sides in the successful Soviet campaigns of 1943–5, especially the concept of 'deep operations'. A clear lesson learned from World War Two was that linear defences were vulnerable and that the retention of mobility offered the best form of defence.

AirLand concepts were also a development of World War Two operational lessons, with a heavy emphasis on ground-support airpower and on enhanced manoeuvrability that also drew on the greater possibilities stemming from the development of helicopters. The latter were an instance of the shift that occurred in the decades after 1945, for – alongside the continued dominance of the weapons types that had been used to wage the war, both long-established, such as artillery, and relatively new, particularly aircraft, tanks and submarines, as well as of much of the doctrine – there were new developments, not least in the capabilities of existing weapons. Thus, the specifications of aircraft by 1980 were very different to those of 1940. The impact of the German and American submarine campaigns in World War Two encouraged NATO to devote much attention to anti-submarine capability in the north Atlantic.

The applicability of the military lessons of World War Two was lessened not only by the spread of atomic capability and the avail-ability of improved weaponry, but also by the fact that most of the wars in the period of the Cold War were very different in type. The closest, in operational terms, were the wars between states where armour and airpower could be used, particularly the Arab–Israeli wars. Indeed Liddell Hart saw Israeli operations as another instance of *Blitzkrieg*. However, the most 'typical' wars were those that involved at least an insurrectionary element. This was true of the conflicts of decolonisation, such as the British in Malaya, Kenya, Cyprus and Aden, and the French in Vietnam and Algeria. Political will and the battle to win or intimidate 'hearts and minds' were as important as conventional military operations. This was also true of the American engagement in Vietnam, a conflict that very much indicated the limited value of doctrine and strategy derived from World War Two and from Cold War confrontation with the Soviet Union. The need to rethink military practice (and history) in order to give due attention to the range of challenges that might have to be confronted by major powers was readily apparent; although all too many commentators continued to place their trust in the paradigm approach to war, with the related assumption that a partic-ular operational method and/or type of military technology would lead to increased capability and success.

## The fate of the defeated

The war was followed by the occupation of the defeated powers and the reconstruction of their civil societies in accordance with the norms of the victorious. Thus, in areas of Germany occupied by Soviet forces, there was a deliberate destruction of the residences of Prussian landowners, as part of an attempt to create a new social politics. In a necessary closure to the barbarity of their regime, Nazi leaders were tried by an international tribunal in Nuremburg, and twelve of the most prominent, including Göring and Ribbentrop, were sentenced to hang. Göring cheated the hangman by committing suicide. Despite the hypocrisy of Soviet membership, the tribunal was important in the development of international jurisprudence and of the concept of 'crimes against humanity', the fourth count or category designed for the indictments.[24]

Other Nazis and collaborators were executed, particularly in Eastern Europe. Few of the German senior commanders captured by the Western Allies were tried, in large part because of a failure to bring home the extent of the German army's co-operation with the killing of civilians,[25] although Manstein served four of the eighteen years to which he was sentenced for war crimes in the Soviet Union by a British military court in 1949, while Kleist was handed over to the Yugoslavs, who imprisoned him for war crimes before handing him over to the Soviet Union, who imprisoned him until he died. The Germans responsible for the execution of American prisoners near Malmédy in December 1944 were tried and sentenced to death in 1946, but none were executed.[26]

Large numbers of particular ethnic groups who had fought for Hitler were slaughtered. Tito's troops killed many of the Croat Fascist militia, which had proved a particularly brutal force, while the Soviets slaughtered Cossacks handed over by the British. At the Yalta Conference (4–11 February 1945), the British and Americans had agreed to hand over to the Soviets those they captured who had been Soviet nationals before the Nazi–Soviet pact of 1939. About 4.25 million people were handed over. Most were sent to the Gulags but many were killed.

Elsewhere, prominent collaborators, such as Laval in France and Quisling in Norway, were executed, while the Vichy leader Pétain was sentenced to death, but reprieved and imprisoned. In France, 1,509 people were executed after trial for collaboration, and about 9,000 were killed by unofficial means.[27] The Tokyo war crime trial from 1946 to 1948 led to the execution of seven Japanese leaders, although Emperor Hirohito was not tried; 920 other Japanese defendants were convicted, sentenced to death and executed for their harsh treatment of prisoners of war, or for crimes against humanity.[28] Mussolini had been killed by partisans shortly before the end of the war.

In contrast, some prominent experts in weapons development were eagerly recruited by the combatants. The Americans were able to gain German expertise in rocketry that was to help them during the space race with the Soviet Union of the 1950s, most prominently Wernher von Braun and his staff, who had been responsible for the V-2. The Americans also gained the scientific data accumulated by Unit 731, a Japanese biological warfare unit established in 1936 that experimented on humans, in return for giving its members immunity from prosecution.[29]

## Political consequences

Germany and Austria, and their capitals Berlin and Vienna, were partitioned between American, British, French and Soviet occupation zones, while Japan was occupied by the Americans (the Soviets remained in the Kuriles and southern Sakhalin). In order to ensure a liberal democratic Japan, the Americans not only pushed through governmental and social changes, including land reform (but not republicanism), but also demilitarisation. As a result, in the long term, the Japanese were able to acquiesce in their own defeat. There were similar changes in Germany, with political and government changes in the Western and Soviet zones matching their assumptions for benign developments. Italy became a republic, while, in France, the Third Republic, discredited by defeat, and brought to an end by Vichy in 1940, was replaced by the Fourth, whose constitution was backed by a referendum in 1946.

There were also significant territorial changes, rather than a return to pre-war boundaries, with Germany losing territory to Poland and the Soviet Union, while Japan lost Korea, Taiwan, south

Sakhalin, the Kuriles and the Pacific islands it had received after World War One. Particularly in Eastern Europe, territorial changes were accompanied by major population moves. In 1945–6, 9 million Germans fled from Eastern Europe, especially from large parts of what had been Germany (Silesia, eastern Pomerania, East Prussia), but also from Czechoslovakia, Poland and other countries. This was an aspect of the widespread displacement that the war had brought and that continued after its conclusion. For example, the Soviet conquest of Karelia and other areas from Finland in 1940 was preceded by the flight of nearly 0.5 million refugees. After Karelia was reconquered in 1941, nearly 300,000 refugees returned, only to flee anew when the Soviet forces advanced again in 1944.

The emigration to British-ruled Palestine of Jewish refugees from Europe, many of them survivors of concentration and labour camps, was an aspect of this wartime and post-war movement of peoples. It exacerbated the British inability to contain the rivalry in Palestine between the indigenous Arab population and Jews. This failure led the British to abandon Palestine in 1948, and resulted in the first Arab–Israeli war (1948–9) and the creation of the state of Israel.

## The new world order

The leading colonial powers, Britain and France, were among the victors of World War Two, but their empires were largely to have disappeared within two decades, one of the most important shifts of authority in global history, and an important aspect of the decline of Europe's place in the world. The war had massively weakened the imperial powers. Two, Italy and Japan, completely lost their empires, but neither empire was treated as the German and Ottoman (Turkish) empires had been at the close of World War One when their colonies had been allocated, as League of Nations' mandates, to the victors. During World War Two, the British occupied both Italian Somaliland and Libya (another Italian colony), and Churchill considered the annexation of the latter, while the French feared British designs on their empire, but such views now seemed anachronistic. The dominant role in the victorious coalition had been taken by the USA and the Soviet Union, both of which, albeit from different perspectives, had anti-colonial ideologies and saw no reason to view the expansion of the European empires with any favour; in fact, they questioned their continued existence. Under American pressure, the Atlantic Charter, issued by Churchill and Roosevelt at the Placentia Bay conference (9–12 August 1941), declared 'the right of all people to choose the form of government under which they will live'.

The United Nations, the body founded in 1945 to replace the League of Nations (which had been moribund during the war), was to show favour for the notion of national self-determination. The inaugural meeting of the United Nations, the United Nations Conference on International Organisation, was, appropriately, in an American city, San Francisco. Held from 25 April to 26 June, the conference was attended by delegates from fifty states. The structure of the United Nations reflected the role of the victors in creating the new world order: the five permanent members of the Security Council – the USA, USSR, Britain, France and (Nationalist) China – had a crucial role to play in the United Nations.

Other bodies founded by the victors were also designed to mould the post-war world. The Bretton Woods conference, held in the USA in July 1944, produced plans for post-war co-operation designed to ensure economic and fiscal stability. Both had been weakened by the 1930s Depression, but this was greatly accentuated by the impact of the war on the trade, credit-worthiness, and industrial production of the combatants bar the USA. Bretton Woods led to the foundation of the International Monetary Fund and the International Bank for Reconstruction and Development (World Bank), both of which had American headquarters. The Americans did not want a return to the beggar-my-neighbour devaluation policies of the 1930s. Free trade was also actively supported as part of a liberal economic order. The General Agreement on Tariffs and Trade (GATT), signed in 1947, began a major cut in tariffs that slowly re-established free trade and helped trade to boom.

In practice, both the USA and the Soviet Union were imperial, if not colonial, powers, and the war strengthened both their systems. Although the Philippines were, as promised before the war by the Americans, granted independence in 1946, American territorial power in the Pacific increased as a result of occupation of Japanese territory and the establishment of military bases, such as Okinawa; under the San Francisco Peace Treaty of 1951, Japan accepted

American control of the Ryūkyū and Bonin chains under a United Nations' trusteeship. More generally, the USA became the dominant military and economic power in the Pacific.[30]

The Soviet state not only maintained its imperial grip on Siberia, Central Asia, the Caucasus and Mongolia, with the independence of the last now recognised by China; the Soviet Union also made territorial gains on its western frontiers, including the Baltic republics (Estonia, Latvia, Lithuania), Bessarabia (seized from Romania in 1940), and parts of Finland, Poland, Czechoslovakia (Ruthenia) and Germany (northern East Prussia: the Poles gained the rest). The renaming of Königsberg, the capital of East Prussia, as Kaliningrad by its new Soviet rulers was symptomatic of a wider transformation. The Soviet Union now also controlled most of Eastern Europe, with a large occupation force in Germany and Austria. This control played a major role in the seizures of power in the region by Communists, which culminated in 1948 with a coup in Czechoslovakia.

Italy and Japan had lost their overseas empires because of defeat in the war, but other powers on the winning side found theirs gravely weakened by the strains of the conflict. There were hopes in some circles of revived imperial military greatness. Imperial authority was reimposed, and rebellions, for example against the French in Madagascar in 1947–8, were suppressed, or at least confronted.

However, in large part due to the accumulated strains of war, as well as to the lessening of support for imperial rule from the colonial population, especially their most influential sectors, there was also a major retreat from empire. The British renounced control over India (1947), which became India and Pakistan, as well as over Burma, Ceylon (now Sri Lanka) and Palestine (1948). Syria was granted independence by the French in 1944, although Anglo-French occupation continued. Fighting began in 1945, and, in 1946, the Anglo-French forces withdrew; Lebanon became independent the same year. The French also faced a growing insurrection in Indo-China; Ho Chi Minh, the Communist head of the Viet Minh, declared the Democratic Republic of Vietnam on 2 September 1945. The French regained control, but conflict began in November 1946.[31] The Dutch proved unable to sustain their attempt to regain control of the East Indies.[32] The war also led to a marked increase in hostility to the British in Egypt, a key part of the 'informal empire'.

This collapse of empire reflected both its failure as an ideology for both rulers and ruled, and the breakdown of the system of consensus that enabled the maintenance of imperial control without a major military presence. Both owed much to the humiliations and demands of the war. Furthermore, the disruption brought by industrialisation and other social and economic trends encouraged by the war helped sap established patterns of behaviour and loyalties. Thus the 'home fronts' that were most affected by the war were those of countries under imperial control, which, however, have received the least attention in work on the subject. This process was readily apparent in Vietnam and the Dutch East Indies, but would also have been more obvious in the Philippines and India had they not received independence.

## China

The Nationalist Chinese government had also been gravely weakened by the long war with Japan. Despite American support, it was defeated in the Chinese Civil War of 1945–9 by the Soviet-backed Communists. This would have been unlikely bar for the war: prior to Japanese attack, the Chinese Communists had been in a vulnerable position. This war was the largest, in terms of number of combatants and area fought over since World War Two, and it proves an instructive counterpoint to the latter, indicating the difficulty of drawing clear lessons from the conflicts of the 1940s; although it ought to be stressed that there has been far less scholarship on the Chinese Civil War than on World War Two, and much of the work published on the former has reflected ideological bias. In China, technology and the quantity of *matériel* did not triumph. The Communists were inferior in weaponry, and, in particular, lacked air and sea power, but their strategic conceptions, operational planning and execution, army morale and political leadership proved superior. They also benefited from having become the dominant anti-Japanese force in northern China. The Nationalist cause was weakened by poor leadership and inept strategy; and, as the war went badly, poor morale, corruption and inflation badly affected civilian support. Until 1948, however, the Nationalists held their own, but, that year, Communist victory in Manchuria led to a crucial shift in advantage and the rapid collapse of the Nationalists the following year. Chiang Kai-shek took refuge in Formosa (Taiwan), which was all he retained control over.[33] In 1950, China signed a treaty of alliance with the Soviet Union.

## Conclusion

Every conflict is different, and civil wars have particular characteristics, but the Chinese Civil War demonstrates, like World War Two, that wars have to be waged and won. Their course and result were (and are) not inevitable, and it is necessary to give due weight to operational history: capability had to be proved successful in conflict.

In 1950, with the USA overwhelmingly dominant in the world economy, as well as the leading global power, China and Eastern Europe Communist, India independent, Fascism defeated, and the states of Western Europe now with far less room for independent manoeuvre, the world was set for the situation that was to prevail until the collapse of European Communism.

### NOTES

1 K. Smith, *Conflict over Convoys: Anglo-American Logistics Diplomacy in the Second World War* (Cambridge, 1996).

2 B. Fischer, *Albania at War 1939–1945* (West Lafayette, Indiana, 1999).

3 J.A. English, *Marching Through Chaos. The Descent of Armies in Theory and Practice* (Westport, Connecticut, 1996), p. 105.

4 A. Mombauer, *Helmuth von Moltke and the Origins of the First World War* (Cambridge, 2001). For earlier planning for war with Russia, see G.A. Tunstall, *Planning for War Against Russia and Serbia: Austro-Hungarian and German Military Strategies, 1871–1914* (Boulder, Colorado, 1993).

5 L.H. Addington, *The Blitzkrieg Era and the German General Staff, 1865–1941* (New Brunswick, New Jersey, 1971), pp. xi, 216–17.

6 M. Matloff, 'The American Approach to War, 1919–1945', in M. Howard (ed.), *The Theory and Practice of War* (New York, 1966), p. 237.

7 This came into operational service in February 1945.

8 R.F. Weigley, *History of the United States Army* (New York, 1967), pp. 467–9.

9 O'Connor to Major-General Sir Percy Hobart, 24 August 1944, LH. O'Connor papers 5/3/41.

10 J.M. Vernet, 'The Army of the Armistice 1940–1942: A Small Army for a Great Revenge', in C.R. Shrader (ed.), *Proceedings of the 1982 International Military History Symposium. The Impact of Unsuccessful Military*

*Campaigns on Military Institutions, 1860–1980* (Washington, 1984), pp. 241–2, 246–7.

11  K.E. Bonn, *When the Odds were Even: The Vosges Mountains Campaign, October 1944–January 1945* (Novato, California, 1994); C. Whiting, *The Battle of Huertgen Forest: The Untold Story of a Disastrous Campaign* (1989); E.G. Miller, *A Dark and Bloody Ground: The Huertgen Forest and the Roer River Dams, 1944–1945* (College Station, 1995); M. Doubler, *Closing with the Enemy: How GIs Fought the War in Europe, 1944–1945* (Lawrence, 1994); P.R. Mansoor, *The GI Offensive in Europe: The Triumph of American Infantry Divisions, 1941–1945* (Lawrence, Kansas, 1999); R.S. Rush, *Hell in the Hürtgen Forest: The Ordeal and Triumph of an American Infantry Regiment* (Lawrence, Kansas, 2001).

12  Manchester, John Rylands Library, Special Collections, GOW/1/2/2, pp. 33, 54, 1/2/1, p. 6.

13  S. Bungay, *Alamein* (2002), pp. 210–12.

14  LH. Alanbrooke papers 6/2/37.

15  O'Connor to Major General Allan Adair, 24 July 1944, LH. O'Connor 5/3/22.

16  LH. Alanbrooke papers 6/2/37.

17  R. Buderi, *The Invention that Changed the World* (New York, 1996); G. Hartcup, *The Effect of Science on the Second World War* (Basingstoke, 2000).

18  D. Hapgood and D. Richardson, *Monte Cassino* (1984).

19  P.K. Grimsted, *Trophies of War and Empire. The Archival Heritage of Ukraine, World War II, and the International Politics of Restitution* (Cambridge, Massachusetts, 2001), pp. 196–209.

20  M. Levene and P. Roberts (eds), *The Massacre in History* (Oxford, 1999).

21  A.J. Aluit, *By Sword and Fire: The Destruction of Manila in World War II* (Manila, 1966).

22  Pound to Admiral Layton, 9 February 1943, BL. Add. 74796.

23  P.S. Dull, *A Battle History of the Imperial Japanese Navy, 1941–1945* (Wellingborough, 1978).

24  G. Best, *Nuremberg and After: The Continuing History of War Crimes and Crimes Against Humanity* (Reading, 1984); T. Taylor, *The Anatomy of the Nuremberg Trials* (1993).

25  D. Bloxham, *Genocide on Trial. War Crimes Trials and the Formation of Holocaust History and Memory* (Oxford, 2001), pp. 156–81, 226.

26  J.J. Weingartner, *Crossroads of Death: The Story of the Malmedy Massacre and Trial* (Berkeley, 1979); F. Buscher, *The US War Crimes Trial Program in Germany, 1946–1955* (Westport, Connectictu, 1980); M. Reynolds, *The Devil's Adjutant: Jochen Peiper, Panzer Leader* (Staplehurst, 1995).

27  I. Deak, J.T. Gross and T. Judt (eds), *The Politics of Retribution in Europe: World War II and Its Aftermath* (Princeton, 2000).

28  P.R. Piccigallo, *The Japanese on Trial: Allied War Crimes Operations in the East, 1945–1951* (Austin, Texas, 1979).

29  P. Williams and D. Wallace, *Unit 731: Japan's Secret Biological Warfare in World War II* (1989).

30 S.R. Fischer, *A History of the Pacific Islands* (Basingstoke, 2002), pp. 210–11.
31 S. Tonnesson, *The Vietnamese Revolution of 1945: Roosevelt, Ho Chi Minh, and De Gaulle in a World at War* (1991); D.G. Marr, *Vietnam 1945: The Quest for Power* (Berkeley, 1995).
32 J.A. Krancher, *The Defining Years of the Dutch East Indies, 1942–49* (Jefferson, New Jersey, 1996).
33 L.E. Eastman, *Seeds of Destruction: Nationalist China in War and Revolution, 1937–49* (Stanford, 1984).

# Selected further reading

The best recent single-volume coverage is *A War To Be Won. Fighting the Second World War* by Williamson Murray and Allan R. Millett (Cambridge, Massachusetts, 2000). Effective shorter studies include A.W. Purdue, *The Second World War* (Basingstoke, 1999), and S.C. Tucker, *The Second World War* (Basingstoke, 2003). An excellent earlier single-volume account is provided by Gerhard Weinberg, *A World at Arms: A Global History of World War II* (Cambridge, 1994), and, for another look at the war in its global context, John Ray, *The Second World War: A Narrative History* (1999). The encyclopedia approach of *The Oxford Companion to the Second World War* (Oxford, 1995), edited by I.C.B. Dear and M.R.D. Foot, offers a mass of well-informed essays. The significant cartographic dimension is covered (with helpful text as well) in *The Times Atlas of the Second World War* (London, 1989), edited by John Keegan, who has also published a single-volume *Second World War* (London, 1989).

The economic dimension is tackled in Richard Overy's *Why the Allies Won* (London, 1995), while long-term perspectives are offered in Paul Kennedy's *The Rise and Fall of the Great Powers* (London, 1988) and Jeremy Black's *Warfare in the Western World 1882–1975* (Chesham, 2002).

The naval dimension can be approached through R.D. Spector, *At War. At Sea: Sailors and Naval Warfare in the Twentieth Century* (London, 2001), C. Barnett, *Engage the Enemy More Closely: The Royal Navy in the Second World War* (1991), and G.W. Baer, *One Hundred Years of Sea Power: The US Navy, 1890–1990* (Stanford, California, 1993). For air warfare, John Terraine, *The Right of the Line: The RAF in the European War 1939–45* (1985), and John Buckley, *Air Power in the Age of Total War* (London, 1999).

For the war in Europe, the series *Germany and the Second World War*, published under the auspices of the Militärgeschichtliches Forschungsamt, and, in English translation, by Oxford University Press, is of great importance. The most instructive of these lengthy volumes is volume 6, *The Global War. Widening of the Conflict into a World War and the Shift of the Initiative 1941–1943* (Oxford, 2001), edited by Horst Boog and others. On German policy, see also Ian Kershaw, *Hitler 1936–1945: Nemesis* (London, 2000), and Gerhard Weinberg, *Germany, Hitler and World War II: Essays in Modern German and World History* (Cambridge, 1995).

For Germany's early successes, see R.A. Doughty, *The Breaking Point: Sedan and the Fall of France, 1940* (Hamden, Connecticut, 1990), and Brian Bond and Michael Taylor (eds), *The Battle for France and Flanders. Sixty Years On* (Barnsley, 2001).

For the Eastern Front, John Erickson, *The Road to Stalingrad* (London, 1975) and *The Road to Berlin* (London, 1987), can usefully be supplemented by David M. Glantz and Jonathan M. House, *When Titans Clashed: How the Red Army Stopped Hitler* (Lawrence, Kansas, 1995) and *The Battle of Kursk* (Lawrence, Kansas, 1999), Richard Overy, *Russia's War: Blood upon the Snow* (London, 1997), and D.M. Glantz, *Barbarossa. Hitler's Invasion of Russia 1941* (Stroud, 2001).

For the war in the Pacific, see R. Spector, *Eagle Against the Sun: The American War with Japan* (New York, 1985), and H.P. Willmott, *Pearl Harbor* (London, 2001).

For the war in North Africa, see W.G.F. Jackson, *Battle for North Africa* (1975), and, in the Mediterranean, C. D'Este, *World War II in the Mediterranean, 1942–1945* (Chapel Hill, 1990).

For the war in Europe, see A.N. Garland and H.M. Smith, *United States Army in World War II: The Mediterranean Theater of Operations: Sicily and the Surrender of Italy* (Washington, 1993), and R.F. Weigley, *Eisenhower's Lieutenants: The Campaign of France and Germany, 1944–1945* (Bloomington, Indiana, 1981).

For Axis occupation and the response, see M. Mazower, *Inside Hitler's Greece: The Experience of Occupation, 1941–1944* (New Haven, 1993), and B. Moore (ed.), *Resistance in Western Europe* (Oxford, 2000).

# INDEX

Abyssinia 5
air conflict 36, 47, 53–4, 81, 98,
    142, 150, 183–4, 190
'Air Gap' 64–5, 145
air power 23–7, 273
air supply 198, 219, 223
airborne forces 26, 153, 170, 175,
    179, 210, 222–3
Albania 56, 59, 166, 234, 267
Aleutian Islands 103, 141, 228
Alexander, General Sir Harold
    153–4, 167–8
Algeria 52, 151–2
Andaman Islands 101
anti-tank weapons 36–7, 48–9,
    120, 208, 270–1, 274
Antwerp 177, 183
Anzio 157, 167–8
appeasement 4–9, 76–7
Arakan 112, 137, 219
Arctic xiii, 227
Arnhem 177
artillery 49, 117, 206, 208, 222,
    270, 272, 279, 281
Athens 61, 235,
Atlantic, battle of the 62–5, 113,
    126, 143–7, 216
atomic bombs 218–19, 221, 275,
    280
Auschwitz 87, 126, 183
Australia 109–10, 99, 221, 227
Austria 5–6, 60, 283

Axis powers *see* Germany, Italy,
    Japan
Azores 67, 146

Bagration, Operation 162–3
Baku 27, 41, 116, 275
Balkans 224, 234; *see also* Albania,
    Bulgaria, Greece, Hungary,
    Romania, Yugoslavia
Baltic Sea 19–20, 38, 164
Baltic states 76, 164–5, 244, 286
Barbarossa 74–87, 229
Barentz Sea, Battle of the 144
Bataan 88, 93, 98
battleships 15–17, 21, 138–9, 215
Beijing 31–2
Belgium 45–6, 176–7
Belgrade 61, 166
Berlin 149–51, 206–9, 212, 278,
Bessarabia 42, 83, 286
*Bismarck* 63, 148
Black Sea 19
Blitz 70
*Blitzkrieg* 11, 25, 35, 48–9, 68, 77,
    86, 103, 162, 198, 222, 241,
    278, 281
Bock, Field Marshal Fedor von
    75, 116
bombing 37, 46, 53–4, 125,
    149–51, 182–8, 207, 210,
    216–18, 240, 276–7

Borneo xiii, 96, 221, 275
Bose, Subhas Chandra 101
Brazil 227
Breslau 207
Brest 63, 65, 147–8
Brest-Litovsk 36
Britain: prior to World War Two
  4–11, 14–18, 20, 24–7; in
  1939–42 38–9, 41, 43–59, 63;
  in 1941 60–71, 83, 92, 94,
  103–7, 273–4; in 1942
  95–101, 112, 119–26; in 1943
  137–8, 143–7, 149–58; in
  1944 166–88, 190, 196–9; in
  1945 209–12, 216, 219–20,
  224; economic aspects 253;
  postwar position 284–6; social
  aspects 252–9
Britain, Battle of 53–4, 150
Brittany 52
Budapest 166, 209
Bulgaria 60, 165, 188
Bulge, Battle of the 177–80, 192,
  202
Burma 40, 96–102, 112, 121,
  137–8, 157, 190, 194, 196–9,
  201, 219–20, 237, 275, 286
Burma Road 98

California 249–50
Cambodia xiii, 89–90, 221
Canada 54–5, 64, 147, 227–8,
  248, 251–2, 259
Canaries 67
Canton 32, 192, 220
carriers, aircraft 15–19, 21–2,
  91–2, 99, 101, 110–12, 138–9,
  141–2, 189–90, 192–6, 215
Casablanca conference 129, 149
casualties xiv, 4
Caucasus 76, 116, 130–1, 286
Ceylon (Sri Lanka) 99–100, 286
Chad 123
Chamberlain, Neville 8, 38, 45,
  52, 70
Changsa 33, 190

Channel Isles 52, 176, 212
Cherbourg 38, 50
China xiii, 2, 31–5, 20, 25, 67,
  98, 130, 157, 190–2, 195,
  198–9, 202, 220, 232, 238,
  243, 261, 287–8
Christmas Island 99, 110
Churchill, Winston xii, 9, 38, 45,
  53, 55, 57, 62, 64, 70, 96,
  121–2, 126, 155, 168, 224,
  254–5, 266, 284–5
Cologne 125
concentration camps 183, 210,
  239
convoys see Atlantic, battle of the
Co-prosperity Sphere 101
Coral Sea, battle of the 101, 110,
  140
Corregidor 93
Corsica 56, 155
Coventry 70
Crete 55, 62, 67
Crimea 82, 114, 135, 162, 165,
  278
Croatia 61, 68, 282
Cuba 226–7
Cunningham, Admiral Sir
  Andrew 62, 69
Cyprus 62
Cyrenaica 57, 120, 122
Czechoslovakia 5, 7–8, 284, 286

Dakar 66, 123
Darwin 99, 110, 228
D-Day 16, 143, 153, 169–71
Denmark 6, 8, 42, 45, 68
Dieppe 124, 171
Dodecanese 155
Dominican Republic 226–7
Dönitz, Admiral Karl 144–5, 212
Doolittle raid 111
Douhet, Guilio 23–4
Dragoon, Operation 174–5
Dresden 185, 207
Dunkirk 49–50, 184

Dutch East Indies 90, 96–8, 109, 237, 286–7

East Prussia 165
Egypt 52, 57, 60, 122, 151, 157, 286
Eisenhower, General Dwight 169, 174–5, 180–2
El Alamein 120–2, 126, 151
Elbe, river 206, 210
Eritrea 58
Estonia 42
Ethiopia 57–9

Faeroes 45
Falaise pocket 164, 174, 180
'Final Solution' 87, 125–6, 183
Finland xiii, 27, 39–42, 77, 82, 83, 115, 164, 254, 284, 286
food 242, 253–4
Formosa (Taiwan) 32, 192, 215, 283, 288
France: prior to World War Two 4–10, 13; 1939–Fall of France 38–9, 41, 42–52, 56; Fall of France to D-Day 66, 103–5, 123, 125; social aspects 260
Fuller, J.F.C. xiv, 10–11, 13, 23, 61–2, 78, 82, 83, 86, 168, 171, 176–7, 185, 275

Gaulle, Charles de 51, 66, 103–5
Germany: prior to World War Two 1–9, 17, 24–5; in 1939–40 35–9, 42–56, 59; in 1941 59–71, 24–88, 105; in 1942 113–26; in 1943 129–37, 143–58; in 1944 161–88, 199–202; in 1945 206–12; brutality of system 228–31, 233, 235, 238, 272, 277; economic aspects 228, 238–42; postwar settlement 282–4; social aspects 239, 257, 261
Gibraltar 66

Gilbert Islands 142–3
Goebbels, Josef 74, 257
Göring, Hermann 18, 25, 118, 240, 277, 282
Graf Spee 63
Greece 41, 56, 59, 60–1, 68, 166, 234–5
Greenland 45
Guadalcanal xi, 110, 138–40
Guam 20, 94, 194
Guatemala 226
Guderian, General Heinz 113
Gulags 243–4, 282
Gustav Line 167
gypsies 126

Haiti 227
Halder, General Franz 126, 280
Hamburg 149–50, 210
Hart, Basil Liddell 10–11, 13, 281
Hawaii 20, 112
'hedgehogs' 114
Hiroshima 217
Hitler, Adolf 2–8, 25, 38–9, 51, 52, 62, 67, 71, 74–5, 76, 80, 83, 84–5, 87, 105–6, 113, 116–17, 129–30, 132–3, 135, 151, 157, 162, 174, 178, 182, 229, 239, 257, 267–8
Honduras 227
Hong Kong 92, 98, 192
Hood 63
Huertgen Forest, battle of the 178, 273
Hungary 7, 60, 83, 131, 165–6, 179, 239

Iceland 45, 67
Imphal 197–8
India 112, 190, 255, 286–7
Indian Ocean 99–101, 141, 182, 227
Indo-China 32, 52, 88, 96, 221
industry 80–1
Iraq xiii, 24, 103, 124, 275
Ireland 6, 67

Italy 56, 57–60, 83, 153–6,
    166–9, 211–12, 242–3, 258
Iwo Jima 216, 218

Japan 20, 83; prior to Pearl
    Harbor 1–2, 15–23, 31–5,
    88–90; Pearl Harbor to end of
    1942 91–103, 109–13, 119;
    1943 136–43, 147–8, 158;
    1944 188–202; 1945 212–24;
    economic aspects 242–3, 248;
    postwar settlement 282–4;
    social aspects 242
Java Sea, battle of the 97
jet aircraft 27, 241
Jews 3, 37, 87, 100, 125–6, 158,
    175, 230, 233, 276, 277
July Bomb Plot 200–1

Karelia 42, 82, 284
Kasserine Pass, battle of the 152,
    272
Kerch 114–15, 116
Khalkhin-Gol, battle of 15, 78
Kharkov 85, 113, 114, 130–1,
    134
Kiev 75, 77, 79, 87, 114, 136
Koh-Chang, battle of 90
Kohima 197–8
Korea 223, 283
Kuriles 223, 283–4
Kursk, battle of xiii, 131–5, 156,
    192, 202, 236
Kwantung army 2, 15

La Rochelle 63
Laos xiii, 89–90, 221
Latin America 227
Latvia 42
Le Havre 50
Lebanon 52, 103, 104, 286
Lebensraum 3, 74
Leeb, Field Marshal Wilhelm von
    75, 85
LeMay, General Curtis 216

Lend-Lease Act 70, 90, 227
Leningrad 20, 76, 79, 85, 114,
    119, 132, 136, 164, 230, 278
Libya 57, 59, 122, 284,
Lidice 235
Lithuania 8, 42
logistics 123–4, 197–8, 215–16
London 54, 70, 183
Lorient 63, 176
Lübeck 125
Lublin 163
Luftwaffe 6, 18, 36, 53–5, 81, 87,
    25, 103, 134, 150, 164, 173,
    183–4,187, 241–2
Lvov 37, 163

MacArthur, General Douglas 93,
    181
Madagascar xiii, 18, 52, 100,
    119–20, 124, 142, 286
Maginot Line 13, 46
malaria 197
Malaya xii, 57, 90, 93, 94–5,
    97–8, 102, 220, 278
Malta 120, 151
Manchuria 1–2, 5, 15, 31–4, 68,
    83, 137, 192, 221–3, 245, 274,
    287
Manila 20, 93, 181, 213, 278
Manstein, Field Marshal, Erich
    von 131, 135, 282
maps 249, 256–7
Mariana Islands 21, 193–5
marines 181, 214–15
Marseilles 176
Marshall, General George 126,
    218
Marshall Islands 21, 143, 193
Mediterranean 65–6, 69, 83, 100,
    121, 150–1, 155, 168–9, 175,
    266
Meiktila 219
Mers-el-Kébir 66
Mexico 227, 267, 272
Midway, battle of 101, 111–12,
    126, 129, 140, 192, 279

mines 65, 217
Minsk 77
Mongolia 15, 151–2, 157, 286
Monte Cassino 277
Montgomery, Field Marshal
    Bernard 121–2, 172–3, 178,
    180–1, 274–5
Morocco 10, 24, 52, 66
mortars 269
Moscow 76–7, 79, 132, 230
Moscow, battle of xiii, 81, 84
music 257–8
Mussolini, Benito 56, 60 77, 79,
    151, 154–5, 157, 187, 283

Nagasaki 216–17
Nanjing 2, 31–2, 34–5, 137
Naples 154
Narvik 43, 45
naval warfare 15–23, 43, 59,
    62–7, 113, 126, 143–7,
    188–90, 192–6, 215–16
Nazi–Soviet Pact 8, 15
Netherlands 45–6, 52
New Britain 109–10
New Guinea 107, 109–11, 140,
    195
New Zealand 221, 227
Nicaragua 277
Nice 56, 261
Normandy 52, 55, 119, 143,
    169–74, 236
Norway 6, 8, 16–17, 41, 42–6,
    52, 62, 68–9, 165, 182, 237
Nuremberg 151, 185–6, 210, 282

Oder, river 207, 278
Odessa 82
oil 27, 60, 84, 89, 98–9, 101, 105,
    115–16, 131, 156, 171, 186,
    207, 210, 251, 266–7, 274–5
Okinawa 218, 223, 248, 285
Oradour 175

Palestine 284, 286
Panama 227

Paris 50, 174, 278
partisans 211, 231–8
Patton, George 154, 181, 223
Pearl Harbor xiv, 20, 22, 94, 102,
    110, 112, 148
Penney, Major-General William
    181, 218, 224, 230
Persia 103, 105, 115, 124, 252,
    275
Pétain, General Henri 51, 53,
    239, 282–3
Philippine Sea, battle of the 193
Philippines 12, 20–1, 55, 90–3,
    94, 96, 98, 101, 109, 143, 164,
    170, 195–6, 199, 201, 213–14,
    221, 227, 237, 287
Phoney War 39, 47
Ploesti 60, 156, 274
Poland 7–9, 14, 35–9, 41, 68, 77,
    206–7, 224, 232, 234, 244,
    284, 286
Port Moresby 100, 107, 109
Potsdam Conference 217
Pound, Admiral Sir Dudley 44–5,
    55, 279
Prague 212, 235, 278
*Prince of Wales* 63, 94
prisoners 96, 143

Quisling, Vidkun 43, 282

Rabaul 141, 193
radar 53–4, 99, 141, 150, 193,
    252, 275–6
Raeder, Grand Admiral Erich 75,
    144
Rangoon 97, 100, 219
Remagen 209–10
Rhine, river 180, 209
River Plate, battle of the 63
Romania 8, 37, 60, 82, 83, 87,
    165–6, 239, 274
Rome 167–8
Rommel, Field Marshal Erwin
    50, 60, 120–2, 278
Roosevelt, Franklin Delano 6,

64, 67, 70, 105–6, 129, 174, 246–7, 250, 285
Rostov 76, 85–6, 116, 130–1
Ruhr 39, 46, 210, 275
Rundstedt, Field Marshal Gerd von 75, 86
Ruthenia 7, 286

Saigon 90
Saipan 188, 194–5, 216
Sakhalin 223, 283–4
Salerno 154, 167
Samoa 20
Sardinia 155
*Scharnhorst* 65, 147
science 275–6
Sealion, Operation 52, 54
Sedan 46
Senegal 52
Sevastopol 19, 117, 165, 278
Shanghai 25, 32, 277
shipbuilding 248–9
Sicily 134, 153, 156
Singapore xii, 20, 66, 94–6, 100, 109, 220, 278
slave labour 238–9, 243
Slim, General William 198, 219
Slovakia 83, 165–6, 209, 236, 239
Smolensk 76–7, 79, 136
Solomon Islands 109, 138, 141, 197
Somaliland 57–8, 284
Southampton 70
Soviet Union (USSR) 39–42; prior to World War Two 11, 15, 19, 26–7; in 1939–40 37, 39–42; in 1941 74–88, 105; in 1942 113–19; in 1943 130–7; in 1944 161–6, 176, 202; in 1945-Europe 206–9; brutality of system 234, 243–4, 272; economic aspects 244–6; postwar position 280–1, 283–4, 286; social aspects 260; war with Japan 221–4
Spain 52, 66–7

Spanish Civil War 11–12, 24–5
Special Operations Executive 234, 237
Speer, Albert 228, 240
St Nazaire 50, 63, 124, 176
Stalin, Josef xi, 75–7, 80, 83, 84, 113–15, 116–17, 130–1, 149, 221, 223, 231–2, 235–6, 239, 267, 275
Stalingrad, battle of xiii, 115, 116–19, 126, 130, 153, 164, 278
submarines 19–20, 63–5, 70, 113, 123, 126, 144–7, 157, 182, 187–9, 212, 215, 230, 279
Sumatra 196, 275
Sweden 6, 8
Switzerland 6
Syria 10, 52, 61, 103–4, 124, 286

Taiwan *see* Formosa
tanks 36–7, 47–8, 81, 84, 115, 120, 122, 164, 172, 207, 245, 251, 269–71, 273–4, 278
Taranto 59, 154
Tarawa 142
Thailand 90, 97, 102
Timoshenko, Marshal Semyon 76
Tinian 194–5
*Tirpitz* 147
Tobruk 67, 120–1, 278
Todt Organisation 241–2
Tōjō, General Hideki 90, 101
Tokyo 111, 216–17
Torch, Operation 120, 122–5
Toulon 125
Tukhachevsky, Mikhail 11
Tunisia 52, 60, 69, 123, 151–3
Turkey 115, 155, 227

Ukraine 76, 79, 130, 161–2, 165, 233, 238, 245, 277
ULTRA 62, 146, 151, 178
United Nations 285; United States: prior to Pearl Harbor

9–10, 12, 16–23, 64, 67, 89–90; Pearl Harbor to end of 1942 91–4, 101–3, 105–7, 110–13, 122, 126; 1943 138–43, 145–58; 1944 166–96, 201, 272–3; 1945 209–18, 224; postwar position 280–1, 283–8; economic aspects 246–52, 256–7; social aspects 250–1, 258–9, 271–2

V rockets 182–3, 186
Versailles Peace Settlement 2, 5, 10, 16
Vichy 47, 51–2, 62, 66, 68, 80, 89, 100, 119, 123, 125, 233–4, 239, 271, 283
Vienna 209
Vietnam 89, 221, 286–7

Waffen-SS 133, 143, 229, 241
Wake Island 94
Walcheren 180
Warsaw 37–8, 158, 162–3, 182, 206, 236, 276, 277–8
Wavell, Field Marshal Sir Archibald 97, 100
Wingate, Orde 137
women 239, 259–61

Yalta Conference 282
Yamamoto, Admiral Isoroku 90, 111–12
Yugoslavia 60–1, 69, 79–80, 166, 234, 236

Zhukov, Marshal Georgi 15, 78, 81, 119, 208